# Autonomy and Independence in Language Learning

# APPLIED LINGUISTICS AND LANGUAGE STUDY

GENERAL EDITOR

PROFESSOR CHRISTOPHER N. CANDLIN

*Macquarie University, Sydney*

*For a complete list of books in this series see pages v–vi*

# Autonomy and Independence in Language Learning

Phil Benson and Peter Voller

**Longman**

London and New York

**Pearson Education Limited**
Edinburgh Gate
Harlow, Essex CM20 2JE
United Kingdom

and Associated Companies throughout the world

*Visit us on the World Wide Web at:*
http://www.pearsoneduc.com

© Addison Wesley Longman Limited 1997

First published 1997

ISBN 0 582 289920 Ppr

**British Library Cataloguing-in-Publication Data**

A catalogue record for this book is
available from the British Library

**Library of Congress Cataloging-in-Publication Data**

Autonomy and independence in language learning / edited by Phil Benson
and Peter Voller.
    p.  cm. — (Applied linguistics and language study)
    Includes bibliographical references and index.
    ISBN 0-582-28992-0 (ppr)
    1. Language and languages—Study and teaching.  2. Independent
study.  I. Benson, Phil, 1955-  .  II. Voller, Peter.
III. Series.
P53.445.A94  1997
418'.007—dc20                           96-33241
                                                      CIP

Set by 35 in 10/12 pt Baskerville

8 7 6 5 4 3 2
05 04 03 02 01

Printed in Malaysia, TCP

# APPLIED LINGUISTICS AND LANGUAGE STUDY

GENERAL EDITOR

PROFESSOR CHRISTOPHER N. CANDLIN

*Macquarie University, Sydney*

v

# Contents

# Contributors

**Guy Aston**, University of Bologna, Italy

**Michael Breen**, Edith Cowan University, Australia

**Edith Esch**, Language Centre, University of Cambridge

**David Little**, Centre for Language and Communication Studies, Trinity College, University of Dublin

**Andrew Littlejohn**, Institute of Education, University of London and University of Lancaster

**William Littlewood**, English Centre, University of Hong Kong

**Sarah Mann**, University of Western Australia

**John Milton**, Language Centre, Hong Kong University of Science and Technology

**David Nunan**, English Centre, University of Hong Kong

**Felicity O'Dell**, Eurocentre, Cambridge

**Alastair Pennycook**, Department of Linguistics and Applied Linguistics, University of Melbourne

**Philip Riley**, CRAPEL, Universite de Nancy II, France

**Stephen Ryan**, Department of General Education, Osaka Institute of Technology, Japan

**Susan Sheerin**, The Bell Language School, Cambridge

**Gill Sturtridge**, Centre for Applied Language Studies, University of Reading, England

# General Editor's Preface

It might be worthwhile setting out a couple of more or less folk assertions as a way in to reading this provocative but informing book. The first, in Mrs Thatcher's (in)famous phrase, is the assertion that: '*There's no such thing as society*', and the second is, as every (language) teacher knows (and sometimes says), '*I can't learn it for you*'. The answers, of course, are: 'there is', and 'you're right'. The point is that for language learning *both* answers are right, it depends on what you're focusing on, and it's also a question of ends and means.

One way of regarding the title of this book is, then, to see it as containing the ultimate tautology; how could there be language learning which wasn't 'autonomous' and 'independent'? In that sense the title might as well be just *Language Learning*. However, if as good pupils of Paul Grice we engage with the Cooperative Principle, we are bound to reflect that to write and print such an apparently tautologous title must contain the implicature of some other meaning. Maybe, language learning isn't autonomous and it isn't independent? Is it or was it for you? That's when the title starts to get interesting and sets you off on the quest. It's probably the best way to start to read Phil Benson's and Peter Voller's timely and challenging collection of original papers from about the most representative and expert group of writers on this theme as one might assemble, and the *Applied Linguistics and Language Study* series is very much in their debt for the idea and for the accomplishment. At the risk of too great a series self-promotion, *Autonomy and Independence in Language Learning* is set to become a classic in applied linguistics.

The editors, like Deep Throat in Watergate, have got it right for the reader: don't follow the money, but follow Holec's five definitional principles for autonomy in language learning: assess the conduciveness of the *situations* (the contexts of learning), the *skills* learners need to refine and develop, the *capacity* or ability that needs to be enhanced, the *responsibility* that needs to be encouraged and the *rights* to learn that need to be asserted. More interestingly, though, consider how each of these acts as a corroboration and also a control on each of the others. If the focus is on context, then the issue of rights immediately engages us in the degree of control the learner can and is allowed to exercise on what she learns, when and how she learns, and how she comes to assess and evaluate the success of her learning; if the focus is on rights, then the issue of responsible exercise of those rights is foregrounded, itself dependent on the missing element (though subsumed) in Holec's list: the *content* of what she learns, necessarily dependent on the degree of language learning skill the learner has been enabled to acquire, and the conduciveness of the contexts of learning. Such skills are, of course, only epiphenomena for learning; what is essential is the enhancement of capacity, that development of cognitive and communicative ability which is itself ineluctably bound up with the recognition by the curriculum of both social and individual aspects of learning.

This perspective of internal validation, autonomy and independence provides a further way of reading the arguments of this book. The Parts and their papers offer a similar and supportive mutually corroborative opportunity. Part Three, with its focus on *Methods and Materials* is challenged by the *Philosophy and Practice* of Part One, mediated by the exercise of participant action characterised by the *Roles and Relationships* of Part Two. In this way, the book takes on a curriculum-defining shape, a critical and reflexive approach to its own subject matter, and the individual papers themselves offer similarly contestable positions when set against each other. Phil Benson and Peter Voller have by this means carefully constructed and achieved an interactive and thus an interpretive but also an explanatory analysis of their subject matter.

More than this, however, the book itself provides an example of how any language learning curriculum that has autonomy and independence as its goal (and which curriculum would not?) needs to provide within itself the sources for its own internal debate; about curriculum content, curriculum process and curriculum evaluation. Autonomy cannot be legislated, independence cannot be wished, in the curriculum as anywhere else in the social polity;

what can be done is to embed their defining principles in the actions of teachers and learners and make such actions not only open for reasoned choice by both, but, much more importantly, to establish the philosophical, purposeful and language acquisitional bases of such choices themselves as part of the subject-matter of the curriculum. After all, deciding what is to be done and why is one of the few genuinely communicative acts any classroom can encourage.

At a risk, then, of distilling the debates of these invigorating papers to their essence, we might (to entangle metaphors) unravel and deconstruct the struggling branches of the tree that marks so appositely the cover of this book. The contesting discourses of the individual and the social are not, ultimately, to be resolved in some bland and homogenised interdiscursivity, neither for learning, nor for language. If learning, despite Mrs Thatcher's maxim, requires the society of other learners, real or virtual, for its successful engendering, language and communication certainly do. Insofar as successful learning requires negotiation by the learner of what she already knows in the face of and in the light of the new, so too does communication. In that sense exploring the meaning potential of utterances is itself a learning as well as a communicative act. The question is how that exploration and that negotiation can be made the mainspring of any curriculum, whether institutionalised or personalised. Achieving autonomy and independence is a matter for the curriculum, not just for the learner or the teacher. But it can never be unattached from its contexts, never cut and dried in cyberspace.

It is perhaps worthwhile remembering that the chief mainsprings to what came, unfortunately perhaps, to be called communicative language teaching are all closely allied to the principles of autonomy and independence outlined here, but with two closely linked differences, one of focus, the other of principle. The difference of principle was that of emphasising *inter*dependence, not just independence in language learning: interdependence of learners, learners and teachers, learners and data, learners and contexts and goals of learning. The difference of focus was that of the central position of *language* as communication, for me the key and perhaps too covertly naturalised construct in these pages, where the goal of the curriculum was to enable and empower learners to make their own meanings. In this sense, the pathways, modes and strategies are less important than the goal: if interdependence can be fostered, and language as meaning potential made the central curriculum principle, then autonomy is how the individual learner (and the teacher) comes to learns *it* for himself and herself, where *it* is both learning and communication, as well as the value of an interdependent autonomy, in language, learning, and, above all else, in living. The how is locally constructable, the why inalienable.

Professor Christopher N Candlin
Macquarie University
Sydney, Australia

# 1

# Introduction: autonomy and independence in language learning

PHIL BENSON AND PETER VOLLER

## Aims

Over the last two decades, *autonomy* and *independence* have taken on a growing importance in the field of language education. David Little (1991: p.2) has described autonomy as a 'buzz-word' of the 1990s, and this is borne out by the number of recent books (Dam, 1995; Dickinson and Wenden, 1995; van Lier, 1995), international conferences (Esch, 1994; Gardner and Miller, 1994; Pemberton *et al.*, 1996) and newsletters (*Independence*; *Learner Autonomy in Language Learning*; *Learning Learning*) connected to the topic. Anita Wenden (1991: p.11) states that 'few teachers will disagree with the importance of helping language learners become more autonomous as learners', but concepts with which we can hardly disagree are often those that stand most in need of clarification. In spite of widespread agreement on the importance of autonomy and independence, there remains a good deal of uncertainty about their meanings and applications for language education. It is the aim of this book both to clarify and to problematize these meanings, in order that they might be opened up to wider debate.

For a definition of autonomy, we might turn to Holec (1981: p.3) who describes it as 'the ability to take charge of one's learning'. In language education, however, the word has been used in at least five different ways:

1. for *situations* in which learners study entirely on their own;
2. for a set of *skills* which can be learned and applied in self-directed learning;
3. for an inborn *capacity* which is suppressed by institutional education;

1

4. for the exercise of *learners' responsibility* for their own learning;
5. for the *right* of learners to determine the direction of their own learning.

There are also differences in the extent to which autonomy is seen as a property of individuals or of social groups: it can be thought of in terms of withdrawal from education as a social process (self-instruction), or in terms of redistribution of power among participants in that social process (learner control). There are differences in the place that autonomy occupies in language learning: it can be thought of both as a means to the end of more effective language learning (autonomy for language learning) or as an end of language learning itself (language learning for autonomy). To add to the uncertainty, 'independence' is used sometimes as a synonym for 'autonomy' (Sheerin, 1991) and sometimes with a distinct sense of its own. Dickinson (1992), for example, associates 'autonomy' with the idea of learning alone and 'independence' with active responsibility for one's own learning. There are also questions about whether autonomy and independence are universal or western culture-bound values in education (Riley, 1988a).

It should be emphasized that there is no canon for concepts such as autonomy and independence in the field of applied linguistics. These are problematic concepts because they carry with them meanings from other discourses and from their applications in particular instances of language education. Because different usages relate to different underlying perspectives, it is unlikely that applied linguists will arrive at single agreed definitions of these terms. In spite of this, there has been surprisingly little debate on the fundamentals of autonomy and independence as concepts in the field of applied linguistics. It is almost as if we have skipped over the debate on what autonomy and independence mean in our haste to move more rapidly on to their implementation. But whenever autonomy and independence figure in concrete language education projects, there is always a risk that underlying conceptual differences will emerge in the form of conflicts over the practical steps to be taken.

This lack of concern with theory and the dangers this has for practice is the primary concern of this book. The three parts of the book reflect the major questions that need to be addressed if the gap between theory and practice is to be narrowed. These questions are: What kinds of autonomy or independence are aimed at and how can they best be achieved (*Part I: Philosophy and practice*)? What changes are envisaged in the roles and relationships of teachers and learners (*Part II: Roles and relationships*)? What specific methods and materials might best contribute to overall goals (*Part III: Methods and materials*)? When discussion of goals, rationales, and appropriate methodologies is informed by a deeper understanding of the meaning potential of autonomy and independence for language learning, the chances of successful implementation will be increased.

The aim of this book is to explore the discourses and applications of autonomy and independence for language learning and clarify where the concepts have come from and where they are going. Its overall message is that autonomy and independence are not simply totems whose evocation can automatically produce 'better language learners' or 'better people' as a result of language learning. It aims to show that there are different *versions* of autonomy and independence and different ways of implementing them, and that each way leads into fields of debate where widely accepted assumptions about language teaching and language learning are open to question.

The chapters that make up the book are based on their authors' experiences of autonomous and independent learning projects in a variety of settings. The authors do not always share the same view of autonomy and independence nor do they necessarily agree on the means of achieving it. In some cases, they are critical of methods and approaches with which they are themselves closely associated. The book does not, therefore, simply aim to promote autonomy and independence in language learning (although the editors are certainly committed to that goal), but to hold these concepts up to critical scrutiny at a time when they are entering the mainstream of language education. In this introductory chapter, we would like briefly to map out the terrain so that readers will better understand why autonomy and independence are so important to language education at the present time.

## The origins of autonomy and independence in language learning

Although autonomy and independence have deep historical roots in both western and eastern philosophies (see Pierson, 1996, on the concept of autonomy in Chinese thought), it is primarily in their western form that we know of them in language education. Autonomy and independence are keywords of twentieth-century liberal western thought in the fields of philosophy, psychology, politics and education. From the eighteenth century onwards, western discourses on society have increasingly emphasized the responsibility of the individual as social agent. In philosophy and psychology, autonomy and independence have come to be associated with the capacity of the individual to act as a responsible 'member of society'. The autonomous individual is, in Rogers's (1969: p.288) words, 'a fully functioning person'. In education, autonomy and independence are associated with the formation of the individual as the core of a democratic society. In this sense, they are by no means radical educational concepts. As Boud (1988: p.18) points out: 'A fundamental purpose of education is assumed to be to develop in individuals the ability to make their own decisions about what they think and do.' The notion of individual autonomy has a certain ambiguity, however, because it implies both responsibility and freedom from constraint. In *Collins COBUILD English Language Dictionary*, one definition of *autonomy* is 'the ability to make your own decisions about what to do rather than being influenced by someone else or told what to do', a definition somewhat ominously illustrated by the phrase: *These parents see autonomy in their youngsters as a threat.* The word *independence* has a similar ambiguity, implying both individual responsibility (independence in a growing child, for example, denotes doing what the family expects without being told to do so) and freedom from reliance on others (an 'independent woman', a person of 'independent means').

A second, and older, sense of autonomy is found in the political field, where it denotes freedom from external control. This is the other sense of autonomy defined by *Collins COBUILD Dictionary*: 'the control or government of a country, organization, or group by itself rather than by others' (illustrated even more ominously by the phrase: *The proposals include the ending of university autonomy*). Unlike individual autonomy, political autonomy and independence are not conditional upon 'responsibility'. They are rights rather than capacities. As Kwame Nkrumah (late President of Ghana) once argued of political independence: 'The best way of learning to be an independent sovereign state is to be an independent sovereign state.' The dictionary example shows that, in the educational context, autonomy is something that institutions may or may not enjoy in relation to governments or other funding institutions. In radical educational theory, autonomy, in the political sense, is a product of socially liberating education. In the work of Illich (1971), for example, the objective is to liberate learning from the restrictions of 'schooling'. In the work of Freire (1970), it is to help learners develop tools for engagement in social struggle. In these contexts, autonomy has a more radical, social content concerned not only with the psychological autonomy of the individual, but also with the autonomy of individuals as they are constituted within social groups.

Although autonomy and independence in language learning currently tend to be conceived in individual and psychological terms, we should bear in mind that the roots of these concepts are both contradictory and complex. We should bear in mind also that those who have done most to develop and popularize these notions were often inspired by the radical educational ideas of Freire, Illich, Châlon, Dewey, Kilpatrick and others. As John Trim (cited in Holec, 1988: p.6) stated in a report on modern language teaching to the Council of Europe the autonomy approach is both 'learner-centred' and 'anti-authoritarian'. Its implementation is therefore often characterized by ambiguities arising from two basic tensions: on the one hand, between responsibility and freedom from constraint; and on the other, between the individual and the social.

## Why language learning? Why now?

The promotion of autonomy in language learning has links to developments elsewhere in the field of education (Boud, 1988; Knowles, 1975; Tough, 1971) and has been sustained and nourished by innovative work in the field of self-directed learning and self-access (for reports, see Dickinson, 1987; Esch, 1994; Gardner and Miller, 1994; Holec, 1988; Little *et al.*, 1989; Riley, 1985; for a historical view of the concept of autonomy in language learning, see Gremmo and Riley, 1995). For the 'real meaning' of autonomy and independence there is a tendency to look towards the European tradition represented at CRAPEL (Centre de Recherches et d'Applications Pédagogiques en Langues), Nancy (Riley, 1985), but important as this work has been, we feel that it is also necessary to look at connections between these concepts and wider developments in language education. The most important of these is the fact that there is far more language education taking place, in more varied circumstances and for a wider variety of purposes, than ever before. The languages of the economically developed western world, English especially, account for the largest proportion of this growth, and it is in connection with the teaching of these languages that the concepts of autonomy and independence have established strongest roots. In the face of the growing scale and complexity of language education, they have emerged as keywords for flexible approaches to teaching and learning and responsiveness to diverse needs and circumstances.

At the same time, autonomy and independence have become linked to the growing role of technology in education, a link which has supported the growth of self-access language learning. For language teaching institutions, self-access often appears to represent an economical solution to large-scale language learning needs, a solution which is justified pedagogically by its association with the keywords of autonomy and independence. For advocates of autonomy and independence also, these terms have often been inseparable from the practice of self-access. Yet there is a good deal of ambiguity in this relationship. Self-access language learning can easily lead to dependence on a narrow range of strategies and materials and a narrowing of perspectives. As many of the authors in this collection are at pains to demonstrate, there is no necessary link between learning a language in a self-access facility and the development of autonomy and independence.

Autonomy and independence in language learning are also supported by three related tendencies in language education: individualization, learner-centredness and a growing recognition of the political nature of language learning.

Autonomous language learning has long been associated with individualization (Geddes and Sturtridge, 1982; Brookes and Grundy, 1988), and the notion that learners each have their own preferred learning styles, capacities and needs (Skehan, 1989). Advocates of autonomy and independence have also drawn upon 'constructivist' approaches to learning, which suggest that learners construct their own systems of knowledge as experience is filtered through 'personal construct systems' (Little, 1991). Proponents of autonomous and independent learning have tended to distance themselves from the implication that they promote individualistic approaches to learning by emphasizing the collective or collaborative nature of effective language learning. Autonomy continues, nevertheless, to be supported by views of learning which emphasize the learner's individuality. Concepts of autonomy and independence have also been promoted by the general trend in language education towards 'learner-centredness' over the last two decades (see, for example, Tarone and Yule, 1989). Learner-centredness is characterized by a movement away from language teaching as the transmission of a body of knowledge ('the language') towards language learning as the active production of knowledge. At the same time, there is tendency to focus on methods of learning rather than methods of teaching. Over the last decade, a number of learner-centred approaches to language education have emerged, all of which include autonomy and independence among their aims: the learner-centred curriculum (Nunan, 1988), the negotiated syllabus (Breen and Candlin, 1980; Bloor and Bloor, 1988), learner training (Ellis and Sinclair, 1989; Dickinson, 1992) and strategy training (Oxford, 1990; Wenden, 1991), the project-based syllabus (Legutke and Thomas, 1991), experiential and collaborative learning (Kohonen, 1992, Nunan, 1992), learner-based teaching (Campbell and Kryszewska, 1992), and so on. Autonomy and independence are, therefore, also supported by approaches that emphasize the role of learners as active agents in their own learning.

Lastly, there is the more recent tendency to emphasize the political element in language learning. Terms such as 'ideology' and 'empowerment' have entered the standard vocabulary of language education theory, and Marxist and post-Marxist theoreticians such as Vygotsky, Bakhtin, Gramsci and Althusser are becoming common figures in applied linguistics bibliographies. Behind this trend is a growing concern with the social implications of language learning and the development of critical approaches to language pedagogy (Pennycook, 1990; Fairclough, 1992b), leading to renewed interest in theories which link language education to social and political liberation. Recent work has also begun to look at the culturally invasive nature of much language education (Phillipson, 1992; Skutnabb-Kangas and Phillipson, 1994; Pennycook, 1994), where issues of autonomy and independence are directly raised. In this case, it is not so much the autonomy of learners as individuals that is at issue, as the ways in which language education supports or threatens the autonomy of the social or cultural groups to which learners belong. This tendency to think of learners not only as individuals but as members of socially constituted groups, adds a dimension to concepts of autonomy and independence for language learning which has yet to be fully explored.

## Issues of debate

The various tendencies that have combined to produce more than one version of autonomy have also generated a number of areas for debate within the field. Here, we would like briefly to map out some of these areas and how they are addressed in this book. (Readers will find more detailed chapter summaries in the introductions to each of Parts I–III.)

One of the most important issues, arising from the more political approaches to language education, concerns the theoretical basis for autonomy and independence as concepts within the field. As we have observed, these concepts have roots in more than one discourse. In the late 1970s they were propelled by political concerns about the organization of educational systems, but in the 1980s psychological issues appear to have become dominant. In the mid-1990s, growing recognition that language education is a political process at both policy and content levels appears once again to be lending a political coloration to autonomy and independence. One of the key issues that is emerging in the field is how to reconcile psychological and political (and individual and social) perspectives in these concepts. These issues are addressed in several chapters (see especially, Chapters 2, 3, 7, 9, 11 and 12).

A closely related issue is the cultural specificity of autonomy and independence. Since Riley (1988a) first asked whether autonomy was not a peculiarly western concept, the question of whether the promotion of autonomy and independence in non-western settings is culturally intrusive or not has been on the agenda. This question is part of a broader set of issues concerned with the export of 'modern' teaching technologies from 'west' to 'east'. Recently, the British Council in Hong Kong has advertised Chinese-language courses for expatriate residents using 'native-speaker teachers and western methods'. The suggestion is that such methods are either intrinsically superior or intrinsically appropriate to 'western learners'. The 'superiority' of western methods and their appropriateness to non-western contexts is questionable, however (Kachru, 1991;

Holliday, 1994). One issue that arises is whether autonomy and independence in language learning embraces the right of learners to opt for methodologies that might be perceived negatively from the western learner-centred perspective. These issues are addressed directly in Chapter 3.

The link between autonomy and independence as broad principles of language education on the one hand and particular methods of implementing them on the other leads into a discussion of the role of self-access and self-instruction. Much of the literature on autonomy and independence in language learning has tended to assume that self-access and self-instruction are natural means for its implementation (Dickinson, 1987; Little, 1989; Sheerin, 1989). Yet there is very little evidence that self-instructional modes of learning are in themselves sufficient to lead to greater autonomy or independence. On the contrary, it appears that learners who are forced into self-instructional modes of learning without adequate support will tend to rely all the more on the directive element in the materials that they use. Doubt has been expressed in recent years about the effectiveness of self-access, and a number of the contributions to this book re-evaluate the relationship between self-access, self-instruction and autonomy in this light (Chapters 4, 5, 6). As in Part I, this theme is also prominent throughout the chapters in Part II, which stress the abiding importance of *teachers* in autonomous language learning, and those in Part III, which emphasize the need for open-ended methods and materials which actively involve learners in the development of their own autonomy.

In regard to the role of the teacher in autonomous language learning, the key issue is whether it is possible to 'teach' learners how to be autonomous without at the same time denying their autonomy. If not, does the teacher have any role to play other than to be a 'resource person' organizing facilities and providing opportunities for learning? If autonomy is identified exclusively with self-instruction, the role of the teacher does indeed seem to be under threat. However, changing roles in autonomous learning are closely bound up with changes in the distribution of power within the learning process. These changes raise problems of identity and adaptation for both teachers and learners, which are addressed in Chapters 5, 7, 8, 9, 10 and 11.

Lastly, there is the issue of autonomy in a changing technological world. New educational technologies are often perceived simultaneously as both a promise and a threat. The new technologies of language learning have tended to latch on to autonomy as one justification for their existence. Computer software for language learning is an example of a technology which claims to promote autonomy simply by offering the possibility of self-study. Such claims are often dubious, however, because of the limited range of options and roles offered to the learner. Nevertheless, technologies of education in the broadest sense (from the textbook to the computer) can be considered to be either more or less supportive of autonomy. The question is what kinds of criteria do we apply in evaluating them? This question is addressed particularly in Chapters 12 to 17, where a number of innovative approaches are described. Attention to the ideologies conveyed by self-instructional materials, and the authenticity and open-endedness of such materials are all emphasized.

## Conclusion

It may be helpful if we conclude this introduction by returning to the 'mainstreaming' of autonomy and independence as a central theme of this book. From time to time, a new concept enters the field of language education as an alternative method or approach, but rapidly grows in significance to the point where it comes fundamentally to condition thinking throughout the field. Such was the case with Communicative Language Teaching (Breen and Candlin, 1980; Legutke and Thomas, 1991), which began life in the late 1960s as an alternative to 'structural' and 'grammar-translation' models of teaching, but rapidly became an axiom of language teaching methodology. The question ceased to be, 'Should we be teaching languages communicatively?', and became, 'How do we teach languages communicatively?'. As part of this paradigm shift, other concepts (authenticity, learner-centredness, negotiation, etc.) began to cluster around a 'communicative' core. The return of structures and grammar was perhaps inevitable, but equally inevitable was the fact that these re-emerged in 'communicative' guises. Behind these changes lay major shifts in the structures of language education on a global scale, of which the most important aspect was the rapid growth of migration and travel with its consequent influence on markets for language education. This new structural framework for language education undermined traditional anglocentric assumptions that the main purpose of learning foreign languages was to broaden the mind, and focused attention on learners who were learning languages because they needed to *use* them in an ever-shrinking world.

A similar pattern of development may well lie ahead for the concepts of autonomy and independence in language learning. The need for learners to become more autonomous is increasingly taken for granted as we begin to turn our attention to how the goal of autonomy can best be achieved. At the same time, autonomy and independence are beginning to act as a focus for other methods and approaches, conditioning their orientations and goals. The changing patterns of language education that support this tendency are essentially a continuation of those which supported the mainstreaming of Communicative Language Teaching: the ever-increasing quantity of language education and the growing importance of media and information technologies. We will do well to consider carefully Gill Sturtridge's picture of the future of language education presented in Chapter 5 of this book, a picture in which language learners are more and more *forced* to rely on their own resources in an increasingly technological world. If this picture becomes a reality, it will become all the more important to reflect upon the meanings of autonomy and independence. In such a situation the question may well be whether learners are to become *personally* and *socially* more autonomous as a result of the *situational* autonomy which external circumstances prescribe for them, or whether they will merely become more dependent on the materials and technologies that support this situational autonomy. In a wider perspective, the technologization of education is also a process in which methods and materials flow from the highly developed economies of the West to the less economically developed, but language-hungry, cultures of the rest of the world. In this context, it becomes important that we reflect also on the links between the personal autonomy of learners as individuals, and the broader issue of cultural autonomy in the world in which they live. Autonomy and independence can no longer be thought of simply as alternative methods or approaches to language teaching. They become conditioning concepts for language education, and the questions become, 'What kind of autonomy do we mean?' and 'How do we go about achieving it?'.

In 1988, Arthur Brookes and Peter Grundy published a milestone collection of papers entitled *Individualisation and Autonomy in Language Learning*, in which they argued that: 'One corollary of learner-centredness is that individualization will assume greater importance, as will the recognition that the autonomy of the learner is our ultimate goal' (p.1). Seven years later, it seems that although the second part of this prediction has been borne out, the close link that was observed between individualization and autonomy is beginning to be broken. This is one aspect of the transition that we are observing. At the same time, as several of the contributions to this collection testify, autonomy and independence are beginning to tie into fields more concerned with the social and political implications of language education: language and culture, critical language pedagogy, language inequalities and rights, world Englishes, and so on. Interestingly, this shift points back to the concern expressed by Brookes and Grundy in their Introduction (based on Riley's opening paper) that individualization and autonomy might be 'ethnocentric' concepts. The attempt to free autonomy and independence from this ethnocentricity is a second aspect of the transition. In a second milestone collection published in 1988, Henri Holec presented a number of reports on autonomous learning projects, in which he observed: 'Among the various kinds of attempt to implement this approach, the most frequent is undoubtedly the establishment of resource centres' (p.10). The third aspect of the transition is a questioning of the efficacy of organizational means towards autonomy (self-access in particular) and an emphasis on the content of learning and relationships between students, teachers and institutions. Self-access resource centres remain an important part of the language education scene, and it is likely they will continue to do so in the future. But proponents of autonomy and independence, it seems, are no longer content simply to promote self-access, they are centrally concerned with how it works and what its influences may be.

Because autonomy and independence are concepts in transition, their future is inevitably uncertain. This book offers a glimpse into that future and shows that there are many involved in this field who are concerned not only to promote autonomy and independence in language learning but also to question and re-evaluate both the concepts and their means of implementation. Our hope, as editors, is that readers will welcome this re-evaluation by joining in the debate.

# PART I

# Philosophy and practice

## Introduction

Two of the most pressing issues for those who argue for autonomy and independence in language learning at the present time
are, first, to define the senses in which these terms are used, and
secondly, to determine how they can be implemented in concrete
educational situations. Neither of these questions avails itself of
easy answers. Monolithic definitions of autonomy and independence have proved elusive, and it is perhaps more productive to
speak of different *versions* of the concepts which correspond to
different perspectives and circumstances. Accepted means of
implementing autonomy and independence through self-access
and self-directed learning have also proved open to question, and
again it may be more productive to think of a range of possibilities for implementation.

The first part of this volume, therefore, deals with questions of
the philosophy and practice of autonomy and independence for
language learning. Chapters 2 and 3 are concerned with the
theoretical grounding of the concepts, while Chapters 4–6 are
concerned with methods of implementation, self-access and self-
instruction. The chapters by Benson and Pennycook with their
analyses of the historical, political and cultural roots of autonomy
contrast with those by Sheerin, Sturtridge and Littlewood, who
emphasize autonomy and independence as a means to the end of
more effective language learning. For Benson and Pennycook a
more overtly political version of autonomy is needed if effectiveness of learning is to be understood in more than narrow technical
terms. By presenting this diversity of viewpoints we hope to bring

into focus the importance of the relationship between the theory and practice of autonomous language learning.

In Chapter 2, Phil Benson identifies three 'versions' of autonomy in language learning (technical, psychological and political) and links them to three approaches to knowledge and learning. He relates the technical version of autonomy, with its emphasis on learning strategies and learner training, to positivism and its paradigm that knowledge reflects an objective reality. The psychological version, with its emphasis on the capacities of the individual is linked to constructivism, where knowledge is seen as subjectively based upon unique personal meaning systems. The political version, with its emphasis on control over both the internal and external contexts of learning, is linked to critical theory, which posits that the construction of knowledge is dependent upon prevailing political and social ideologies. Benson's aim in making these connections is to show the historical development of the concept of learner autonomy and to unravel some of the complexities inherent in it, in order to argue for a 'more explicitly political approach'.

In clarifying what such an approach might mean, Benson argues for the inadequacy of the technical/positivist position and the relative failure of the psychological/constructivist position to question the ideological contexts in which learning takes place. He argues for a learning framework in which learners are encouraged to explore relationships between individual beliefs and actions about language and second language learning and the social contexts in which they occur. He concludes by defining eleven areas of activity in which this kind of exploration can be conducted, while providing the caveat that a version of autonomy in language learning based on critical theory is virtually uncharted territory.

For Alastair Pennycook (Chapter 3), critical awareness is crucial to autonomy in language learning as autonomy is fundamentally about 'authoring one's own world'. Like Benson, he is concerned that the concept of autonomy in language learning has become 'psychologized, technologized and universalized', and he argues forcefully for a version of autonomy that stresses the importance of 'voice' and 'cultural alternatives'. Pennycook first examines the notion of autonomy in philosophy and political science and explains how it is open to criticism as a particular cultural and historical product. He shows how autonomy has become an unquestionable goal in language education, and how the main-streaming of the concept has emptied it of its radical cultural and political content. In the process, autonomy has been attached to the psychological and to 'progressive' concepts such as 'learner-centredness' and 'learning how to learn'. Pennycook warns that there is a danger in this that autonomy will simply become a question of learners focusing on narrowly defined personal needs. Meanwhile, educators become preoccupied with appropriate strategies, materials and technologies while disregarding the broader cultural context in which language learning takes place.

Pennycook also points to the risk that autonomy will be seen as another example of the free and enlightened West bringing emancipation to the backward and authoritarian classrooms of the world. He argues that there is a need for acute awareness of local cultural, political and economic contexts, and that autonomy should be seen not as 'learning how to learn', but as 'learning how to struggle for cultural alternatives'. The language educator's role is to help learners develop their own 'voice' in order to transform their cultural contexts through their understandings of society. Pennycook ends his chapter with examples from colonial and gender contexts of how educators can help learners become 'voiced', illustrating how autonomy in language learning is dependent, in his view, on an awareness of the cultural contexts of language learning.

Self-access resource centres are the most typical means by which institutions have attempted to implement notions of autonomy and independence over the last 20 years to the extent that 'self-access language learning' is now often used as a synonym for 'autonomous language learning'. Chapters 4–6 directly address the relationship between these two notions. The authors of Chapters 4 and 5, Susan Sheerin and Gill Sturtridge, are well known for their work in the field of self-access while William Littlewood will be better known for his work in general language education. For each author there is a concern to emphasize that self-access and autonomous learning are not the same thing. For both Sheerin and Sturtridge, it is the way that we do self-access that determines whether it promotes autonomy or not. For Littlewood, the place that self-access occupies within a student's overall programme of learning is the crucial factor.

Sheerin makes a distinction between 'learner independence', which refers to a set of dispositions and abilities, and 'self-access' which refers to materials and organizational systems. Her argument is that self-access can either inhibit or promote independent learning, according to the way it is organized. In other words, there is no automatic relationship between studying in a self-access centre and the development of independence. Her chapter goes on to analyse some of the factors in self-access which can contribute to positive or negative outcomes. Sheerin argues first, that in order to help learners develop independence, it is important that we are able to help them identify their own entry levels and provide appropriate preparation and support. She then makes an important distinction between 'training', which can cover basic skills needed to work in a self-access mode, and 'development', which involves increasing one's self-awareness as a learner. Learner development she argues, is not something that teachers do to learners. It is something that only learners can do for themselves, although there are ways in which teachers can facilitate the process through materials design and organization and through learner support systems.

Sheerin's discussion of materials design points forward to issues discussed in more detail in Part III of this book. Her central argument is worth emphasizing, however. Self-instructional materials, she argues, can actually be antithetical to learner independence if they do no more than transfer the authority of the teacher to the materials selected by the learners. She suggests that it is important that such materials give feedback in ways that encourage learners to accept a degree of uncertainty. A similar theme is explored in her discussion of access and retrieval systems and the role of teachers and counsellors.

Sturtridge (Chapter 5) begins from the assumption that, for reasons connected with the growing quantity of language learning worldwide and the technologization of learning, self-access and the self-access resource centre are here to stay. She argues forcefully that unless such centres are organized in ways that promote autonomy and independence, they will tend to fail. In other words, promotion of autonomy is not only essential to the survival and success of self-access, it is vital to the future of language education, for which self-access modes of learning are likely to become the norm. Sturtridge isolates six factors that lead to successful self-access: (1) good management with support and involvement of learners, (2) suitable location and facilities, (3) staff training and development, (4) learner training and development, (5) using

the cultural strengths of the learners, and (6) appropriate materials. Pointing forward to the concerns of Part II, Sturtridge discusses how these factors depend upon institutional reassessment
of the roles of teachers and learners. Like Sheerin, she argues that
learning materials can be just as directive as teachers, and that
independent learners need to develop the kinds of skills which
enable them to be aware of different types of materials, to see the
purpose of tasks, to assess the value of tasks, and to make use of
teachers and peers as 'resources'. It is in this sense that learner
independence is seen to be essential to the success of self-access.

In the concluding chapter to this part, William Littlewood offers a perspective on autonomy and self-access based on his recent
involvement with EAP (English for Academic Purposes) courses
that include a substantial self-access component. His concern is to
define what is involved in autonomy for language learning and to
elaborate a model to evaluate how self-access work and classroom
work can combine to contribute to this goal. Littlewood offers an
original interpretation of autonomy in language learning involving the notions of 'autonomy as learner', 'autonomy as communicator' and 'autonomy as a person'. Using an 'integrated' model
of language learning, he proposes that different forms of self-
access work can be located along a continuum on which 'analytic'
and 'experiential' activities ('learning' and 'acquisition') stand at
opposite ends. In his view, self-access work is strongest at the analytic/
learning end of the continuum, and weakest at the experiential/
acquisition end. This is also equivalent to a weakness in regard to
the 'productive' skills. Littlewood's experience does not lead him
to conclude that self-access work can promote autonomy in isolation from classroom work, but he leaves open the question of
whether or not self-access should aim to cover what he sees as the
full continuum of language learning. Some of the weaknesses in
self-access and self-instructional materials identified by Littlewood
are taken up in the chapters that make up Part III, and readers
will be able to judge for themselves whether innovative methods
and new technologies are able to take on the challenge that
Littlewood proposes.

# 2

## The philosophy and politics of learner autonomy

PHIL BENSON

### Introduction

Recent thinking on language teaching methodology has been informed by two notions in regard to learner autonomy: first, that greater autonomy is a legitimate goal of language education, and secondly, that autonomous learning is more or less equivalent to effective learning. There has been relatively little discussion of the meaning of autonomy within the field of language learning theory, however, even though it has been defined in more than one way. In this chapter, I want to suggest that there are, in fact, three major versions of learner autonomy for language learning (technical, psychological and political) which roughly correspond to three major approaches to issues of knowledge and learning in the humanities and social sciences (positivism, constructivism and critical theory).

In the first part of the chapter I want to suggest that by drawing out links between theories of knowledge, approaches to learning and versions of autonomy we may be able to arrive at a better understanding of the ways in which learner autonomy for language learning has developed. This is not a disinterested exercise, however, and in the second part of the chapter, I will attempt to unravel some of the political implications of the apparently 'apolitical' stance taken in technical and psychological versions of autonomy, in order to argue for a more explicitly political approach based on critical theories of knowledge and learning. In the last part of the chapter, I will tentatively outline what a more political concept of autonomy might mean in practice.

# Versions of autonomy

In 'technical' versions of learner autonomy, the concept is defined simply as the act of learning a language outside the framework of an educational institution and without the intervention of a teacher. Autonomy is seen in terms of situations in which learners are obliged to take charge of their own learning (for example, at the end of formal schooling) and the main issue is how to equip learners with the skills and techniques they need to cope with such situations when they arise. 'Psychological' versions define autonomy as a capacity – a construct of attitudes and abilities – which allows learners to take more responsibility for their own learning. The development of autonomy is seen as an internal transformation within the individual that may be supported by situational autonomy without being dependent on it. Lastly, 'political' versions of learner autonomy define the concept in terms of control over the processes and content of learning. The main issue for political approaches is how to achieve the structural conditions that will allow learners to control both their own individual learning and the institutional context within which it takes place.

Although each of these versions of autonomy could easily be supported by example definitions from the literature, to do so would be misleading. It would risk identifying particular versions with particular writers when, in fact, most adopt a position representing a mixture of elements from each of the three. Nevertheless, technical, psychological and political positions can be found within the literature and, as ideal constructs, these 'versions' serve as a useful starting point for investigating relationships between autonomy in language learning and theories of knowledge and learning.

# Learner autonomy and philosophies of learning

The three categories that I will be using – positivism, constructivism and critical theory – do not represent clearly articulated theories of knowledge or philosophies of learning. Nor can they be mapped unproblematically against the three versions of autonomy outlined in the previous section. They are nevertheless useful in characterizing dominant approaches to problems of knowledge and learning within the modern humanities and social sciences. They are equally useful in characterizing implicit approaches within applied linguistics to problems of language and language learning. In this section, I will discuss each of these approaches in turn, first in relation to theories of knowledge and learning, and secondly in relation to language and language learning. The assumption is that ideas about how languages are learned are related to particular conceptions of the kinds of knowledge that language represents, and that these are in turn based on particular conceptions of the constitution of knowledge itself. At the end of the section I will summarize how each of these approaches connects up with the issue of learner autonomy.

Positivism constitutes the dominant approach to issues of knowledge and method in twentieth-century western social sciences, and has similarly dominated the field of applied linguistics virtually from its inception (Raimes, 1983). Positivism is based essentially on the assumption that knowledge is a more or less accurate reflection of objective reality. According to this view, knowledge – whether 'known' or still awaiting discovery – is already given within objective reality. The process of learning, therefore, can take one of two forms depending on the status of the knowledge to be acquired. Learning can consist simply in the transmission of knowledge from one individual to another. In this sense, a positivist view of knowledge is fundamental to the maintenance of traditional teacher–learner relationships in which the learner's mind is seen as a container to be filled with the knowledge held by teachers. On the other hand, positivism also supports the notion that 'new' knowledge is discovered through the 'hypothesis-testing' model that is so widespread in the field of applied linguistics. The positivist research model also underpins models of discovery learning where the knowledge to be acquired is predetermined but withheld from the learners, in the belief that it will be more effectively acquired for the fact that it is 'discovered' rather than 'taught'.

Positivism supports conceptions of language as a direct representation of objective reality. To the extent that this representation is 'accurate', language can be said to express meaning transparently. Positivism also supports descriptive approaches in which language is represented in terms of structures, patterns, words, and so on, and presented to the language learner as a predetermined system or code. Positivist conceptions of language therefore constitute the underlying framework for structural, drill and practice approaches to language teaching methodology. But they can also provide a framework for more communicative or inductive methodologies, if the ultimate objective of learning is seen as the mastery and internalization of a given set of linguistic structures and forms that will subsequently be used in communication.

Constructivism is a term that has been used in the context of adult learning by Candy (1989) to link together approaches in fields such as ethnomethodology, symbolic anthropology and post-structuralist literary theory, in which knowledge is represented as the construction of meaning. In the field of applied linguistics, this approach is probably most strongly associated with Halliday (1979) and others who discuss language acquisition in terms of the construal of experience and construction of meaning. Candy refers to two key elements in constructivist approaches to knowledge and learning: 'discourse about the world is not a reflection of the world, but is a social artefact' and 'knowledge cannot be taught, but must be constructed by the learner' (p.96). In contrast to positivist approaches, constructivism posits a relativist view of knowledge according to which individuals construct their own unique personal meaning systems on the basis of the same objective reality. Learning, therefore, consists in the reorganization and restructuring of experience rather than the gradual internalization or discovery of predetermined knowledge. At one extreme, constructivism could be taken to represent a position where individuals are assumed to be free to think as they wish and act according to their thinking, but in practice it is widely argued that construction of meaning is subject to social constraints.

Constructivism supports conceptions of language as the raw material of meaning. Language does not reflect reality; rather, through devices such as categorization and metaphor, it constitutes the means by which subjective realities are constructed. Consequently, a language cannot be described adequately by reference to its forms and structures unless these are related to the meanings conveyed in specific interactions. Similarly, language learning does not simply consist in the internalization of a given set of structures and forms. In principle, each learner constructs his or her own version of the target language and the process of learning is one in which the language itself is potentially reconstructed. Learners are, in the main, responsible for their own learning in constructivist approaches. Creativity, interaction and engagement with the target language and negotiation of meaning are all emphasized in such approaches.

Critical theory has evolved as a generalized approach within the humanities and social sciences on the basis of work by Marxist and post-Marxist thinkers such as Gramsci, Althusser, Habermas and Foucault. Critical approaches of various kinds are becoming increasingly influential in language studies (Kress and Hodge, 1979; Fairclough, 1992b) and are also beginning to find a place in the field of language teaching methodology (Pennycook, 1990; Benesch, 1993). While critical theory tends to share with constructivism the view that knowledge is constructed rather than acquired, it places a much greater emphasis on the social contexts and constraints within which the process of learning takes place. In contrast to positivism, critical theory argues that knowledge is not a neutral reflection of objective reality, but rather consists of competing ideological versions of that reality expressing the interests of different social groups. In versions of critical theory based on Gramsci's notion of hegemony, positivist 'truths' are seen as expressing particular configurations of ideologies corresponding to relationships of power between the dominant and the dominated at particular moments in time. In contrast to the rationalist hypothesis that 'knowledge is power', critical theorists are inclined to argue that 'power is knowledge'. Critical approaches to education and learning therefore tend to emphasize issues of power and control. The process of learning is conceived in terms of 'criticism' or the uncovering of the fundamental social relationships that underlie the ideological surface of things. Learning is also seen as a process of engagement with social context which entails the possibility of political action and social change.

Critical approaches to language argue that language *is* ideology. In other words, linguistic form is inseparable from the social meanings it expresses and the social interests it supports. Moreover, language plays the particular role of ideologically constituting other kinds of knowledge. In this sense, language is not a neutral means of expressing knowledge constituted elsewhere, language is knowledge and vice versa. Critical approaches to language pedagogy therefore tend to emphasize issues of power and control within language. Learning to use a language also involves learning about the language and its social contexts and how both can be changed. Critical approaches to language learning also problematize the barriers between language learners and target language communities by asserting the rights of learners to exercise control over the languages they learn and the ways they are used.

How do these three approaches to issues of knowledge, language and language learning connect up with the concept of learner autonomy? It will be clear that learner autonomy is not unique to any one of the approaches outlined above. It is not in itself a positivist, constructivist or critical notion. On the contrary, as an essentially political concept imported into applied linguistics, autonomy is a highly flexible notion that is easily adapted to different approaches. We can therefore ask how the concept of autonomy is likely to be constructed within each of these broad approaches.

Positivist approaches to language learning would appear to support what I described at the beginning of this chapter as 'technical' versions of learner autonomy. If language learning consists in the acquisition of predetermined structures and forms, autonomy can be defined simply in terms of the situational conditions under which this acquisition takes place. As positivism strongly supports 'teacher–learner' models of learning, there is a tendency to view the classroom as a natural site for learning. Autonomy tends to be defined as 'learning outside the classroom', a situation that calls for a new set of skills primarily concerned with the management of learning. I have called this version of autonomy 'technical', because of its concern to equip learners with the technical skills they need to manage their own learning beyond the walls of the classroom. Technical versions of autonomy are found particularly in the literature on learner strategies and learner training (see Benson, 1995). Positivism also supports notions of autonomy or independence within the classroom. Dickinson (1992: p.1), for example, defines independence as the degree to which learners involve themselves in making decisions relevant to their learning and argues that this can be promoted within the framework of classroom learning. Such a version of learner independence would be supported by the positivist view that discovery learning is a more effective method of acquiring knowledge that is 'already known' than direct transmission from teacher to learner.

In contrast, constructivist approaches to language learning tend to support 'psychological' versions of autonomy that focus on the learner's behaviour, attitudes and personality. Constructivism is associated with the notion that autonomy is an innate capacity of the individual which may be suppressed or distorted by institutional education (Candy, 1989: p.101) and it tends to support versions of autonomy that are couched in terms of individual responsibility for decisions about what is learnt and how. Constructivist approaches to language learning also tend to value interaction and engagement with the target language. This encourages a positive view of situational autonomy, which is seen not as a problem that learners must cope with, but as an opportunity for more appropriate and authentic learning. Consequently, constructivism tends to support self-directed learning and self-access as a positive means of promoting autonomy (cf. Holec, 1988) and an emphasis on authentic interaction with the target language community (cf. Little, 1991).

Lastly, critical theory encourages versions of learner autonomy that are more social and political in character. Autonomy grows as learners become more critically aware of the social context of their learning and the constraints it implies, the contingency of what is presented to them as the 'target language', and the potential for social change implicit in language learning. It can be argued that a good deal of what goes under the heading of 'critical language pedagogy' aims at a form of autonomy, even if the term is not often used. Outside the field of language learning, however, there has been a tendency to re-evaluate self-directed learning in more critical terms (Hammond and Collins, 1991; Brookfield, 1993). While critical pedagogy has tended to focus on issues of content, this recent literature has begun to look again at issues of control of the learning process from a social point of view (for a more detailed discussion, see Benson, 1996).

In exploring relationships between theories of knowledge, approaches to learning and versions of autonomy, there is an inevitable risk of over-simplification on two counts. First, the divisions between positivism, constructivism, and critical theory are by no means as clear cut as I have implied. Purely positivist approaches are difficult to find, and all theories of knowledge must engage at some level with issues of 'fact' and empirically verifiable 'truth'. Purely subjectivist versions of constructivism are also rare, and to the extent that ideological and sociological constraints are recognized, constructivism tends to merge with critical theory (Candy, 1989: p.101). It is questionable, too, whether we can really posit a unified 'critical theory' from works as diverse as those of Gramsci, Althusser, Habermas and Foucault. Secondly, we need to be wary about relationships among theories of knowledge and philosophies of learning and autonomy. Although a certain view of what knowledge is may imply a corresponding view of how it is acquired, we cannot assume that such correspondences are necessarily consistently applied in the formulation of learning methodologies. The usefulness of the categories, however, lies in the extent to which they may help in unravelling complexities of this kind. In the following section, I will use them to attempt to explain how the different versions of autonomy have arisen and what their political implications are.

## The political implications of learner autonomy

The notion that language teaching methodologies have political implications has gained considerable ground in the field of applied linguistics since Judd (1984) first declared TESOL to be a 'political act'. However, the idea of language teaching as a political project remains closely identified with critical pedagogy. While other approaches may acknowledge the political nature of language and make use of political terminology, they often present the practice of teaching and learning in ways that are far from political. To summarize from the previous section, we are dealing with three basic definitions of autonomy in language learning:

1. autonomy as the act of learning on one's own and the technical ability to do so;
2. autonomy as the internal psychological capacity to self-direct one's own learning;
3. autonomy as control over the content and processes of one's own learning.

In the political field, from which the term has entered applied linguistics, autonomy denotes self-government. Comparing the three definitions above with this usage, it is evident that only the third definition is in any real sense political. In the first and second definitions, the concept has undergone some kind of change. In order to fully understand the political implications of different versions of autonomy, we therefore need to examine the nature of this change in more detail.

The reduction of the political concept of autonomy to a technical version within applied linguistics can be explained by the overwhelming dominance of the positivist paradigm in language teaching practice. Raimes (1983: p.545) has illustrated this dominance in a discussion of the assimilation of communicative methodology by the early 1980s:

> The current emphasis on communication has, I believe, been absorbed neatly into our positivist traditional framework. Far from superseding tradition, it has been assimilated into it. It opens up a variety of classroom procedures, such as interactive drills, while for the most part leaving undisturbed the underlying approach to language and language teaching.

The reduction of the concept of autonomy to a technical level can similarly be seen as an assimilation of the surface features of a radical innovation to a dominant positivist paradigm. We may even go further to suggest that there is a sense in which this paradigm tends towards a systematic depoliticization of concepts of this kind. So dominant are the positivist truths of language teaching methodology – among them the view that language learning is an apolitical activity – that it seems almost impossible to imagine language learning as anything other than what it is now. However, closer examination suggests that prevalent practices are constructed in ways that systematically *divorce* language teaching from politics:

1. As Widdowson (1983: pp.6–7) has pointed out, language education is usually organized so that language teachers are concerned solely with achieving the 'objectives' of a language learning course ('pedagogic intentions of a particular course of study to be achieved within the period of that course'), while the 'aims' of language learning ('the purposes to which learning will be put *after* the end of the course) are the concern of educational management.
2. Textbooks, teaching materials and tasks systematically avoid social and political issues and often occupy an entirely fictional world of conflict-free personal relationships.
3. Language learning very often takes place without any real social engagement with the target language or the target language community: artefacts of the language are cast in the role of learning materials while native or expert speakers are cast in the role of teachers.

Language teaching methodology tends to promote the view that learners want to learn how to use the language but not learn about the language or its social contexts of use. Behaviourist and naturalistic approaches in particular have promoted artificial distinctions between 'knowing what' and 'knowing how' that have encouraged forms of language learning in which learners are actively discouraged from thinking *about* the languages they learn.

In these and other ways, language learning is reduced to a technical activity divorced not only from politics but also from social relationships of any kind. This in turn encourages a view of autonomy in which the social character of language and language learning is subordinated to the technical goal of developing learning skills.

What are the political implications of the view that language learning is an apolitical activity? It is clear that, although the process of language learning can be conducted in an apolitical way, it is almost always embedded in a political context of some kind. Judd (1984: p.265) has listed a number of political and moral issues connected with language teaching. He argues that:

> Those of us who are engaged in the teaching of English to non- or limited-English speakers are, in addition to teaching, also directly or indirectly implementing a stated or implied language policy as well as promoting a form of language change in our students. Because we are engaged in all of these activities simultaneously, we are involved in a political process.

However, we might go further than this and suggest that teachers of EFL (English as a Foreign Language) and ESL (English as a Second Language), in particular, are more often than not engaged in political processes of a distinctive kind. First, the decision to make English (or any other language) available as a language to be taught in educational institutions is always a political decision that implies a rejection of other possibilities. The acceptance of English as a second language very often implies the acceptance of the global economic and political order for which English serves as the 'international language'. Secondly, learning foreign languages (and again English in particular) is more often than not premised upon inequalities between learner and target language communities. Social and economic inequalities (within and between communities) are invariably underlying motivations for language learning in situations of societal multilingualism, migrant education, and in EAP and Business English. Learners' desires to redress inequalities by gaining access to the benefits that membership of the target language community brings is often met by resistance in the form of teaching methodologies that aim to maintain distance and assimilate 'non-native speakers' into subordinate roles (Auerbach, 1986; Benesch, 1993).

The spread of languages is a process that goes on more or less independently of institutionalized language teaching. However, language teaching methodologies constitute the framework within which the spread of languages can be structured and controlled. If we accept the argument that dominant structures of language teaching serve the interests of dominant social groups within target language communities, we can begin to see the depoliticization of language learning in terms of an avoidance of issues that might threaten these interests. The introduction of an explicitly political concept such as autonomy into the field of language learning also threatens vested interests and its reduction to a technical level can therefore be seen as a political act. The assimilation of methodological innovations to a positivist paradigm does not, therefore, simply reflect the dominance of a particular theory of knowledge. We also need to understand the ways in which this theory serves to maintain vested interests embedded within social relationships of inequality. It would be wrong to suggest, however, that proponents of technical versions of autonomy are engaged in an ideological defence of inequalities simply because they work within a positivist framework. Clearly, their intentions in adopting the concept of autonomy are quite the opposite. Their reduction of autonomy to a technical concept is an attempt to make it work within the framework of a practice that is seen to be fundamentally unconcerned with politics. It is for this reason that it is important to emphasize that the apolitical character of language learning is not an 'objective fact' but rather an ideological construction that is contingent upon a particular view of knowledge and learning.

In the case of psychological versions of autonomy, there has been a transfer of the concept of autonomy from a social level to the level of the individual. From the political sense of the self-government of social bodies, there has developed a psychological sense of 'individual self-government' – a sense which implies both freedoms and responsibilities. This sense of the term is by no means unique to applied linguistics, however. Indeed, it can be seen as an aspect of a more general trend towards the individualization and personalization of western public discourse, and towards the politicization of private life. This merging of the private and public in discourse is ultimately to be explained in terms of changes in the nature of labour, material production and the social relationships they entail, which have led to the emergence of new forms of social control. Arguably, we are now more than ever before called upon to act as agents of our own socialization and subordination to prevailing social norms, a process in which concepts such as individual autonomy, or the self-definition of the individual's social role, play an important part.

It can be argued that psychological versions of autonomy avoid the political by reducing social problems to the level of the individual. In one sense they may seem to blame individuals for the social conditions in which they find themselves, and to disempower them by directing attention away from the option of social or collective action. In another sense, however, psychological autonomy can be seen as developing the confidence of the individual, who thereby becomes more able to participate in processes of social change. Similarly, psychological versions of learner autonomy for language learning can be seen as promoting qualities in individual language learners that will be of value in the process of independent language use. In its wider applications, the concept of psychological autonomy is both double-edged and highly ambiguous, primarily because it represents both the growing power of the dominated within western societies *and* the tendency for that power to be controlled through individualistic ideological forms. Learner autonomy represents a recognition of the rights of learners within educational systems. In the context of ELT, it also represents a recognition of the rights of the 'non-native speaker' in relation to the 'native speaker' within the global order of English. The political ambiguity of psychological autonomy, however, can easily obscure the fact that these rights belong to social groups by channelling them into individualistic programmes of self-direction and improvement.

To illustrate the political ambiguity of psychological autonomy, I will quote at length some comments from Willing (1987: p.273), made in the context of the Australian Migrant Education Programme and arguing for a greater emphasis on learning skills in ESL:

> For the past few years it has been generally acknowledged in ESL teaching circles that an increased emphasis on helping learners learn how to learn would be valuable. Every teacher has encountered students who, although intelligent and adequately exposed to apparently useful and meaningful material, nevertheless seem to learn very little. Such instances of non-learning are attributed to a

number of possible causes: the student may be disoriented by the formal learning situation or by Anglo-Saxon cultural assumptions in general; there may be a clash of the student's personality with the teaching approach; the material may be perceived to be irrelevant; the student may be under excessive emotional stress; he may have poor language aptitude; and so on.

Another common way of stating the cause in many of these cases is to say the student uses inadequate or inappropriate learning strategies.

The concept of learning strategy is beginning to be recognized as central to the teaching of ESL in Australia. Given the inevitable limitations on time and resources for teaching specific language content, it is now clear that learners could benefit greatly in the long run if a substantial proportion of the formal learning time available were given over to training students in ways of learning for themselves. Given the opportunities for exposure to English which lie all around them, it would be wise to help learners develop their ability to take advantage of those resources for their own learning purposes.

In terms of the categories elaborated above, Willing's comments can be recognized as containing elements of both the positivist-technical version of autonomy (learners can turn unavoidable situations of autonomy to their advantage by acquiring learning strategies) and the constructivist-psychological versions (external social constraints can be compensated for by the development of internal psychological abilities). Political ambiguity arises in the counter-position of individual strategies for self-improvement to what are in effect social constraints on the process of learning. The question can be posed: what happens if the students *are* subject to widespread ignorance and neglect of their own cultural assumptions, if the teaching approach takes no account of their personalities, if the material really *is* irrelevant and the students *are* genuinely under excessive emotional stress, if they genuinely have poor language aptitude? Is it the primary responsibility of the teachers to help the students find a way around these problems (by helping them acquire individual learning strategies) or should they also join with them to find real *social* solutions to the problems that they face? One interpretation of Willing's argument might be that by helping the students as individuals to develop psychological autonomy teachers are doing what they can to help them into a position where they will be able to tackle such problems on their own. Another interpretation might be that by failing to address political issues that are fundamental to the situation of migrant language learners, teachers become implicated in the reproduction of ideologies of immigration that insist that it is the responsibility of the immigrant to adapt to the host community (primarily through language and culture learning) and never the reverse. I suspect that such an interpretation was very far from the author's intention. Yet it has to be recognized that psychological versions of learner autonomy very often contain such elements of ambiguity that could be resolved by a more explicit political stance.

To draw together the strings of the argument in this section, I have tried to show that although critical theory appears to be alone in proposing an explicitly political programme for language learning, other approaches and other versions of autonomy are far from being free of political implications. This may appear to be an 'if you are not with us, you are against us' type of argument, but I would argue that there is a little more to it than this. Many teachers have turned towards practices such as self-access and learner training out of dissatisfaction with conventional teaching methodologies which are seen as socially oppressive or simply too constraining for effective and appropriate learning to take place. Yet, as they become more deeply involved in these practices, they discover that students are often being encouraged to apply the same conventional methods, materials and techniques to themselves. Such experiences point to the fundamental problem that technical and psychological versions of autonomy tend to encourage students to assimilate themselves to established methodologies and ideologies of learning unless alternative political frameworks are offered. Moreover, this tendency is seen to be supported by positivist and individualist-psychological approaches to learning. It is in this sense that an understanding of relationships between theories of knowledge, philosophies of learning and versions of autonomy can play an important role in determining our own approach as teachers to the issue of autonomy in our own work.

## Elements of a political version of learner autonomy

It will be evident from my argument so far that my own position favours what I would call an explicitly political version of autonomy supported by critical theories of knowledge and learning. I would like to conclude this chapter by considering what exactly such an approach might mean in practice. One objection to political approaches is that in many language learning situations students may neither want nor need to be concerned with political issues. To force these kinds of issues on students who simply want to 'learn a language' may be both ethically questionable and counter-productive. Moreover, certain learning situations are more politically charged than others. For example, while the relevance of a political orientation to English in South Africa might be clear (cf. Peirce, 1989), it is less obvious how a similar orientation would work with, for example, European EFL students enjoying a summer holiday course in a language school on the south coast of England. In order to deal with these objections, I will look at three related questions: first, what is meant by the 'political'; secondly, how political engagement can be achieved at different levels; and lastly, at the importance of autonomy as a means for students to find the level of engagement most appropriate to themselves.

I have argued that language learning as an activity divorced from politics is, in the first instance, an ideological construction. Nevertheless, this depoliticization of language learning is embedded within real practices and tends to appear as an objectively given fact. Depoliticization also has the effect of reducing the realm of the political so that we are accustomed to think of politics in terms of elections, parties, revolutions, and so on while neglecting the political content of everyday life. Similarly, we are inclined to think of the politics of language teaching in terms of language planning and educational policy while neglecting the political content of everyday language and language learning practices. In proposing a political orientation for learner autonomy, therefore, we need a considerably expanded notion of the political which would embrace issues such as the societal context in which learning takes place, roles and relationships in the classroom and outside, kinds of learning tasks, and the content of the language that is learned. To give one example of an activity that would be political in this wider sense without necessarily touching on 'politics' in the more traditional sense of the word, a group of language learners might simply spend time discussing the validity of conventionalized reasons for learning languages and evaluating those reasons in the light of their own personal experiences and goals. Through activities of this kind, learners are encouraged to explore relationships between individual beliefs and actions and the social contexts within which they are framed. They are already taking steps towards a more political approach to their own learning and towards greater autonomy.

Working with an expanded notion of the political, we can conceive of a number of levels of engagement ranging from greater awareness of the social context of one's own learning to direct involvement in social and political change. In a similar way, we can also conceive of a number of areas of activity through which autonomy can be promoted at different points on the scale of political engagement. These would include:

1. authentic interaction with the target language and its users
2. collaborative group work and collective decision making
3. participation in open-ended learning tasks
4. learning about the target language and its social contexts of use
5. exploration of societal and personal learning goals
6. criticism of learning tasks and materials
7. self-production of tasks and materials
8. control over the management of learning
9. control over the content of learning
10. control over resources
11. discussion and criticism of target language norms.

Many of these are already areas of concern in fields such as self-access and learner training and a political orientation towards autonomy can therefore be seen as a question of emphasis within existing practice. For example: Do we favour group work over individual work? Do we engage students in criticism of the tasks they carry out? Do we allow student control over the acquisition and production of self-access resources? At 'lower' levels of political engagement, it will primarily be our approach to issues of this kind that determines how far we succeed in promoting autonomy. The important point is to determine what point on the scale is most appropriate for the particular situation in which learners and teachers find themselves.

Lastly, we need to be aware of the importance of concepts of autonomy and self-direction in fostering awareness of the political character of language learning. As Brookfield (1985: p.10) has argued in the context of adult education, one of the problems of self-direction is that it can easily lead us to become 'trapped in our own history' unless we are helped towards the realization that there are alternative ways of interpreting the world. He argues, therefore, that it is a task of the teacher to encourage 'students to view knowledge and truth as contextual, to see value frameworks as cultural constructs, and to appreciate that they can act on their world individually or collectively and that they can transform it'. It is through such realizations that the road to autonomy (in its political sense) lies, yet it is also the case that it is only through their own experiences that learners can come to this awareness of the contextuality of knowledge: we cannot *teach* learners to reconnect language learning with its social and political context. Autonomy, in the narrow sense of the learners' right to choose levels of engagement appropriate to their own situations, clearly remains important. Yet at the same time we as educators must provide learners with the kinds of structures, input and challenges that will encourage them to move towards autonomy in its broader political sense. In so doing we will always tread a fine line between propagandizing on the one hand and the abandonment of responsibility on the other. It is chiefly for this reason that debate on the concept of autonomy and how to achieve it is so important.

## Conclusion

I began this chapter by outlining correspondences between three versions of autonomy (technical, psychological and political) and three approaches to issues of knowledge and learning (positivism, constructivism and critical theory). I went on to use this framework to suggest that the 'apolitical' stance of technical and psychological versions of autonomy represents a reductive approach to a concept which is at root highly political. I concluded by exploring some of the implications of a more explicitly political approach to autonomy in different social contexts of learning. At this stage it must be emphasized that the conclusions of this chapter are highly tentative. The application of critical theory to education is a recent development, its extension to the field of language learning more recent still. Although exploration of the links between critical language pedagogy and concepts of autonomy and self-direction in learning has barely begun, the potential for connecting two of the more radical educational innovations of the late twentieth century is clear.

# 3

# Cultural alternatives and autonomy

ALASTAIR PENNYCOOK

## Introduction

'The fundamental idea in autonomy', suggests Young (1986: p.19), 'is that of authoring one's own world without being subject to the will of others.' Drawn from philosophical debates concerning the notions of autonomy, liberty and free will, this notion of 'authoring one's own world' seems to have particular significance when related to language learning. How, as language educators, can we help students to become authors of their own worlds? In pursuing this challenging notion, I shall look first of all at the general notion of autonomy in philosophy and political science before discussing some of the limitations of the concept of autonomy as it is commonly understood in language education. My principal concerns are that in moving into the mainstream of applied linguistic thinking, autonomy has become a psychologized, technologized and universalized concept. Following a critical discussion of mainstream autonomy, I shall discuss autonomy in language education from a rather different perspective, emphasizing the importance of looking at language learning in terms of 'voice' and the struggle for 'cultural alternatives'.

## Autonomy in context

One initial observation worth making is that it is not only in language education that the notion of autonomy has become particularly salient but also in a number of other contexts:

> For many years we have been hearing that *autonomy* is important. Immanuel Kant held that autonomy is the foundation of human

dignity and the source of all morality; and contemporary philosophers dissatisfied with utilitarianism are developing a variety of new theories that, they often say, are inspired by Kant. Autonomy has been heralded as an essential aim of education; and feminist philosophers have championed women's rights under the name of autonomy. Oppressive political regimes are opposed on the grounds that they deny individual autonomy; and respect for the autonomy of patients is a recurrent theme in the rapidly expanding literature on medical ethics. Autonomy is a byword for those who oppose conventional and authoritative ethics; and for some existentialists, recognition of individual autonomy is apparently a reason for denying that there are objective moral standards. Both new right theorists and the modern social contract theorists maintain that their theories best affirm autonomy. Finally, and not least in their esteem for autonomy, well known psychologists speak of autonomy as the highest stage of moral development. (Hill, 1991: p.43)

The concept of autonomy is central to western liberal thought. There are two main uses of the term, one referring to group autonomy, particularly in the political context of self-rule, the other referring to the autonomy of the individual. Although it is the second version that is of interest to the discussion here, it is worth noting in passing that Hong Kong, where I taught until recently, is about to become a Special Administrative Region within China, and a crucial question for many Hong Kongers is what such autonomy will entail: will Hong Kong enjoy economic, social, political and cultural autonomy; or only some of these, or perhaps even none of these? These are concerns of group autonomy. In this chapter, however, it is the second, individual version of autonomy that is of primary interest.

The concept of individual autonomy, as Lindley (1986) points out, has been central to European liberal-democratic and liberal-humanist thought. It refers to a form of self-mastery, both mastery over one's self (an internal, psychological mastery) and freedom from mastery exercised over oneself by others (an external, social and political freedom). Thus it is based on a belief in a developed self – a self-conscious, rational being able to make independent decisions – and an emphasis on freedom from external constraints – a sense of liberty bestowed by social and political structures. The question of autonomy has long intrigued western philosophers, and arguments such as Kant's on rationality have been crucial to this view since autonomy in the Kantian tradition is a product of the rational independence of human beings, the ability of humans to rationally apply moral principles to their daily lives. In this view – to which have been added variations such as J.S. Mill's insistence on the importance of individuals' inclinations being genuinely their own – there is an ideal of autonomy in which the purely rational individual makes independent decisions within a purely democratic state.

Such a view, however, has come under severe critical scrutiny from a number of quarters. As Heller and Wellbery (1986: p.10) suggest:

> Much of the intellectual history of the present century can be read in terms of a fundamental tension in the representation of the individual, a dismantling of the classical figure and a simultaneous effort to reconceive it. For structural analysts from various disciplines, the development of autonomous individuality has passed from its initial categorization as the telos of modernity to become the principle ideology of an illegitimate mass culture.

The questioning of the autonomy of the individual has a long history, from Marxist analyses of ideology to Freudian accounts of the subconscious. Political analyses of the individual within the state have suggested that the notion of the freely acting political agent within a democratic state has been one of the great obfuscatory myths of liberal democracy. Looking at how certain states stress the importance of individual freedoms, for example, Meyer (1988: p.212) emphasizes the need for such states to regulate individual autonomy:

> Only in individualist societies is it so important to control what individuals are and how they behave and think. There it is understood that the society's success or failure, its integration or breakdown, is ultimately determined by the competence and conformity of the individual. As a result much of the effort of modern society goes into constructing appropriate individuals.

In a different vein, but still opposing the view of the rational political subject, Castoriadis (1991: p.164) argues that autonomy cannot be conceived as the following of laws discovered by reason but rather must be a more fluid, boundless activity, since autonomy is

> the unlimited self-questioning about the law and its foundations as well as the capacity, in light of this interrogation, *to make, to do* and *to institute* (therefore also, *to say*). Autonomy is the reflective activity

of a reason creating itself in an endless movement, both as individual and social reason.

Other critiques have suggested that rather than being categories that already exist in nature, the very notions of 'man' or the 'individual' are in fact products of the discourses of modernity (see Foucault, 1970). Post-structuralist critiques of liberal humanism have suggested that far from being autonomous actors, subjectivities are in fact *produced* by discourses. That is to say, rather than being autonomous, rational beings who choose freely how we wish to behave and think, we are all *subjects* of discourses in which we take up subject positions. Whether from a Marxist view of the ideological regulation of classes, a psychoanalytical understanding of the role of the subconscious, or a post-structuralist version of subjectivity as discursively produced, the notion of the free-willed, rational and autonomous individual has become highly suspect.

Beyond these general critiques of the notion of the autonomous individual, more specific work has looked at the notion of the individual as both a culture-specific and a gender-specific construction. Clearly, if the autonomous individual, making rational decisions on his or her own is a construction of western cultures, this notion may have limited applicability to other cultural contexts. I shall return to this point later since it is crucial to the applied linguistic project of autonomy in language learning. An interesting critique of the gendered nature of the notion of autonomy has come from Gilligan (1988). Criticizing the way psychological theories have constructed the notion of autonomy as a criterion for full psychological development, Gilligan suggests that this view ignores alternative, more communitarian approaches to psychological development:

> The values of justice and autonomy, presupposed in current theories of human growth and incorporated into definitions of morality and of the self, imply a view of the individual as separate and of relationships as either hierarchical or contractual, bound by the alternatives of constraint and co-operation. In contrast, the values of care and connection, salient in women's thinking, imply a view of the self and the other as interdependent and of relationships as networks created and sustained by attention and response.

To summarize, the view of the autonomous individual constructed by liberal humanism is a very particular cultural and historical product, emerging from the western model of enlightenment and modernity. Such a notion of the rational individual is open to criticism from a number of quarters. Important questions have been raised about how notions such as the 'individual' or 'rationality' are not so much pre-given, natural categories as they are products of the discourses of European modernity. Other critiques have suggested that as both political and psychological beings, we have far less control over what we do or say than is suggested in the model of the rationally autonomous being. Furthermore, this version of rational autonomy reflects the cultural and gendered origins of its development. Lest this critique seems to leave us only with a version of individuals as passive subjects of social, cultural, psychological and ideological forces, however, I want to argue, by contrast, that such limitations make it all the more imperative to try to understand how forms of autonomy may be sought out. Autonomy in this sense, then, is not something achieved by the handing over of power or by rational reflection; rather, it is the struggle to become the author of one's own world, to be able to create one's own meanings, to pursue cultural alternatives amid the cultural politics of everyday life.

## Mainstream autonomy

It is not an easy task to write critically about learner autonomy in language learning, principally because autonomy seems such an unquestionably desirable goal. Surely the idea of giving students help in becoming more independent language learners is not one that any right-minded liberal-thinking language educator would want to oppose, linked as these ideas are to concepts of democracy in the classroom, learner-centred pedagogy and independence. But it is this very unquestionability that I want to start to question, for once ideas start to become unquestionable givens – whether these ideas are critical or conservative – we need to become more wary than usual. My first concern, then, is that autonomy has moved into one of those areas of ELT theory and practice that seem to claim a moral high ground. Like other common terms such as 'communicative competence', 'authentic materials', or 'student-centred education', it has rapidly achieved a moral status backed by dominant beliefs in liberal, progressive education. By questioning any of these concepts, we apparently betray ourselves as old-fashioned teacher pedagogues interested only in teacher-centred, authoritarian teaching in which students have little or no chance to use the language, where inauthentic language use is the norm, and where the main goal is to hold on to educational power for as long as possible. I would like to suggest, then, that as autonomy attaches itself to the list of 'progressive' forms of education, we should usefully pause to ask ourselves quite how such dichotomies have been constructed and what ends they serve.

Alongside this problem, there are several other concerns I wish to address here that relate to this process of autonomy becoming a mainstream concept. That this is now the case can be seen by the burgeoning number of articles, books and conferences on the topic (including this book). Speaking of self-directed learning in North American adult education, Brookfield (1993) suggests that it 'is now comfortably ensconced in the citadel, firmly part of the conceptual and practical mainstream' (p.227). With respect to language education, Little (1991) points out that autonomy is fast becoming one of the new buzz-words of ELT, the 'communicative' and 'authentic' of the 1990s. Such mainstreaming of the notion of autonomy presents a number of concerns: first, its reduction from a more radical social and political concept which questions the nature of schooling to become an issue principally of individual development, learner strategies or 'self-access'; secondly, its attachment to other mainstream concepts, particularly learner- or student-centred education, which tends once again to emphasize the liberal-humanist and individualist elements of current language education orientations and to give the notion of autonomy in language learning an underlying normative basis; and thirdly, its position in the globalizing discourses of applied linguistics, which tend to suggest that autonomy is a universally 'good thing' for everyone, irrespective of the social and cultural context in which it is applied.

Turning to the first concern, it is clear that in some ways the concept of autonomy has a fairly radical potential. Little (1991), for example, relates its development to Illich's (1971) book *Deschooling Society*, which argues for informal education outside the institutionalized and conservative frames of formal education systems. For Illich, autonomy in education is liberatory not merely in the sense of self-development but more importantly in the sense of a questioning of the nature of education and a search for alternative forms of knowledge and action. But this more radical concept of autonomy is one from which many language educators shy away. Allwright (1988: p.35), for example, suggests that autonomy is a term 'typically associated with a radical restructuring of our whole conception of language pedagogy, a restructuring that involves the rejection of the traditional classroom and the introduction of wholly new ways of working', and goes in search of forms of autonomy that already exist in traditional classrooms. Little (1991: p.11) too shifts his argument from 'education as an inescapably political process' to the psychological, suggesting that the barriers erected by education, which 'are potentially tools of oppression and manipulation', are nevertheless 'erected in the first instance not by political but by psychological factors'. Thus, even in a text which goes a long way towards trying to maintain a sense of the political within the notion of autonomy in language learning, Little mirrors the broader trend in applied linguistics to shift from the wider social, cultural and political concerns of language education and to focus instead on the psychology of the language learner in cognitive isolation.

The idea of autonomy has therefore moved rapidly from a more marginal and politically engaged concept to one in which questions are less and less commonly asked about the larger social or educational aims of autonomy. Broader political concerns about autonomy are increasingly replaced by concerns about how to develop strategies for learner autonomy. The political has become the psychological. Wenden (1991: p.15), for example, discusses autonomy in these terms:

> In effect, 'successful' or 'expert' or 'intelligent' learners have learned how to learn. They have acquired the learning strategies, the knowledge about learning, and the attitudes that enable them to use these skills and knowledge confidently, flexibly, appropriately and independently of a teacher. Therefore, they are autonomous.

Autonomy in language learning has become increasingly concerned with techniques, strategies and materials. Summarizing criticisms of self-directed learning in adult education, Brookfield (1993: p.28) refers to the 'tendency of humanistic adult educators to collapse all political questions into a narrowly reductionist technical rationality'. In the field of language learning, one of the most common areas where this depoliticizing and technologizing of the notion of autonomy can be seen is in the equation too easily drawn between autonomy, 'self-access' and 'centres' or 'laboratories' of various kinds. In such facilities, autonomy is too often reduced to choices about which video to watch or which tape to listen to.

The second, and closely related, aspect of the mainstreaming of autonomy is its definition according to the dominant concept of student-centred education. This move from a more social to a more individual definition clearly parallels the move from the political to the psychological. A central problem here is that so-called student- or learner-centred education has become firmly tied to a very particular version of 'progressive' education whose origins lie in the romantic individualism of the late eighteenth century and especially in the educational ideals expounded by Rousseau (see Skilbeck, 1976). This view of the natural development of the child – the young child, like the 'noble savage', being in a pure and innocent state uncorrupted by the constraints of society – has come to dominate a great deal of current educational thought, from romantic individualism to Piagetian developmental psychology. While usefully rejecting the traditional, classical humanist version of education, with its emphasis on the teaching of a fixed canon of knowledge, this learner-centred version of education, by laying claim to being 'progressive' and at the same time focusing centrally on the psychological development of the individual, unfortunately allows no place for a more politically orientated version of education. Thus, recent work on second language curricula (see Clarke, 1987; Nunan, 1988; White, 1988) has dismissed on the one hand forms of education that aim to teach a fixed body of knowledge, but on the other hand also forms of education that have broader transformative goals. Meanwhile, by trumpeting itself as 'progressive', this line of thinking has come to claim that a version of student-centred, individualistic education is the only path to progress.

The problem here, then, is the way in which concern for our students, and thus the notion of student autonomy, has now become firmly ensconced within this liberal-individualist ideology of learner-centredness. If student-centred education is understood as a pedagogy that takes into account students' lives, desires, wishes, cultures, experiences, backgrounds and so on, it may form a very important part of a broader pedagogical initiative, but it is the fervent belief in the tenets of progressivist ideology, which bifurcates the individual and society, that leads to a diminishment of the potential of the concept of student-centred pedagogy and of autonomy. Hammond and Collins (1991: p.15) warn that what they term 'laissez-faire self-directed learning' can be a 'potentially individualistic, even elitist educational approach'. They go on to suggest:

> In many cases, self-directed learners pursue narrowly defined personal learning needs, taking no account of broader social issues or the roles of educators and learners as either change agents or perpetuators of the status quo in their society.

It is this narrowing of the possibilities of a more socially and politically orientated version of autonomy that the individualistic orientation of student-centred education has now brought about.

The close connection between the notion of autonomy and student-centred education also leads to a normative basis for the notion of autonomy in language learning. Since the notion of progressive, student-centred education relies on a dichotomy between student-centred and teacher-centred education, there is frequently an assumption that 'teacher-centred' education is inherently bad and student independence from the teacher inherently good. Leaving aside the rather important question of whether so-called 'teacher-centred' education is necessarily such a bad thing, there is a problem in the way that autonomy is framed in terms of observable acts of independence from teacher direction. I emphasize 'observable' because there does not seem to be much space for a consideration of student independence in terms of how they take up, resist or ignore what a teacher is doing. Is there a space in the concept of learner autonomy for silent, unobserved resistance? I emphasize 'independence from teacher direction' because there does not seem to be much space for the possibility of a student who independently chooses to come to a teacher to learn and would prefer that teacher to teach in a 'teacherly' way. My concern is that such a move on the part of a student might not be considered 'autonomous' if autonomy is only understood in terms of independence from teacher direction.

My third concern is that the universalizing discourses of applied linguistics have not only given sanction to the notion of student autonomy but have also now taken it up as a universal need for all students. One immediate danger here is that the promotion of learner autonomy around the world may become yet another version of the free, enlightened, liberal West bringing one more form of supposed emancipation to the unenlightened, traditional, backward and authoritarian classrooms of the world. Masemann

(1986, p.18) discusses how the evolutionary model of development that permeates much educational thinking replicates the traditional/modern dichotomy with its simple assumptions that education passes from 'rote' to 'structural' to 'open'. Within this context, the promotion of another version of 'openness' – after humanist and communicative language learning, there is now an even more libertarian and democratic educational approach: autonomous language learning – needs to proceed with far more humility, sensitivity and caution than is often the case when the supposedly new and best ideas that flow from the applied linguistic centres are vigorously marketed around the world.

The universalizing discourses of applied linguistics also tend to promote ideas regardless of local contexts. Psychologized and individualized, learner autonomy becomes something that can be established independent of cultural, political, social or economic constraints. Clearly, as I suggested earlier, the notions of student-centred education, individualism and autonomy derive from a very particular cultural context. These concepts will be structured and valued differently in other cultural contexts. As Riley (1988a) argues, there are serious concerns that the principles and practices of autonomous or self-directed learning may be ethnocentric. While the work that Riley uses to support his argument – such as Hofstede's (1983) global model of cultural differences in educational orientations – operate with rather simplistic dichotomies (individualism versus collectivism, for example) and run the risk of being over-deterministic, his point is nevertheless well made that the ways in which autonomy is theorized and practised may be very much based on an ethnocentric western view of education. This is not to say that autonomy as a concept or an educational goal does not exist elsewhere, but rather that a notion of autonomy will be very different in different educational contexts. To encourage 'learner autonomy' universally, without first becoming acutely aware of the social, cultural and political context in which one is working, may lead at best to inappropriate pedagogies and at worst to cultural impositions.

## Voice and autonomy

Having expressed these doubts about the notion of autonomy in language learning, I now want to return to the question of how we might be able to help our students become authors of their own worlds, of how a notion of autonomy may nevertheless be usefully taken up. The concerns I have expressed above relate particularly to the way I see learner autonomy developing within current theories and practices of language teaching, a notion based very much on developing strategies, techniques or materials (indeed vast and expensive 'self-access centres') in order to promote individual self-development. As my criticisms above have probably made clear, the version of autonomy that interests me is one that relates far more clearly to the social, cultural and political contexts of education. To become the author of one's world, to become an autonomous language learner and user, is not so much a question of learning how to learn as it is a question of learning how to struggle for cultural alternatives.

When similar questions emerge in educational contexts, it is common to take them up in terms of 'empowerment'. Indeed, Hammond and Collins' (1991: p.14) version of 'critical self-directed learning' operates with the understanding that while the immediate goal of critical self-directed learning is 'to help learners take greater control of their learning', the ultimate goal is to 'empower learners to use their learning to improve the conditions under which they and those around them live and work'. Yet there are a number of problems with the notion of empowerment as it is commonly used, a brief discussion of which can help highlight the argument I want to make here. First, of course, empowerment has suffered the same fate as autonomy by moving from its more radical origins to a more mainstream concept, even becoming linked these days to the same discourses of liberal individualism that inform student-centred pedagogy. But it is to two other aspects of the notion of empowerment, particularly when applied to language learning, that I want to draw attention. Ruiz (1991) points to these problems when he argues that empowerment is frequently used in a transitive sense as if it is something done to students, and that 'language' is frequently used when the term 'voice' would be far more appropriate.

This first problem was addressed long ago by Paulo Freire (1970: p.53) when he argued that 'not even the best-intentioned leadership can bestow independence as a gift'. That is to say, if our goal is to bestow a degree of autonomy on our students, we cannot do so by trying to hand it over as if we as teachers hold power in our hands and can simply turn it over to students. Too often, versions of autonomy that start to deal with questions of power still do so from a position that understands power simply in terms of control. Thus, to develop student autonomy in language learning is merely a matter of handing over the reins, of giving students greater control over the curriculum, of giving them greater control over or access to resources, of letting them negotiate what, when and how they want to learn. Of course, such concessions may be very valuable moves but they still seem to operate on the one hand with a version of autonomy that does not encourage students to question the status quo and on the other with a reductive version of power as something that can simply be handed over. As Freire (1970) suggests, a critical pedagogy that aims to emancipate students must aim to help students to develop the tools to engage in the struggle themselves. According to Ruiz (1991: p.223): 'The radical educator who treats empowerment as a gift is not yet radical.' We need, therefore, to incorporate an idea of struggle into any notion of empowerment, and to have ways of thinking about both the limitations and the possibilities that confront students.

Earlier in this chapter, I pointed to the inadequacy of the liberal-democratic and liberal-humanist versions of choice and autonomy, and suggested that it can never be possible to achieve more than partial cultural or ideological autonomy. We can never step completely outside the cultural and ideological worlds around us. But we can learn to question, to become aware of those worlds, to search out other possibilities and to pursue cultural alternatives. Thus, a critical version of autonomy must have not merely a language of critique but also a vision of possibility and alternatives. In trying to pursue a form of education that both acknowledges the cultural and ideological frames that limit our lives and avoids the pessimism of deterministic positions on education as social and cultural reproduction, Roger Simon (1987: p.372) has developed the idea of a 'pedagogy of possibility'. He proposes that 'as educators both our current problem and our future project should be an educational practice whose fundamental purpose is to expand what it is to be human and contribute to the establishment of a just and compassionate community within which a project of possibility becomes the guiding principle of social order'. Such an educational project, he argues must be 'rooted in a view of human freedom as the *understanding of necessity and the transformation of necessity*' (p.375). A lot of work in critical pedagogy tends to talk rather grandiosely in terms of 'social transformation' as if our teaching could and should aim to dramatically transform the social structure. What Simon is getting at here is the importance of aiming primarily not at the transformation of society in the first instance but the transformation of the cultural, of how society is understood. A pedagogy of possibility, he suggests, must pay attention to 'the "social imaginary", the way of naming, ordering and representing social and physical reality whose effects simultaneously enable and constrain a set of options for practical action in the world' (Simon, 1992: p.37).

Like Simon, I am interested in the cultural domain as a site of pedagogical intervention. By 'culture' here I do not of course mean culture in the sense of artistic endeavour, or 'high' and 'low' culture, or culture as defined according only to national or ethnic boundaries. Rather, this is culture in the broader sense of how we make sense of our lives. In my view, too, culture is not some secondary domain, some superstructural response to the socio-economic infrastructure, or certain beliefs and behaviours that take second place to the realities of social life. Rather, culture determines how social reality is understood; it is a site of primary importance. This is not to deny the importance of a material world, of social or economic relations, but to emphasize that these have no meaning outside their cultural interpretations. What I want to pursue here, then, is the notion of a *pedagogy of cultural alternatives*, an educational project that seeks to open up alternative ways of thinking and being in the world. It is in the development of such alternatives that a useful notion of autonomy (or perhaps heteronomy) can be understood.

Refocusing attention more clearly on the question of auto-nomy in language learning, I want to suggest that it is important, as Ruiz (1991) points out, to consider ourselves to be concerned with *voice* rather than language. Versions of autonomy in language learning that operate with a reductive notion of power as some-thing a teacher can hand over to students and a reductive sense of language learning as the acquisition of a system miss an important site of pedagogical intervention. My understanding of language and language learning suggests that language cannot be isolated from the particular contexts in which it is used. I have elsewhere (Pennycook, 1994) referred to this as the 'worldliness' of English, arguing that English needs to be understood not only in terms of its global position but also in terms of the specific social, cultural, economic and political contexts of use. Thus, in the particular contexts in which we teach, the notion of being an autonomous language learner cannot be considered merely within the psychological and individualistic frame of 'language acquisition' but must start to pose questions about what it means to be an autonomous user of language. Such a notion is centrally concerned with voice, with how a language user can come to express cultural alternatives, with becoming the author of one's own world.

The notion of voice is intended to suggest that language use and language learning are about finding means of articulation and that this is inevitably a struggle amid the cultural politics of language. Voice here is not being used to refer simply to non-silence, a mouthing of words, or a mastery of lexis, pronunciation or syntax; neither is it being used to describe an individual phenomenon in isolation, a question of merely using language, or enunciating a 'true self' or a cultural essence (cf. hooks, 1988). Rather, I am using voice here to refer to a contested space of language use as social practice, as language users struggle to negotiate meanings between subjectivities, language and discourse. This, then, is a notion of 'voice' that emphasizes the political nature of the subject and searches for ways in which students can come to voice that are not so much celebrations of individual narration as they are critical explorations of how we are speaking subjects. The notion of voice, therefore, suggests a pedagogy that starts with the concerns of the students, not along the lines of 'humanist' or 'student-centred' concerns with the 'inner feelings' of students, as if this were a sufficient end-product in itself, but rather through an exploration of students' histories and cultural locations, of the limitations and possibilities presented by languages and discourses. For Giroux (1988: p.199), voice refers to 'the means at our disposal – the discourses available to use – to make ourselves understood and listened to and to define ourselves as active participants in the world'. As Walsh (1991) suggests, voice can be understood as the place where the past, collective memories, experiences, subjectivities and meanings intersect. It is a site of struggle where the subjectivity of the language user confronts the conditions of possibility formulated between language and discourse. The notion of voice, therefore, is not one that implies *any* language use, such as the often empty babble of the communicative language class, but rather must be tied to an understanding that to use language is not so much a question of mastering a system as it is a question of struggling to find means of articulation amid the cultures, discourses and ideologies within which we live our lives. Within a pedagogy of cultural alternatives, then, the voices that we are seeking to help students to find and create are *insurgent* voices, voices that speak in opposition to the local and global discourses that limit and produce the possibilities that frame their lives.

Let me try to pull the different strands of this argument together. I have been arguing for a more socially, culturally and politically engaged version of language education than that commonly assumed by what I see as the mainstream version of learner autonomy. I have been suggesting that the question of what it means to be an autonomous language user is more important than dealing with autonomy only in terms of helping students to take charge of their own learning. If as language educators we start to see our goal in terms of helping students to find a voice, and if we understand the notion of voice as I have described it above as a site of struggle between language, subjectivity and discourse, then the goal of autonomy in language learning becomes one of helping students in a struggle towards alternative cultural definitions of their lives. In this view, language is no longer taken as a given, a code that students need to learn, but rather as a major aspect of the cultural domain in which our lives are constructed and reconstructed. Thus, while accepting the partiality of all autonomies, our goal as language educators becomes an attempt to teach language in a way that opens up cultural alternatives for our students, that allows them to become authors of at least part of their worlds.

## Teaching culturally alternative Englishes

A version of autonomy that focuses on the cultural contexts of language use will emphasize voice as a struggle towards partial cultural autonomy rather than the psychological processes of learning or techniques to promote independence. If we focus only on the learner as individual and on language as a code to be acquired, we may as teachers be avoiding the responsibility we owe our students to help them to become voiced language users. Unlike the more universalized concept of learner autonomy, which as a psychologized and individualized concept is assumed to have global applicability, the version of autonomy that I am putting forward can only be understood in terms of the specific context of the language user. In this final section, therefore, I shall endeavour to clarify my argument by discussing how I understand language learner autonomy in specific contexts.

Earlier in this chapter I suggested that a key aspect of the liberal-humanist idea of autonomy was the idea of self-mastery. The possibility of such mastery seems highly questionable, however, from a point of view that questions the versions of the Human and the Rational that were developed during the age of European Self-importance ('Enlightenment'). A similarly problematic notion of mastery is often used in language education, suggesting that the ultimate goal of language learning is to 'master' the language. Searle (1983: p.68) raises concerns about this notion of mastery, arguing that 'when we talk of "mastery" of the Standard English, we must be conscious of the terrible irony of the word, that the English language itself was the language of the master, the carrier of his arrogance and brutality.' English, Searle suggests,

> has been a monumental force and institution of oppression and rabid exploitation throughout 400 years of imperialist history. . . . It was made to scorn the languages it sought to replace, and told the colonized peoples that mimicry of its primacy among languages was a necessary badge of their social mobility as well as their continued humiliation and subjection.

The challenge for us as teachers, Searle argues, is 'to grasp that same language and give it a new content, to de-colonize its words, to de-mystify its meaning, . . . to rip out its class assumptions, its racism and appalling degradation of women, to make it truly *common*, to recreate it as a weapon for the freedom and understanding of our people'. Searle is not altogether clear on where such 'class assumptions, . . . racism and appalling degradation of women' lie in relationship to English: are they somehow part of the language itself or are they outside the language? The arguments I have made above, however, suggest that it is not predominantly in the language system per se that relations of class, race and gender can be found but rather in the relationship between English and its contexts of use, between English and the cultures and discourses it is used to express. Developing a voice in English, therefore, needs to be seen as a struggle for cultural alternatives.

In Hong Kong, for example, where I taught from 1992 to 1995, a central concern for me became how the discourses and cultures of colonialism silenced our students. This was nicely articulated by a first year Arts faculty student, who argued in an essay that,

> the compulsory learning of English in schools is one of the British government's political strategies. . . . By enforcing the compulsory education, more people in Hong Kong are ready to accept the British culture, customs and of course, the government policy. And if the majority of the English speakers in Hong Kong regard the language as superior to Chinese, it is reasonable or rational for them to support the government policy. In other words, the teaching of English is a kind of cultural intrusion in Hong Kong and may be regarded as a political weapon. (Ma Wai Yin, Hong Kong University, 1993)

It is, I believe, the colonial context of English that presents the greatest obstacle to students' finding a voice in English in Hong Kong. While on the one hand it is clearly the language of social and economic prestige, the gatekeeper to tertiary education, it is also the language of a colonial government, the language in which 150 years of colonial exclusivism have been articulated.

The effects of English as a colonial language have been noted in many other contexts. Discussing American colonization of Puerto Rico, for example, Walsh (1991: p.5) argues that,

> it is partially through the battle for voice that the war of colonization is waged; it is through language imposition and practices in schools that colonization is, in part, effectuated . . . Through the social and linguistic policies of English imposition, deculturation, and the implantation of American values, schools have attempted to refashion the voices of the Puerto Rican masses, debilitating their history and national identity and promoting a dependence on and an alliance with imperialist rule.

As Walsh suggests, it is not merely a question of two languages in competition with each other 'but the taking over of both the public and personal functions of language, that is, the means of communication and the consciousness behind this communication, including self-concepts, identities, and voices' (p.43). This should not be seen in terms of some simple cultural imposition (a view that is often more insulting to the colonized than to the colonizers) but rather a closing down of the choices available. According to Clignet (1978), 'the colonized is deprived of the choices that he should have in terms of his relation to his past and his present, to himself, to his peers, and to the outside world' (p.128).

As Searle (1983) suggests, however, as teachers our struggle is to decolonize the language, to change its class, race and gendered assumptions. While the discourses and cultures associated with English may close down the possibilities of our students to articulate the world differently, it is also possible to struggle against this. As Walsh (1991) observes, 'While colonialism has exercised the power of language to suppress cultural (and national) unity, language, as a dynamic and dialectic force, has also stimulated antagonism and opposition' (p.4). The struggle for a voice in English can indeed be fought but it must be acknowledged as a struggle, an attempt to create new spaces in an insurgent, post-colonial English.

A similar argument applies to discourse of gender. An important site of struggle for women's equality is not only for socially and politically determined rights but also for different cultural definitions of women and men. Women need to redefine not only the social, political and legal definitions of their lives but also the *cultural* definitions of who they are (matched by a concomitant need for men to redefine the cultural definitions of masculinity). Women have had to struggle against what Coser (1991: p.135) calls their 'cultural mandate':

> the cultural mandate for women to be committed to the family first has not changed much in its manifestations – from watching mother in the kitchen to being excluded from boys' games to being told that mathematics is not for girls and that girls must stay close to home.

For women to achieve some sense of autonomy, therefore, the significant struggle is not only for equal pay, access to jobs, day care, and so on, but also for a form of cultural autonomy, a freedom from 'women's cultural mandate'. Equality and autonomy for women is a struggle amid the cultural politics of gender to find cultural alternatives for how our lives can be lived. A pedagogy of cultural alternatives in English would need to address not only issues of colonialism and gender but a broad range of cultural representations of Third World people, lesbians and gays, people with disabilities, working-class people, and many other groups. Indeed, it must be concerned with how any of us come to be represented, and how those representations can be changed.

As a language educator, therefore, my attempts to help my students to achieve more autonomy, to find a voice in English, involves an understanding that they confront a range of cultural constructions as they learn English. I hope to help my students to find cultural alternatives, to find meanings in English that run against the class, gender, race and cultural assumptions linked to different contexts of language use. Promoting autonomy in language learning, therefore, needs to take into account the cultural contexts of the language learners, to open up spaces for those learners to deal differently with the world, to become authors of their own worlds. If language educators take up the notion of autonomy in language learning merely in terms of developing strategies for self-directed learning, or, in its most reductionist version, sending students to a self-access centre to study on their own, they may be denying their responsibilities as language educators to help students to find the cultural alternatives they deserve.

# 4

# An exploration of the relationship between self-access and independent learning

SUSAN SHEERIN

## Introduction

The presence of self-access facilities does not necessarily ensure that independent learning is taking place. The term 'self-access' refers to learning materials and organizational *systems* (designed for direct access by users), whereas the term 'independent learning' refers to an educational *philosophy* and *process*. It is the way teachers and learners *use* self-access facilities which determines whether independent learning takes place, or – in the words of Riley *et al.* (1989: p.38) – 'who does what to whom and who takes the decisions'. This chapter seeks to explore the nature of learner independence and to examine ways in which teachers (or advisers) and self-access facilities can promote or inhibit its development.

## Reasons for the provision of self-access

Brookes and Grundy (1988: p.2) talk of the 'Janus-like nature' of individualized instruction programmes in that they have, on the one hand, high face validity for teachers and learners , and yet, on the other hand, implications for changing roles which are often not so acceptable. The face validity comes from the fact that individualization represents a *pragmatic* solution to the problem of diversity of need, but the changing roles for teachers and learners that this solution entails calls for an *ideological* change in the way the education process is viewed. This is also true of self-access in that, on a practical level, teachers and learners alike can instantly appreciate the potential usefulness of good self-access facilities, but the fact that traditional modes of learning and teaching may need to be modified is less apparent.

Broadly speaking, proponents of self-access put forward two main reasons for their advocacy. These reasons reflect the two 'faces' of self-access described above: the pragmatic – individualization; and the ideological – promotion of learner independence.

## Individualization

One of the main reasons for setting up self-access facilities is to cater for learners' individual needs. Individual learners have particular weaknesses which they may wish to work on alone or in small groups with similar needs. Learners differ in their learning styles and preferences in terms of types of activity, and they may have particular language requirements arising from their occupation or from their studies. There may also be time constraints or other factors which prevent learners from attending regular classes.

These reasons, which concern the varying needs of individuals, are pragmatic and practical in nature. They are reasons which are easily understood by, and have high face-validity for, learners, teachers and finance providers. Moreover, it is clear that good self-access facilities create the opportunity for highly effective individualization of learning. However, as Trim (1977) pointed out, it is possible to pursue individualization in a thoroughly authoritarian framework. In terms of self-access this means that it is possible to have a marvellously well-stocked self-access centre and for student activity to be totally directed within that centre. In this situation self-access materials are being used as an extension of teaching, as a teaching aid, in fact, on a par perhaps with the language laboratory. The question we need to ask is whether effective individualization of learning is sufficient pay-off and justification for self-access.

## *Promotion of independent learning*

The other reason for providing self-access facilities is the promotion of independent learning, which involves learners taking responsibility for their own learning and developing effective learning strategies; in other words, learning how to learn.

The reasons for the desirability of promoting independent learning are less transparent to those outside (and some within!) the language-teaching profession. They are philosophical and psychological in nature. They arise from a general belief among educators – and not just language educators – that learning is more effective when learners are active in the learning process, assuming responsibility for their learning and participating in the decisions which affect it. Knowles (1975: p.143), for example, writes that proactive learners

> learn more things and learn better than do people who sit at the feet of teachers, passively waiting to be taught (reactive learners) ... They enter into learning more purposefully and with greater motivation. They also tend to retain and make use of what they learn better than do the reactive learners.

In my view, Knowles sets out here the most compelling and universally valid reasons for encouraging learner independence – reasons which stem from the psychology of learning and human motivation. For many educators there are also strong moral and political reasons for promoting learner independence, but one has to beware here of the dangers of cultural imperialism or at the very least insensitivity. Independence, a quality which may not be valued as highly in all cultures as it is in the West (see for example Riley, 1988a), should not be an end in itself but rather the means to an end, namely more effective learning. It is important to be clear, therefore, that the reasons for encouraging learner independence are to do primarily with the psychology of learning rather than any moral or political imperative alone.

Other reasons for promoting independent learning in self-access mode spring from an appreciation of the fact that the ability to use language is not a *product* you can acquire simply by buying a book, a set of video cassettes or a course. None of these aids which are for sale, no matter how expensive and 'good' they are, can have the magical effect of turning non-proficient language users into proficient language users if the learners themselves are not engaged in and do not take responsibility for the learning *process*. Since money can buy most things these days, this realization can come as something of a shock to some would-be language learners!

# Factors in independent learning

Learner independence is a complex construct, a cluster of dispositions and abilities to undertake certain activities. It is important to distinguish between disposition and ability because a learner may be disposed to be independent in an activity such as setting objectives, but lack the technical ability (the activities 7–12 in Figure 4.1), which means that he or she could be characterized with respect to that activity as an independent learner in intention but not in practice. The activities involved in independent learning include at least: analysing needs; setting objectives; planning a programme of work; choosing materials and activities; working unsupervised and evaluating progress. Each activity can be thought of in terms of a cline ranging from teacher dependence to learner independence (see Figure 4.1).

Learners could be at differing points on each of the twelve clines shown in the figure – teacher dependent on some, independent

| | | DISPOSITION TO | |
|---|---|---|---|
| D | 1 | ← Analyse one's own strengths / weaknesses, language needs → | I |
| | 2 | ← Set achievable targets and overall objectives → | N |
| E | 3 | ← Plan a programme of work to achieve the objectives set → | D |
| P | 4 | ← Exercise choice, select materials and activities → | E |
| E | 5 | ← Work without supervision → | P |
| N | 6 | ← Evaluate one's own progress → | E |
| D | | ABILITY TO | N |
| E | 7 | ← Analyse one's own strengths / weaknesses, language needs → | D |
| N | 8 | ← Set achievable targets and overall objectives → | E |
| C | 9 | ← Plan a programme of work to achieve the objectives set → | N |
| E | 10 | ← Exercise choice, select materials and activities → | C |
| | 11 | ← Work without supervision → | E |
| | 12 | ← Evaluate one's own progress → | |

**Figure 4.1**   Activities involved in independent learning

on others. At the lowest level of independence a learner might be willing and able to work unsupervised but in every other respect be dependent on a teacher or advisor for direction. Included in any initial needs analysis of learners there should be an assessment of that learner's readiness for independent learning. Such an assessment would be based in the first instance on the results of enquiries (questionnaires or interviews) designed to ascertain the learner's educational background and learning experience to date. One would obviously need to know whether the educational model the learner had come into contact with previously was, broadly speaking, based on principles of the authoritative transmission of society's received wisdom (associated with activities such as rote learning and copying written texts), or on principles of the development of individual potential (characterized by such activities as discovery learning and creative writing).

One would also need to investigate the learner's own individual attitudes towards learning, which will reflect past experience of education to some extent but which will also be influenced by personality factors. Willing (1989: pp.22–3), for example, has devised a questionnaire designed to ascertain a student's learning style within a matrix consisting of the following learning styles: 'Communicative'; 'Authority-orientated'; 'Concrete'; 'Analytical'. The questionnaire consists of a number of statements with which the learner agrees or disagrees. The statements concerning the 'Authority-orientated' learning style are:

> I like the teacher to explain everything to us.
> I want to write everything in my notebook.
> I like to have my own textbook.
> In English class, I like to learn by reading.
> I like to study grammar.
> I like to learn English words by seeing them.

By gauging the learner's responses to a set of statements such as the one above teachers can discover much about his or her *disposition* to be independent. Figure 4.2 provides an example set of attitudinal statements relating to factors 1–6 in Figure 4.1, where learners are asked to say in each case which of two statements (reflecting the two extremes of dependence/independence) they agree with most. Many learners say they cannot agree with either statement and it is then useful to ask them to explain what they

*Put a tick beside which statement you agree most with, the one on the left (a) or the one on the right (b):*

| | |
|---|---|
| (a) I think it's the teacher's job to correct all my mistakes. | (b) It's good for me to find out my own mistakes wherever possible. |
| (a) I want my teacher to tell me what I have to do to learn better English. | (b) I want to find out for myself what I have to do to learn better English. |
| (a) My teacher should tell me what exercises to do and what books to read, etc. | (b) I want to choose for myself what exercises to do and what books to read, etc. |
| (a) I don't think it's useful to do speaking activities in pairs or groups if the teacher isn't listening to my group all the time. | (b) I think speaking activities in pairs or groups are useful, even when the teacher isn't listening to my group. |
| (a) The teacher should give us lots of tests and tell us how well we've learned. | (b) Tests can't tell you everything. You know yourself if you've been learning well. |

**Figure 4.2** Attitudinal statements on independent learning

agree and disagree with in the two statements as well as asking them to formulate a statement that they can agree with.

Learner independence should not, then, be viewed as an absolute which is present or absent in any one learner, but rather as a complex cluster of attributes. In what ways can self-access help to develop these attributes in learners?

## Promotion of independent learning through self-access

A self-access centre which is geared towards promoting independent learning will make provision in some way for preparation before learners begin work in self-access mode and ongoing learner support during self-access work. The centre will provide materials which themselves foster learner independence rather than providing teacher direction by remote control, and the materials will be arranged in such a way that they are physically and cognitively accessible to learners.

### Learner preparation and support

Learner preparation and support can be categorized as either training or development (Sheerin, 1989: p.34). The word training implies the imparting of a defined set of skills and it also implies something that is done by someone to someone else. Certain basic self-study skills would fall under the heading of learner training, such as using a cassette or video recorder, looking up items in an alphabetical list; using a dictionary effectively; recording new vocabulary; using a grammar reference book, and the like. Learner development, on the other hand, is cognitive and affective development involving increasing awareness of oneself as a learner and an increasing willingness and ability to manage one's own learning. Above all, it involves accepting responsibility for one's own learning and being willing to be proactive in that process. Learner development is not something that teachers 'do' to learners, although there may be ways the process can be encouraged and facilitated. Learners develop themselves.

These two processes of learner training and learner development can be seen to reflect the two faces of self-access discussed above. Learner training is practical and relatively straightforward. Its usefulness is evident to both teachers and learners. The learner development which needs to accompany the promotion of independent learning is, however, much less easily defined, much more gradual and, all in all, more complex and problematic, but it is the process in the end which brings the greater reward and advancement.

## Materials design

Learning materials for use in self-access mode can very easily be antithetical to the concept of learner independence. Self-access material needs to provide feedback to the learner on the work he or she has done, and the easiest way of doing this is to give the learner the correct answer in a situation where there is only one possibility. Such materials are self-administered objective tests, of necessity involving discrete item practice rather than whole task practice. The authority which used to be invested in the classroom teacher has simply been transferred to the answer key. Self-testing materials can satisfy the aim of 'individualization' very well, but they do very little to promote learner independence.

The possibilities of self-access materials are much greater than this and can take many forms. The following list is taken from Sheerin (1991: p.150):

- guided discovery tasks based on authentic data (see Sheerin, 1989: pp.128–9);

- questionnaires designed to help learners clarify their own beliefs concerning language learning or to challenge their beliefs, provoke thought and raise awareness (see Sheerin, 1989: pp.134–5);
- study guides containing suggestions for language practice activities not based on didactic materials;
- fluency activities for pairs and groups together with checklists and guidelines for self- and peer evaluation (see Ferris *et al.*, 1988 and Sheerin, 1989: pp.137–43);
- suggestions for different ways of using learning materials, for example, different ways of proceeding with tapescripts or comprehension questions when engaged in listening practice (see Sheerin, 1989: pp.83–6);
- student-generated materials (see Carver and Dickinson, 1982);
- standard reading and listening exercises (comprehension questions designed for a particular text genre rather than for individual texts (see Dickinson, 1987: pp.170–5 and Sheerin, 1989: pp.86–8).

Fundamental to those self-access materials which encourage greater autonomy is the notion that feedback to learners can take other forms apart from 'the right answer'. For example, a questionnaire aimed at getting learners to think about how they like to learn vocabulary can give feedback in the form of a commentary with further suggestions (see Sheerin, 1989: pp.170–1). However, the less objective the feedback in self-access materials, the more prepared learners have to be to accept a degree of uncertainty. The use of such materials then further promotes learner independence.

## Access and retrieval

The organization and retrieval systems of self-access can be key factors in inhibiting or promoting independence in learners. To maximize independent selection, materials need to be physically accessible, that is to say easily visible and 'browsable' (not shut away in a filing cabinet) and organized in clearly signposted and appropriate sections, with each item individually classified and labelled or colour-coded. Answer keys (and other forms of feedback) also need to be easily accessible, which can best be achieved if they are kept together with worksheets. Where activities involve multimedia it should be possible to see at a glance which items go together.

When first setting up self-access facilities very careful consideration needs to be given to what categories of material there will be, since this is a very important way in which choice can be maximized or limited. The division of materials into various levels, for example, will immediately limit choice, as students are usually very reluctant to try materials which they feel may be below or above their level. In fact, there are many kinds of materials which are suitable for a range of levels and there are circumstances in which learners can benefit from working on materials which are above or below the level they normally work at. In order not to limit choice artificially it is advisable to keep the number of levels to a minimum, between three and six depending on the range of proficiency of your learners.

Similarly, the division of materials into sections can limit access if account is not taken of the needs and levels of sophistication of potential users. For example, a doctor who is studying English because he or she needs to write articles for medical journals may be looking for a section on 'Medicine' and/or 'Writing academic papers'. If materials are not shelved according to topic and there is no form of topic index then this learner's ability to select according to his need will be severely limited. If he or she then looks in the 'Writing' section and discovers subcategories which refer to sub-skills, such as 'Linking sentences and paragraphs', rather than text types, such as 'Academic Papers', he or she may come to the conclusion that there is no material to help him or her, even though this may not be the case. In other words, inappropriate categorization and inadequate indexing can have the effect of hiding material from learners.

Another way in which materials can be made cognitively accessible to students is to ensure that the metalanguage in rubrics, classification headings and the like is appropriate to the learners who use the system. This implies not only the control of language level in terms of structures and vocabulary, but also the avoidance of overly technical language and jargon. Access and retrieval systems – whether they are computer-based or card-indexed – should be as explicit as possible about the attributes of all materials in order to facilitate learner choice. This means that besides the level (for example, intermediate) and the main and subsidiary language focus (for example, grammar: past tense) there should also be information concerning topic if appropriate, and concerning activity-type (for example, multiple-choice exercise, dictation, study guide, discovery task). In an ideal world the aims of any piece of material would also be apparent. (For a comprehensive discussion of these and other issues concerned with the organization of materials see McCall, 1992.)

## The role of teachers and counsellors

It is the paradox of independent learning that almost all learners need to be prepared and supported on the path towards greater autonomy by *teachers*. Before learners can engage meaningfully in self-access work there needs to be an initial analysis of needs so that short- and long-term objectives can be set, a programme of work planned and suitable activities and materials selected. Once self-access work is underway, learners need support in evaluating their progress, reanalysing their needs and setting further object-ives. Teachers, in other words, have a crucial role to play in launch-ing learners into self-access and in lending them a regular helping hand to 'stay afloat'.

If teachers give guidance to students in this way there may be a danger that learner autonomy will be jeopardized. It is easily possible for teachers – the 'experts' – to be too dominant in their roles of facilitator or consultant. This may occur because they them-selves are ill-prepared for such roles in teacher training courses, or because the learner is reluctant or unable to assume greater responsibility for decision making. Whatever the cause, if teachers take all the decisions for the learners and do not attempt to wean them, however gradually, away from teacher dependence, then learners may be working unsupervised (on material selected by teachers) but not independently in any other respect. In this case, there is a danger that learning will be very limited, since effective language learning has to involve learning about oneself as a lan-guage learner and learning to function as a language user inde-pendently of a teacher.

If, on the other hand, in the interests of promoting greater autonomy, a teacher withholds support and advice from a learner who is as yet ill-equipped to assume the mantle of independent learning, there is great danger that learners may lack direction or may waste time heading in the wrong direction. This may well have the opposite effect to the one intended since learners who are abandoned to their own devices too soon tend to seek out activities and materials which they know. They do not, therefore, broaden their horizons and develop as learners. Another danger of under-advising learners is that this may cause them to feel frustrated, isolated and discouraged so that, in the 'worst case scenario', the attempt to learn may be abandoned.

The role of the teacher is, then, a difficult one requiring great skill and sensitivity. Teachers need to assess learners not only with regard to their language needs but also with regard to their readiness to become independent learners. At each point in the preparation and support process the teacher needs to make a judgement as to where the learner stands on the various dependence/independence clines (illustrated by Figure 4.1), both in terms of ability and disposition, so that he or she may be encouraged along the clines towards greater independence by appropriate degrees in ways that neither threaten nor cosset. Learners need the professional guidance of a teacher or adviser so that they can take *informed* decisions for themselves.

## Conclusion

Although the mere existence of self-access facilities does not ensure independent learning, well-organized self-access materials (of the right *sort*) can do much to facilitate and encourage self-directed learning. Even in a fairly traditional context where teachers see their role as directive and/or learners are disposed to seek direction, the choice afforded by self-access can subtly change teacher/learner roles even when this is not the primary intention. Teachers become resource managers rather than resource providers, focusing of necessity on the needs of individuals. Learners become aware that there *is* a choice, and as they become more experienced users of the facilities, the chances are they will begin to explore and browse and eventually start making their own suggestions during consultations or tutorials with a teacher. Such a learner is becoming more active in the learning process and beginning to exercise choice. A change of this nature can be seen as progress in one limited area of learner independence but does not in itself represent a significant development in the superordinate metacognitive learning strategies such as 'self-monitoring' and 'self-evaluation' (see O'Malley *et al.*, 1985, for a list and description of metacognitive learning strategies). Such a development, which many would argue is the true hallmark of independent learning, is to a considerable extent dependent upon the facilitative skills of a teacher or adviser.

Although self-access does not necessarily ensure learner independence, it provides the *practical* means whereby learners can take a more active part in determining their own objectives and their own learning programmes. Learners may initially be attracted towards self-access because of the opportunities for individualization it represents, but the practical imperative can very naturally entail a more broadly educational imperative, in other words learning to be a better learner. The very practical nature of self-access lends point to learner training and learner development activities which, without the end-goal of self-access, can seem pointless to learners. In this way, the dual nature of self-access – the pragmatic and the idealistic – can smooth the path towards learner independence.

# 5

## Teaching and learning in self-access centres: changing roles?

GILL STURTRIDGE

### Introduction

In the last years of the twentieth century a number of factors have combined to make the provision of self-access language learning centres an attractive option for educational institutions worldwide. As this new wave of centres is being set up in an educational climate which may change the roles of centres, teachers and learners, it is crucial to learn from the successes and failures of the past. This chapter looks at the factors contributing to the spread of self-access and discusses why centres succeed and why they can fail. It argues that appropriate methodology, involving a recognition of the changing roles of teachers and learners in self-access, is critical to the success of centres.

### Factors affecting change

As we approach the end of the century, four factors are contributing to an educational climatic change, and producing a microclimate in which the self-access centre can flourish. These factors will influence the role that such centres play and affect the roles of teachers and learners in them. They are the information explosion, the electronic revolution, the explosion of student numbers and the current state of thinking on language learning and language acquisition.

The first two factors come from outside the field of language learning and could bring about a radical re-organization of our teaching institutions, and a far greater use of self-access provision. The information explosion will affect teaching and learning procedures across the curriculum in the next century. At university level there is already 'too much' to teach for the student's timetable. The amount of information available in any one field means that tertiary level institutions will focus more on whatever is defined as 'core' courses and will have to provide some sort of access to other information for those who seek it. Rising staff costs may mean a re-assessment of teacher–student contact time and a re-assessment of materials production costs. The live lecturer addressing two hundred students for an hour today, may not be regarded as economic tomorrow: We have already seen how the recorded versions of such lectures, together with prepared support materials, can reach wider audiences, in centres and students' homes, while in-house materials are already being produced at the tertiary level to maximize staff time and make input sessions more readily understandable and available to students who cannot follow a fixed timetable.

The electronic revolution makes the delivery of teaching possible either in the learner's home or in his place of work, and it is feasible that self-access centres will become more providers of distant learning than library-like places to go to study. The advent of multimedia hardware means the extension of the type of feedback available to learners and a reconsideration of how they can best use that feedback. Though the materials produced on multimedia often do not live up to the potential of the technology at present, that potential is there and could produce materials of design and intention which differ significantly from the design of the paper and taped materials we know.

The third and fourth factors come from within the field of language learning. Probably the most important of these is the worldwide increase in demand for foreign language learning which is making self-access provision a matter of expediency. In some countries it is quite impossible to train the numbers of language teachers required in the time available. Furthermore, the cost of employing professional teachers may be prohibitive. Consequently, the traditional idea of the teacher and his or her students in a class held at a fixed time may no longer be feasible. A different sort of language learning provision must be made, and in situations where numbers have increased suddenly there has been a trend towards self-access provision. Mexico is one such example where the universities are setting up self-access facilities for language learning. At the time of writing, thirty-four well-resourced centres are in operation, each one planned to meet the particular learning needs and flexible working hours of the thousands of students on its campus. Regional work groups and frequent conferences have established a network between the universities to exchange ideas and discuss problems.

The fourth factor is changing views on language learning in the last ten years. These have already had a positive wash-back effect on self-access centres. An awareness of the research on learning strategies has given a fresh impetus to the provision of facilities which allow learners to work in their own way. The work of Willing (1987: p.3), O'Malley and Chamot (1990: pp.137–9) and Oxford (1990: pp.16–21), has given a practical framework with which teachers can design their own learner development programmes. We now accept that few learners learn well by themselves without language awareness and learning awareness development programmes. We also recognize that considerable support and personal contact is necessary, not only initially, but throughout their work at the centre.

Current views on language acquisition also lend support to self-access provision. If language is not acquired in a step-by-step linear progression and if what is taught systematically is not necessarily systematically taken up by learners, then it would seem essential that learners should be able to have access to language input of any type they choose to further their own language learning.

The information explosion, information technology and increasing student numbers may not only mean the integration and acceptance of self-access centres within the traditional classroom-based teaching institution, but also the complete re-assessment of the mode of delivery of education generally. Institutions could become total providers of self-access learning and the traditional classroom could disappear entirely in some institutions. What is critical is the recognition that alongside the organizational changes there must be an appropriate methodology which directs those changes and ensures their success.

## Why centres succeed or fail

Self-access centres have been in existence now for nearly three decades, and the issues of learner independence and autonomy have been widely discussed (Holec 1981; Dickinson 1987; Wenden 1991). There are examples worldwide of well-implemented self-access provision, catering successfully for learners of varying ages, backgrounds and needs. In spite of this, such centres are not a usual feature of language teaching institutions, nor has the potential of self-access provision been fully recognized. In some instances, self-access centres have been set up and have then either been closed down to make way for the next innovation or simply withered away. In the hope of our avoiding a repetition of such past failures and also to encourage the proliferation of successful centres, I would like to consider some reasons why centres succeed and why they can fail.

It is not easy to evaluate the success of a centre in terms of the whether the work done there has contributed more to learners' proficiency than work they did in class. Learners who come to centres are often the self-selected good language learners who are able to exploit the resources well. Even where there is a wide spread of students, learner variables make it difficult to attribute language improvement directly to working in the centre. User questionnaires can reveal the degree of popularity the centre has, but do not measure the contribution independent learning is making to the learner's progress in comparison with the contribution of classroom teaching. One obvious way of defining the success of a centre is by the amount of student use. Most institutions are aware of the percentage of their student population that uses the centre and its materials over a period of time. High attendance figures show a good return on the investment in staff time, space and equipment and satisfy those in authority, even though such figures may not be a true measure of the value of a centre. Failure, then, is an empty centre, or one where student numbers are consistently low, or where out of a large student population the same few students attend. A centre must also consider itself a failure if it is full of students who are not there to learn languages, but who use it merely as a convenient place to do other work.

The centres which have grown and developed appear to have had a flexibility which enabled them to respond to needs and to evolve; they have been able to avoid all or at least some of the pitfalls. Where centres closed down it appears that they lacked this ability to evolve, and that they failed in one or more of the following areas.

## 1.   The management of the innovation

Sometimes the idea of establishing a self-access centre originated from, and was imposed by, the top management with insufficient consultation with all the teaching staff. In such cases there was almost certainly no consultation with the students either. This meant that no clear role was established for the centre within the institution. There was no true integration with the teaching timetable, nor did teachers take their classes to the centre during class hours to introduce them to the facilities. The change of role was not made clear to the teachers. In some instances the teaching staff, being inadequately briefed about the innovation, saw the introduction of a self-access centre as a threat to their jobs and therefore regarded it with animosity. In other cases, the teaching staff only saw the educational reason for the centre's existence, whereas the management saw it primarily in terms of good publicity for the institution and possibly as a way of saving salaries. There was no shared philosophy underlying the centre nor any attempt to help teachers develop a methodology for the new mode of working.

Nor was the change in their role made clear to the learners; they were not involved in the introduction of the innovation. There was no attempt to make them aware that the centre was part of the teaching-learning package on offer. There was no publicity to encourage them to use the centre or give them a clearer idea of how it could help them. Often centres were not open at times when learners would have liked to work in them. Finally, there was no attempt to make learners feel they could contribute to the centre, to collect or make materials, or help in its running.

Thus we can say that the initial step towards the success of a self-access centre lies in the successful management of its introduction into the institution or educational system.

## 2.   The provision of a suitable location and facilities

A highly-resourced centre and a low-resourced centre have an equal chance of success or failure: a centre can be successful without an enormous budget. Waite (1994: p.236) reports on a successful low-cost, low-tech centre in Nicaragua where needs were met on a low budget. Indeed, where the other conditions for the successful introduction of self-access provision are not met, money alone will not ensure success. However, available resources need to be imaginatively used. Low student use of a centre can be a result of poor location. Centres must be in locations where learners notice them and which are easy to reach. Their existence must be allowed to make impact on the student population. Where lack of funds does not allow for the glamour of new furnishing and modern hardware to enhance a centre's image, much can be done with good planning and continual up-dating of materials.

## 3. The training and development of the staff

Successful centres have a sound initial training and development programme for all staff so that the workings of the centre and its role are fully understood throughout the institution. There must also be an on-going development programme to encourage growth and change. We are still in the early stages of our knowledge of the delivery of flexible learning and a centre has to keep its approach and materials under review constantly by making good use of feedback mechanisms and action research from centre staff. Centres may fail because there have been no programmes to ensure all staff members become stakeholders, or because only a small cadre of teachers have received training to enable them to run the centre while the remainder of the staff are not given the opportunity to became familiar with the role and purpose of the centre and its organization and materials. There is a need for development programmes to help teachers become aware of their new role as facilitators when working in the centre; teachers need to be trained to *stop teaching* students.

## 4. The training and development of learners

Learners must be helped to consider their own working styles and strategies and to relate these to the work they are doing. This process often takes far longer than teachers expect. Some centres only provide initial training to learners when they first come to use the centre, and at its worst this training is limited to showing the learner how to find his way around, rather than how to work independently. A successful centre will attempt to make learner development an ongoing cycle of action and reflection and to offer a development programme that keeps pace with the learners as they work.

## 5. Using the cultural strengths of learners

Different cultural backgrounds and different educational systems foster different strengths and weaknesses in learners. A good
centre must be able to use the strengths. Ignoring traditional
learning styles completely can make learners feel ill at ease. One
example of this would be not making allowance for learners to
work in groups in a country where learners work well together but
feel threatened when working alone. In such a case materials and
modes of working in the centre should be geared to maximize the
value of learning in groups. Similarly, where rote-learning is an
accepted practice and students have a facility for learning by heart,
work should be provided in the centre which makes a positive use
of this strength.

## 6. Suitable materials

Centres are accepted or rejected by learners on the relevance of
the materials they have on offer. Where centres have failed it was
often because the organizers were obsessed by the *quantity* of materials they thought were needed, rather than the quality and as a
result the materials bank was never evaluated, weeded or revised.
Some contained materials which were intended for classroom use
and which had not been adequately adapted for self-access work.
This meant that sometimes learners were expected to 'teach
themselves' from class textbooks which had been designed to be
teacher-led. In a successful centre the materials should not only
make allowance for the learners to improve linguistically but also
to develop their way of working.

Lack of learner development, cultural mismatching of approach,
and poor materials provision, are only three area where centres
can fail and they reveal that though effort may be put into the physical environment of the centre, sufficient thought must also be
given to the approach to learner independence. In many cases,
the centres that closed were those which had no clear approach.
It is essential that a distinction is made between what I shall call
*the student explorer* and *the student practiser* and that centre organizers ensure that allowance is made for the students to develop
from being practisers to being explorers.

The self-access centre which provides only *language practice*
is one where the materials are largely graded grammar exercises,

examination practice and controlled activities, all with keys. It is more likely to be found in an institution where classroom contact is regular and a course book and syllabus are closely followed. Such a centre has the role of supporting work done in class and giving learners extra time to work on weaknesses. Learner training is likely to be limited to learning how the centre works and how to find materials; there may be little attempt to develop the learner's own learning strategies.

The materials are likely to be teacher-directed, and primarily form-focused. The learners are likely to see each piece of work as a single task, and as an end in itself, to be entered on a record card. Most learners are *student practisers* when they first start using a self-access centre because it is a secure role and they see traditional practice exercises as valuable. They realize over a period of time that they can integrate different activities into their self-access work, and make different demands on the materials. Thus the practice centre does not meet the learners' changing expectations.

*The student explorer* prefers to work in a *language learning* centre rather than a language practice centre because he wants materials which encourage the use of language, as opposed to the study of it, and he wants to extend his own range of language through play or open-ended tasks. Of course, the explorer can at any time become a practiser again, so a language learning centre must be flexible enough to provide for and encourage both types of learning.

A language *learning* centre is more likely to be found in an institution where learners cannot attend classes on a regular basis, or where they are encouraged to extend their language work beyond the areas covered in the classroom. The teachers are required to re-examine their role and the materials they are offering because of their learners' mode of working. The centre has to include practice materials and packages, but these are likely to be regarded in a different light from the way they are regarded in a practice centre. The completion of the activities are not seen as an end in themselves, but as part of the progress towards an identified goal. Learner development materials are more likely to be an integral part of this type of centre's induction programme. In a true learning centre the learners know why they have selected a piece of work to do, and how it will help them towards the goal they have chosen. There are a range of simplified and authentic materials with accompanying translations, glossaries, recordings and transcripts for which no tasks have been developed. These are the materials that the student explorer can roam through, constructing his own tasks as he goes. It appears to be the centres which come into the learning centre category which not only survive, but grow.

The reasons for failure raised earlier must still be recognized as dangers to the successful introduction and development of centres, even though the educational climate has changed in ways that make it more probable that self-access provision will be a permanent part of language learning programmes. This makes the development of an appropriate approach even more important. Such an approach must involve a review of the changing roles of the centre, the teacher and the learner.

## Changes in the role of the self-access centre

In a sense, a self-access centre has two roles. The first is the public role relating to its place in the institution and the community and the second is the more private role of providing a learning environment for an individual learner. Within an institution the centre usually has an ancillary role in relation to classroom teaching. In its public role outside the institution, the self-access centre is sometimes used to demonstrate that particular institution is up-to-date in its thinking and its facilities; it reflects well on its sponsors. Its private role is very different. When it comes to provision of a learning environment the roles of the self-access centre and the teacher and the learner are interdependent and symbiotic. A change in any one of these elements inevitably affects the other two. A centre can change its role by providing a different type of material, by changing the type of learner preparation it provides and by changing the ways it sees its staff and how it prepares them.

A self-access centre is restricted in some areas by its very nature and if it is to replace classroom teaching then these restrictions have to be addressed. Two obvious examples are speaking and listening. Providing for fluency practice has always presented organizational problems because live contact is essential and groups or conversation sessions have to be arranged at fixed times. Developments in methodology mean that similar problems have arisen with listening. The majority of listening materials in self-access centres are monologues or dialogues to which learners respond by taking notes or making some response on a worksheet, a computer screen or by recording an answer on tape. This is obviously useful work for the learner, but does not account for the fact that the teaching of listening skills has moved on. Rost (1990: p.172) points out that listening task procedures 'should include ways of dealing with non-understandings and possibilities for negotiation'. The absence of live speakers makes this impossible and that means the learner is deprived of the opportunity of being a participant. A whole range of tasks available in the classroom are not available here. The independent learner needs and wants these types of tasks and a centre must be flexible enough to find ways of providing them. This is essential where the self-access centre is designed to be the sole provider of language learning opportunities.

## Changes in the teacher's role

When teachers first moved from the classroom to the self-access centre they recognized that their role had become a facilitating one. However, the facilitator's job has evolved over the years. Originally, the teacher in the self-access centre guided and advised learners on the location and choice of materials and gave language support where needed. This was when self-access centres were in their infancy and were designed on the 'Find it. Do it. Check it.' principle. Learners were expected to be able to locate the type of activity they wanted to do, to work through that activity and to be able to evaluate their performance with the aid of some type of answer sheet or key. As soon as it was recognized that learners working independently needed help to enable them to work effectively in this new mode, the facilitator became involved in the development of learners' own learning skills through development programmes. If, in the future, the classroom vanishes and self-access provision is all that the learner has, an element of the teacher's role may change. The teacher may become a personal tutor, revert to being a 'true teacher' and become a resource to a far greater degree than now. This change has already taken place in some centres. The teacher is still a facilitator and has the facilitator's familiarity with the materials and a knowledge of hardware and software but he or she applies this more actively and has to develop tutoring skills rather than whole-class teaching skills. Without being over-directive, the teacher is learning to give more focused advice, such as when and how to remotivate a student or alleviate the anxiety of the 'lonely learner'. Tutorial time, rather than class time could be given or sold to centre users and the learner would have to learn how and when to make the best use of the teacher.

## Changes in the learner's role: the learner–teacher

The coming of new learning materials will mean that learners have to extend their strategies for working alone. In language learning centres, video and computer-based materials are now available, bringing to the learner not only the environment where the language is spoken, but access to tools for further understanding through the sound-track, transcript, translations and explanations of what is seen and heard. However, many of these materials are very teacher-directed in the sense that the materials are doing the direction rather than a live teacher; learner freedom is an illusion. In the case of some materials it can also be implied that the feedback given on a learner's performance is sufficient even though the limited range of types of feedback available in such packages can mean that the learner is often provided with little more than a key to the right answer and very little clarification about why he was wrong. Learners will need to learn how to recognize unsuitable materials, how to extract the best value from them by using them in a different way, and when to reject them. Just as a teacher develops the skills of rejecting or exploiting materials on behalf of learners, so successful learners need similar skills so they can know how to handle materials, of whatever kind, and use them to their own advantage.

Those who have received learner development or training will have already been made aware of the need to be aware of their own goals, to be able to monitor their own progress and evaluate their own performance. All these skills were formerly in the province of the teacher. To these I would add an understanding of learning materials and I would include the following knowledge about materials and resources.

## 1.   An awareness of material type

Learners should be able to distinguish materials designed for language learning from raw authentic materials. They should be able to recognize to what extent they are being directed through the material.

## 2.   *Perception of the purpose of a task*

If learners are going to apply their own tasks to raw materials, then they should have a clear idea of the purpose of those tasks and be able to evaluate them. They need to know how the work they are doing is helping them. For example, if a student's goal is to improve his listening and notetaking skills, then listening and transcribing recorded cassettes is not an activity that is going to help him, though it may have other benefits. Task recognition is one of the independent learner's key skills. Learners should be able to see how the performance of a task is intended to help them. This is particularly relevant where tasks have been provided by others and where learners need to understand what the materials designer had in mind. They can then decide whether or not they wish to spend time doing or adapting the activity.

Learners should also be able to recognize when there is task interdependence through a unit of materials so that they do not skip vital activities that will help them with the final task.

## 3.   *Evaluation of a task*

Learners often pick up the design of exercises and tasks from textbooks or from their classroom experience and apply these types of activity to other materials. It is useful therefore for them to be able to assess the value of what they are doing for their own language learning. They should be able to decide whether a task was enjoyable, and at the right level of challenge to them personally. Learners need to be able to perceive that different types of task will help them at different stages of their development so as not to be over-ambitious or over-cautious when selecting the work they do. Learners should be able to assess the value the task has in help-ing them towards their goal, whether short or long term.

## 4.   *Use of the resource person and peers*

Learners should be able to decide how to use the precious time with a facilitator and should be able to report back on learning strategies and materials, discuss them and seek advice.

They should be able to recognize the type of materials and tasks which they could work on more profitably with friends.

They should be helped to structure their working in pairs and groups to maximize the benefit gained from such work and to develop teacher-like skills in organizing and preparing such group activities.

We do not expect a carpenter to learn to handle the tools of his trade but to learn nothing of the properties of wood. At the moment, the bulk of the stuff our learners work with is made up of designed exercises and tasks. Just as the carpenter is taught how to use the different woods, so we should prepare our learners to work with the stuff of their trade, the language teaching materials.

## Conclusion

In many countries it is now expedient for educational institutions to establish self-access provision because of the pressure of student numbers, and with this new wave of centres it is crucial to avoid the mistakes made in the past and focus on successful models.

We must also be aware of the nature of the interrelationship between the self-access centre, the materials, the teacher and the learner. As roles change, learners will need to have further development programmes to help them to learn effectively. Independent learners need to recognize what can be used as learning materials and have an understanding of their own learning management in relation to those materials. Where there is no teacher the good learner is someone who teaches himself well and becomes a 'learner–teacher'. To do that he must take up more of the skills and insights that have traditionally been assigned to teachers.

# 6

## Self-access: why do we want it and what can it do?

### WILLIAM LITTLEWOOD

## Introduction

In some respects we can compare the spread of self-access centres with the spread of language laboratories in the 1950s and 1960s. Then, as now, language teachers found at their disposal a resource which at first seemed to have almost magical qualities. It enabled students to work at their own pace and to devise their own programmes; it enabled institutions to solve staffing problems by time-tabling students to learn without a teacher; it 'never grew tired'; in principle, at least, it could provide students with interesting, up-to-date stimuli which would sustain their motivation to learn and use language.

There is a major respect, however, in which the rise in popularity of self-access centres has differed from that of the language laboratory. The spread of the language laboratory was strongly theory-driven. Its use was justified in terms of specific theories of language and language learning (structural linguistics and behaviourism), which provided the rationale for the wider audio-lingual approach within which the language laboratory seemed to take its natural place (see for example Brooks, 1964; Rivers, 1964). The decline of these theories was also one of the major factors leading to the decline in popularity of the language laboratory in the late 1960s. When it regained some of its status in discussions about language-teaching methodology in the early 1970s, this was in the context of a more cognitive-based approach, within which it could provide opportunities for varied exposure and problem-solving as well as (or in place of) repetition and intensive drilling (Dakin, 1973).

Self-access has not been underpinned to the same extent by specific theories of language learning and teaching. In this respect, the nature of its rise has reflected a more general trend in language teaching, which nowadays tends to be 'eclectic' rather than driven by single, clearly defined theories or methods (Littlewood, 1994; Stern, 1983).

This independence from specific theories does not mean, however, that theory is not relevant. Like any other component of our teaching, self-access needs to be guided by a theoretical framework which justifies its existence, accounts for its procedures and clarifies its relationship with other elements in a programme of language learning. Without a framework of guiding principles, it will lack direction and may even, at its worst, become little more than a set of random interventions into the students' learning processes.

The present chapter seeks to contribute to such a framework by considering self-access activities from two complementary perspectives:

The first part of the chapter considers self-access within the broader context of current interest in 'autonomy' as the goal of all forms of education. It discusses the concept of autonomy in relation to second language learning and proposes a methodological framework for the development of autonomy in language learning. This framework offers a justification for self-access in terms of students learning needs (both general and specific to language learning). It should also enable us to determine how self-access can function within a general pedagogical strategy for furthering autonomy.

In contrast, the second part of the chapter adopts a more differentiated perspective. Starting from an integrative model of second language learning, it considers how particular forms of self-access work correspond to particular aspects of the second language learning process. This is a prerequisite to perceiving how specific self-access activities relate to each other, to other activities and to the students' overall learning process. It should also help us to evaluate both the potential and the limitations of self-access for the development of students' second language proficiency.

What is presented, then, is a double perspective on self-access. First we look *at* self-access and see it globally in relation to an overall strategy for developing learners' autonomy. Then we look *into* self-access and see its different forms in relation to an overall conception of second language learning.

Because self-access exists in such a wide variety of forms, I will base the discussion on a number of contextual assumptions which reflect, in the main, my own experience. First, I will assume that self-access work takes place in an organized resource centre rather than, say, at home or in the community. Secondly, I will assume that the students' course includes not only self-access work but also classes taught directly by a teacher. The overall objectives and strategies of the course do not therefore have to be decided by the students. Thirdly, I will assume that opportunities exist for the students to receive guidance in their self-access work, either from their regular teacher or from a language counsellor. They can therefore seek help in the selection of materials and specific learning strategies.

## Self-access work and the development of autonomy

The most compelling arguments in favour of taking deliberate steps to integrate self-access work into students' learning experiences do not come from specific language learning theory but from wider educational theory, in particular the concept of 'autonomy' (cf. Little, 1991). As Candy (1988: p.59) points out, 'the development of autonomous individuals [that is, graduates who exhibit the qualities of moral, emotional and intellectual independence] . . . is the long-term goal of most, if not all, educational endeavours'. Working within the scope of this higher-level goal, specific subjects in the curriculum recognize the narrower goal of 'developing autonomous students; that is, people who accept more and more responsibility for their own learning, for setting goals and objectives, for finding resources, and for evaluating the outcomes of their learning activities'. In the course of this learning, students may develop 'subject-matter autonomy', a term which Candy uses to refer to the ability to function independently within a particular area of knowledge and to apply personal frames of reference to it.

If we apply Candy's account to language teaching, we can distinguish three kinds of autonomy which are relevant to our work:

1. With respect to our subject, we aim to help learners develop their ability to operate independently with the language and use it to communicate personal meanings in real, unpredictable situations.
2. We aim to help them to develop their ability to take responsibility for their own learning and to apply active, personally

meaningful strategies to their work both inside and outside the classroom.

3. As we help them to increase their ability to communicate and learn independently, we also serve the higher-level goal of helping them to develop greater generalized autonomy as individuals.

In all domains, autonomy is possible only to the extent that students possess both the *willingness* and the *ability* to act independently. More specifically:

- students' willingness to act independently depends on the level of their *motivation* and *confidence*;
- students' ability to act independently depends on the level of their *knowledge* and *skills*.

With respect to language teaching, then, one way of defining our task is to say that we need to help students develop the motivation, confidence, knowledge and skills that they require in order (a) to communicate more independently, (b) to learn more independently and (c) (by extension) to be more independent as individuals. This definition is represented in Figure 6.1. Here, the centre box contains the four components which contribute towards a learner's willingness and ability to act independently. The three outside boxes show the three (overlapping) kinds of autonomy which students can develop.

The six additional labels placed around the circle show some of the concrete ways in which these three kinds of autonomy are expressed in language learning. They are placed next to the kind of autonomy to which they relate most closely. For example, when students use language creatively or devise communication strategies in order to convey their meanings, they demonstrate (and develop) their independence as communicators; when they apply personal learning strategies or engage in independent work, they demonstrate (and develop) their ability as independent learners; and so on. In practice, however, all of these aspects are interconnected. For example, communication strategies are not only an aspect of a student's autonomy as a communicator but also open up a range of learning strategies (e.g. by enabling him or her to cope with more complex texts or to engage in conversations); in this way they also further a student's autonomy as a learner. Similarly, linguistic creativity is most obviously related to students' autonomy as communicators; in addition, however, by enabling them to express

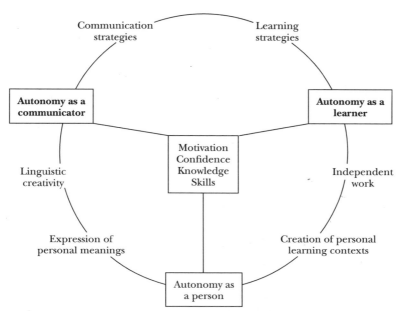

**Figure 6.1**   Developing autonomy through language teaching

personal meanings, it furthers their autonomy as persons, which in turns helps them to create their own contexts for learning, and so on. All of the items shown around the circle in Figure 6.1 can be shown to be linked in similar ways.

The diagram in Figure 6.1 should be perceived as three-dimensional, rising up from the page in the form of a cylinder. Along this third dimension, we can mark the different degrees of autonomy which individual students have acquired in relation to each component and each domain. At a particular stage of learning, for example, it is possible that one student might have acquired a considerable degree of autonomy as a learner in terms of motivation and confidence, but still lack some of the knowledge (e.g. about learning strategies) that would ensure that learning is maximally effective. Because of this and also because the other components of the course may not provide adequate practice, this student's overall autonomy as a communicator may still be low. Another student might have developed the necessary knowledge and skills for autonomous communication but lack sufficient confidence to interact effectively with others in the class.

As teachers, we need to develop systematic strategies for furthering students' motivation, confidence, knowledge and skills in each domain of autonomy. Sometimes we may adopt a global strategy, for example, seeking to develop students' overall confidence by creating an atmosphere which supports exploration and independence. At other times the strategy may be more specific, for example, when we use teaching techniques which encourage the expression of personal meanings or when we make students aware of a range of approaches to learning vocabulary.

Within the framework presented in Figure 6.1, the most important role of self-access work in language learning is that it provides a context for the domains of autonomy on the right-hand side of the diagram: for exercising and developing personal learning strategies and engaging in independent work. Since independent work involves the creation of personal learning contexts, self-access also performs an important role in the development of the learner's autonomy as a person and thus affects the domains on the left-hand side of the diagram. By a similar process of extension, the learning strategies developed in self-access work lead to wider range of communication strategies and thus further the learner's autonomy as a communicator.

## Self-access and models of language learning

The first part of this chapter has adopted a global view of self-access and examined how it fits into an overall framework for language learning and teaching. Self-access work was related in particular to the notion of autonomy, which has achieved an important status not only within language teaching but also in other domains of education. In the present section, we will focus more explicitly on the contributions that different forms of self-access work can make to language learning. These potential contributions will be examined in the light of what we currently understand about the processes that underlie language learning.

According to one commonly recognized model, language learning is a form of skill-learning. As with other skills such as dancing or swimming, the language skill that has to be acquired is analysed into separate procedures (e.g. for articulating sounds, forming structures or expressing functions). These procedures are presented to the students, who practise them separately until they can use them fluently. From time to time, they also practise using a range of procedures in integrated ways, for example, in order to hold a conversation or write a text. This model of learning is familiar to most people who have learnt a language in formal educational settings, where it has usually occupied a dominant position. It characterizes what has sometimes been called an 'analytic' language teaching strategy, which Stern (1990: p.98) describes as follows:

> The learner stands away, so to speak, from the language in use, examines it, or rehearses and practices it in some way. The language item or usage, presented and practised through an analytic technique, makes no pretense of being real communication.

According to a different model, language learning is a process of natural growth. The learner develops an ability to use the language by natural processes, as a result of exposure to real language in communication. Just as a child develops competence in his or her mother tongue without the help of explicit teaching, so the second language learner constructs an internal representation of the system of the other language. This model underlies what has sometimes been called an 'experiential' language teaching strategy, described by Stern (1990: pp.102–3) as follows:

> Experiential activities are arranged in such a way as to engage the learner in some purposeful enterprise. . . . Experiential teaching creates conditions for real language use.

These models correspond to different ways in which people do in fact learn second languages and therefore reflect different aspects of the language learning process. These aspects are not necessarily in conflict but can together form part of the overall learning process. Similarly, with respect to teaching, Stern (1990: p.106) argues for a 'balanced approach':

> In order to achieve the highest degree of effectiveness, the two orientations should be considered complimentary.

One way in which the two models of learning and teaching can be integrated into one composite model is represented in Figure 6.2 (adapted from Littlewood, 1992, where the issue is discussed in more detail). This model shows two main routes by which language can enter the repertoire used for communication. The left-hand route is associated mainly with activities in which learners are

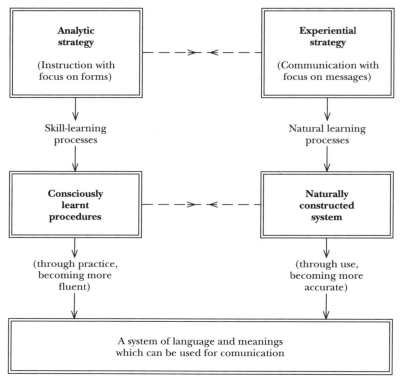

**Figure 6.2**    An integrated model of language learning and teaching

conscious of the procedures they are learning. Learning occurs as, through practice, the procedures involved in using language become increasingly automatized, so that they can eventually operate even when attention is focused on meaning. The right-hand route is associated mainly with activities where the learners focus on the communication of meanings. Learning occurs naturally as the learner develops more and more accurate internal representations of the language. In pedagogical terms, these routes correspond to the 'analytic' and 'experiential' teaching strategies described above. Two other terms are also used which convey a similar distinction: 'learning' and 'acquisition'. Here 'learning' refers to the conscious kinds of internalization that result from instruction, whereas 'acquisition' refers to the subconscious processes of internal construction that take place during natural language use (cf. Krashen,

1985, and critical discussion in, for example, Larsen-Freeman and Long, 1991; Barasch and James, 1994).

From the viewpoint of a student engaged in a particular learning activity, the crucial difference between the routes towards internalization lies in the extent to which he or she focuses on formal aspects of language use (in analytic activities) or on messages which these forms convey (in experiential activities). In the last resort, it is the individual learner who determines this focus and, even within the same organized activity, different learners are likely to have different degrees of focus on the two dimensions. For example, in a question-and-answer session or listening activity, some learners may attend almost entirely to the content of the language, while others try also to 'stand away' (in Stern's terms) and take conscious note of its formal features. However, in planning our courses, we need to try to predict the kind of focus that will be encouraged by different kinds of activity, so that we can involve learners in a range of activities which stimulate a full range of language learning processes.

In order to shape a student's course so that it includes a balanced range of activities along the continuum from form-focused (analytic) to meaning-focused (experiential), we need to work with categories which locate learning activities along this dimension. One such categorization (discussed further in Littlewood, 1993) is presented in Figure 6.3. Here, the triangle occupying the bottom

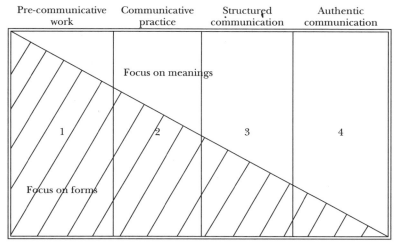

**Figure 6.3**   Focus on forms and focus on messages

left section of the diagram represents focus on the forms of language; the triangle occupying the top right section represents focus on messages to be conveyed. Within the diagram, boxes 1 to 4 represent four categories which differ according to the extent to which they encourage learners to focus on forms or meanings. Thus, box 1 (labelled 'Pre-communicative work') consists of activities where the focus is almost entirely on formal features, such as pronunciation practice and pattern drills. Box 2 (labelled 'Communicative practice') consists of activities where the focus is mainly on formal features but shifts also towards meanings; these would include more meaningful types of drill and simple information gap exercises. In box 3 ('Structured communication') the focus shifts mainly onto the communication of messages, but in situations which have been specially structured to ensure that learners need only language which they have learnt; these might include less controlled information-sharing activities or graded texts. Box 4 ('Authentic communication') consists of activities in which the focus is almost entirely on the communication of messages, such as discussion or reading for content.

Referring back to Figure 6.1, the activities towards the left-hand side of the continuum in Figure 6.2 are predominantly 'analytic', adopt a skill-learning perspective, and involve the students mainly in conscious learning. The activities on the right-hand side of the continuum in Figure 6.3 are predominantly 'experiential', adopt a natural-growth perspective, and involve students mainly in subconscious acquisition.

At this point we are faced with major decisions with regard to self-access work. Should it attempt to embrace the full continuum represented in Figure 6.3? Or should it define its role as falling into the left-hand side of the continuum, leaving the more meaning-focused areas of structured and authentic communication to be dealt with in other parts of the course? More specifically, at different parts of the continuum, what can self-access work contribute to the overall learning process?

On the left-hand side of the continuum, the contributions of self-access work are well-established. Controlled learning through recorded exercises, computer programs, and so on, forms part of a self-access 'tradition' that reaches back to the early days of the language laboratory. On the right-hand side of the continuum, self-access work can also contribute in important ways in the domain of receptive skills, where the initiative for generating meanings lies within the printed or recorded materials rather than with the student. The most problematic area is on the right-hand side of the continuum in the domain of *productive* skills, where the learner requires the kind of message-based feedback that a human respondent normally provides. Until cost-effective ways are found of simulating the essential aspects of the human response (in particular, its creativity and unpredictability), self-access work will be most effective when it complements other forms of learning experience within an integrated language course.

## Conclusion

This chapter has indicated two main dimensions that must be included in a theoretical framework for the role of self-access work in language learning. These two dimensions correspond to the two main sections of the chapter.

The first dimension addresses the role of self-access work in developing *different kinds of learner autonomy*. The first part of this chapter presented a model which distinguished four main components of autonomy and three main domains: communication, learning, and life in general. These components and domains provide a framework within which we can shape and co-ordinate the various aspects of our overall strategy for helping students to develop independence. The model also indicated (under six labels) some of the more specific domains within which this strategy can operate. By its nature, self-access work can provide a context for helping to nurture students gradually from a state of dependence on external support (e.g. from the teacher) towards a greater capacity to act independently in their communication, in their learning and (by extension, we hope) in other aspects of their behaviour.

The second dimension addresses the role of *different kinds of self-access work* in the overall process of learning to communicate. The second part of this chapter outlined two main routes towards the internalization of language, one reflecting a model of language learning as skill-learning and the other reflecting a model of learning as natural growth. It presented a composite model and suggested a categorization of learning activities along a continuum from pre-communicative work, through communicative language practice and structured communication, to authentic communication (which represents the goal of language teaching). Within a course as a whole, we need to balance activities from various parts of the continuum. In self-access work, there is a wide variety of activities from the first two categories. The development of a wider range of techniques for creating activities in the other categories is one of the most challenging tasks that lies ahead.

The difference between these two dimensions can be made clear if we take as an example one particular kind of language learning which, in spite of the attacks which have been directed at it over the years, remains in widespread use: performing pattern drills.

Within the first dimension outlined above, we may encounter a group of learners who are completely dependent on a teacher to select and administer suitable pattern drills for them at appropriate points in their learning process. We may believe that the learners will perform the drills more usefully and enthusiastically if they select them for themselves and perform them independently. We may therefore encourage the learners to see this as a domain in which they can make their own choices (i.e. we try to increase their *motivation* and *confidence*), help them to diagnose their own needs, and show them how to carry out the practical procedures (i.e. we try to increase their *knowledge* and *skills*). Within this limited domain, the students may achieve a high degree of autonomy. If so, we have helped them to take important first steps in developing autonomy in their learning.

Turning to the second dimension, we consider what role the activity performs in helping the students to develop independence in communication. Even if the students have chosen the activity in complete freedom, once they are engaged in it, they have little scope to make choices and are not involved in communicating meanings. Their learning follows primarily the left-hand route shown in Figure 6.2 and the activity is located clearly in the left-hand section of the continuum shown in Figure 6.3. This does not mean that we should reject the activity in terms of the second dimension, since pre-communicative work can also play an important role in a learning programme. We need, however, to be realistic about the extent of its contribution to autonomy in communication and ensure that such activities do not form the major part of a student's programme.

The two dimensions of this framework are obviously closely related. In particular, autonomous communication forms a major part within the first dimension and is also the governing principle within the second. The above example illustrates, however, that it is also useful to view the dimensions separately. A student could reach a high degree of autonomy as a learner in terms of the first dimension but make only limited progress in language learning, if he or she does not make an appropriate range of choices within the second dimension.

It is in order to deal with situations such as the one just described, that self-access needs to be located within a clear theoretical framework. Such a framework should also help us to be aware not only of the strengths of self-access as a means for encouraging autonomy in learning and communication but also of its limitations. Thus, at present, self-access is strong in the domain of receptive skills and, so far as productive skills are concerned, it is strong in the domains represented in the left-hand side of the diagram in Figure 6.3 (i.e. 'pre-communicative work' and 'communicative language practice'). However, as we move towards the right-hand side of this diagram towards the domain of 'authentic communication', its limitations become clear. This means that, in the present state of the art, there are important aspects of the learning process which cannot be catered for by self-access alone. However, as other contributions in this collection make clear, this is an area in which teachers involved in self-access are accepting the challenge and in which new technologies promise to enable exciting breakthroughs to be made.

# PART II

# Roles and relationships

## Introduction

In the context of language education, autonomy and independence are qualities normally expected of learners rather than teachers. But as Gill Sturtridge has shown in Chapter 5, autonomous modes of learning imply a re-evaluation of the roles of both learner and teacher, the relationships between them, and the relationship of both to institutions of learning. These roles and relationships can be complex and are not reducible to simple expectations of behaviour or distributions of power. It is not uncommon for autonomous learning projects to run into problems because of mismatched expectations in the area of learner – teacher roles. Clearly, both learners and teachers need to know who they are, what they can expect from each other and what their respective attitudes are towards the institutional and social context of learning if autonomous learning is to work.

The five chapters in this part deal with five aspects of roles and relationships in independent learning. Peter Voller (Chapter 7) and Philip Riley (Chapter 8) both provide overviews of the issues in this area, Voller evaluating the variety of teacher roles that have been proposed for autonomous learning and Riley looking at counselling for autonomous learning. Michael Breen and Sarah Mann (Chapter 9) look at autonomy in the classroom from both learners' and teachers' perspectives, and raise a number of questions about what is involved in developing a pedagogy for autonomy. Felicity O'Dell (Chapter 10) and Edith Esch (Chapter 11) provide case studies that focus on the roles of teachers and learners respectively.

Traditional teacher training, even 'learner-centred' teacher training, tends to prescribe a leading intellectual and managerial role for teachers and ill-prepares them for the demands of learner autonomy. One problem often encountered in autonomous learning projects is that teachers may, in spite of enthusiasm for the principle of autonomy, experience a degree of disorientation and insecurity resulting from a feeling that they have suddenly become marginalized. Voller, however, takes issue with the view that autonomy necessarily implies the marginalization of teachers and argues for a 'negotiated' approach.

In the literature on learner-centredness, the variety of terms available to replace 'teacher' ('facilitator', 'helper', 'counsellor', 'resource') reflects a need for teachers to find roles for themselves within the process of autonomous learning. But these roles may be less than attractive, particularly if they carry the implication that the teacher is there to be 'used'. This suggests that the change from 'transmission' teaching to 'interpretative' teaching also represents a shift in the balance of power from teachers to learners, which is potentially threatening to teachers and their perceptions of their roles. There may also be the perceived threat that autonomous learning is introduced at the institutional level in order to 'teacher-proof' the learning process – experienced, in Voller's words, as a feeling among teachers that they have become 'tour guides or event organizers'. He argues that the most appropriate approach to 'teaching' autonomous learning is one based on negotiation both with learners and with the discourse communities to which they aim to gain admittance.

While Voller analyses roles mainly in terms of interpersonal relationships, Riley offers a view of counselling for language learning in terms of the processing and distribution of social knowledge. Based on his work at CRAPEL, Nancy, Riley argues that we need to frame a new discourse in which it is possible to 'counsel' language learners without reference to discourses of teaching or therapy. He deals with ethical issues of counselling, namely whether we have the right to meddle with matters related to personality, and whether we can counsel without violating the principle of individual autonomy. Like Voller, Riley argues that the relationship between learner and counsellor is one in which both parties have something to contribute. The aim of counselling in Riley's terms is to establish 'inter-subjectivity'. But this in itself calls for considerable skill because the asymmetry of knowledge which is inherent in the situation may put pressure on both sides to reproduce the teacher–pupil relationship.

Both Voller and Riley offer suggestions on training teachers and counsellors for autonomous language learning. Voller urges us to keep in mind three fundamental principles: (1) that language learning is an interpretative process and that autonomous learning requires a transfer of control to the learner; (2) that teaching for autonomous learning must be based on negotiation; (3) that we need constantly to self-monitor our own strategies. Within the broad framework of these principles, Riley provides a useful list of techniques that are used in 'counsellor training' at CRAPEL.

Breen and Mann focus on autonomy in the language *classroom* from the perspective of the teacher, the learner and the social context. They investigate the potential for autonomous language learning as classroom practice by looking at the qualities autonomous language learners may need to be effective in the classroom, and by discussing how teachers need to rethink their classroom practices in order to develop a pedagogy for autonomy. They argue that teachers may be turning to autonomy as a reaction against the 'culture of authority' that has permeated the educational structure and they see autonomy as a way to bring about innovation, but only if teachers are prepared to research their own classrooms and learners themselves. They suggest that teachers need to look at such issues as power relations, the ethics of seeking cultural change in our learners, the dynamics of the classroom – especially in terms of the 'problematic' stages that may develop for individuals and groups when attempting to create an autonomous learning environment – and innovative but valid ways to assess autonomous language learning. They conclude by suggesting some of the attributes, such as self-awareness, and some of the actions, such as decision sharing, that teachers will need to employ if they are to attain a positive measure of autonomy within the classroom.

A number of the points raised by Voller and Riley, and Breen and Mann, are exemplified in O'Dell's case study of teachers' difficulties with self-access work at Eurocentre, Cambridge. O'Dell (1992) has previously written on the importance of teacher orientation for autonomous learning. In this chapter, she reports on a study of teachers' apprehensions about working with students in self-access. Her study comes to the interesting conclusion that whereas new teachers in the school tend to report worries about students' reactions to self-access, their own pedagogical skills in the self-access centre and the operation of technology, more experienced teachers predominantly report worries about their familiarity with the resources of the centre. It seems that as teachers become more experienced with more independent modes of learning, self-expectations in regard to expertise grow in proportion to self-confidence. This observation would seem to support Voller's and Riley's contentions that the roles and discourses of teaching for autonomous learning need to be distinguished from those of more conventional classroom teaching. The question that arises, however, is how teachers can be trained for autonomous learning if their perceptions of their own roles are embedded in a set of beliefs about what it means to be a 'good teacher'. This kind of problem becomes more complex where teachers are required to act both as classroom teachers and self-access counsellors, often with the same groups of students. Again, it seems that 'negotiation' and 'establishing intersubjectivity' are important in establishing relationships between 'trainers' and 'trainees'. Part of the answer, as Breen and Mann propose, is for teachers to research their own classrooms/working environments *themselves*.

In Esch's case study, the role of the teacher appears at first sight to be minimal. Like Benson and Pennycook (Chapters 2 and 3), Esch is concerned by the tendency towards individualism and psychologism in the development of concepts of autonomy. She is especially critical of the notion that there are 'autonomous language learning skills' in which learners can be trained, and she reports on a short course organized for independent learners of French at the University of Cambridge in which participants essentially 'trained themselves'. Sessions were organized on the pattern of a 'learning conversation' in which the participants themselves discussed and reflected upon their learning experiences from week to week without the direct intervention of a teacher. Esch reports that the programme was successful in terms of attendance and in terms of her own analysis of developments in the discourse of the participants. She is herself sceptical, however, about whether the experience could be generalized. The initial motivation was clearly high, as all the participants were already engaged in independent study. Although their intervention was minimal, the programme was nevertheless initiated by teaching staff, who were present as observers throughout. We may speculate on the importance of this initiating and observing role in the success of the course.

We know that language learning can and does take place inde-pendently of institutionalized education. Indeed, formal language education can itself be considered as an invasion or colonization of a non-formal realm which has been in existence for many thou-sands of years. In focusing on the role of the teacher in auto-nomous language learning this part makes clear that autonomous language learning does not simply mean that learners learn on their own. We have in mind processes within formal education, in which roles and relationships of power and control are called into question and modified. Autonomous language learning tends to fail if teachers and learners do not take account of these neces-sary modifications. It also tends to fail if teachers see autonomy as simply leaving learners to their own devices. The chapters in this section point the way to an exploration of the area in between these two extremes.

# 7

## Does the teacher have a role in autonomous language learning?

### PETER VOLLER

## Introduction

Most teachers would agree with the simple proposition that teaching is something they do in order to bring about changes in learners, and that their aim is to do so effectively. However, what those changes might be, and how they can be effectively brought about, are determined by a complex set of interrelated factors that depend upon what the learner and the teacher perceive their respective roles to be, and upon a set of decisions, both taken by them and imposed upon them, and experiences, both past and present, that they bring with them to any given learning situation. So complex is the relationship between these factors that one feature of many methodologies of language learning is to ignore, or at least marginalize, the teacher's role. This has been true both of language acquisition theory and of some methods associated with communicative language learning and the learner-centred classroom.

My intention in this chapter is to try, first, to isolate the most important of these interrelated factors in the context of autonomous approaches to learning, specifically those factors that are related to *beliefs* about language and learning, and the issue of who has *control* over the language learning situation; secondly, to look at the way these factors are related to the definitions of the teacher's role in the literature on independent learning; thirdly, to suggest that these factors are best addressed by adopting a negotiated approach to autonomous language learning; and finally, to examine how the principle of negotiation has been applied in differing language learning situations that have aimed to promote learner autonomy. As a preliminary, however, it is important to understand what notion of autonomy is being dealt with in this chapter. I am not going to discuss the notion of autonomy as an integral part of all learning nor as a general goal of education, for these are givens in almost all cultures and ideologies of education. The notion of autonomy with which I am primarily concerned in this chapter is that which Boud (1988: p.1) describes as an approach to educational practice that emphasizes learner independence *and* learner responsibility.

## Factors determining the teacher's role

> Teacher roles are . . . related ultimately both to assumptions about language and language learning at the level of approach. Some methods are totally dependent on the teacher as a source of knowledge and direction; others see the teacher's role as catalyst, consultant, guide, and model for learning; still others try to 'teacher-proof' the instructional system by limiting teacher initiative and by building instructional content and direction into texts or lesson plans. (Richards and Rodgers, 1986: p.23)

Wright (1987: pp.45–6) summarizes language teachers' and learners' roles as a complex set of interacting factors, both interpersonal and task-related. The interpersonal factors he discusses are: social role, status and power, which determine the social distance between teachers and learners, and attitudes, beliefs, personality and motivation. He also discusses three task-related factors: the extent to which any learning task activates individuals' personal goals, how it stimulates their affective and cognitive faculties, and what the topic (subject matter and skills) inherent to it is. On the basis of this analysis, he defines a teacher's role as having two functions: a *management* function, which is related to the social side of teaching, particularly to motivation and control of learners, and an *instructional* function, which is related to the task-orientated side.

Wright, in stressing the importance of teachers' assumptions about the nature of language and learning, suggests that it is possible to categorize any individual teacher as lying somewhere along a continuum between what Barnes (1976) characterized as *transmission* teachers and *interpretation* teachers. Wright (1987: p.62 fn.) summarizes the two extremes as follows:

*transmission* teachers believe in subject disciplines and boundaries
between them, in content, in standards of performance laid down by
these disciplines that can be objectively evaluated; that the teacher's
role is to evaluate and correct learners' performance; that learners
will find it hard to meet the standards; *interpretation* teachers believe
that knowledge is the ability to organize thought, interpret and
act on facts; that learners are intrinsically interested and naturally
inclined to explore their worlds; that the teacher's role is to set up
dialogues in which learners reorganize their states of knowledge;
that learners already know a great deal and have the ability to refash-
ion that knowledge.

These different sets of beliefs about the nature of knowledge
and the process of learning, and the teacher's role in the process,
are mirrored in the literature on autonomous learning. This also
makes explicit what is implicit in the continuum between the two
extremes: *a transference of control to the learner.* Boud (1988: p.24)
characterizes the varying approaches to teaching and learning as
ranging from the highly didactic, where students make few decisions about learning, to the highly responsive, where students make
most of the decisions about learning. In terms of teacher beliefs
and the locus of control it would appear that writers on autonomy
are firmly positioned at the responsive, *interpretation* end of the
continuum.

Tumposky (1982: p.5) reflects these concerns in her discussion of teacher and learner roles in individualized learning. She
cites Stevick's (1976: pp.91–3) discussion of the four prototype
patterns of authority. Transmission teachers are likely to follow
a 'rational-procedural' pattern, invoking 'impersonal authority'
(external constraints such as the syllabus or teaching materials),
or a 'paternal-assertive' pattern, setting themselves up as authority
figures, in order to maintain social distance from their learners.
Interpretation teachers, on the other hand, are more likely to follow a 'fraternal-permissive' model. In this:

> the teacher consciously minimizes status differences between him-
> self [*sic*] and the students. In this new role, the teacher is more of
> a resource person or consultant than an authority; he is a facilitator,
> rather than an arbiter, of classroom activities; he is concerned with
> his own sensitivity to the learners and to their individual differences
> in learning styles and rates of learning; above all he wants to train
> his students to develop their own learning strategies so that they will
> not be dependent on him.

It is this view of learning, as a dynamic process rather than the mechanical digestion of a body of knowledge, and this view of where power should reside, that has led to the emphasis (i) on learning styles and learner strategies in learner training, on 'learning how to learn', and (ii) on the importance of *negotiation* between learner and teacher, in the literature on individualization, self-direction and autonomy in language learning. To show how widespread this view of the teacher's role has become (and how prescient Tumposky's use of 'resource person, consultant and facilitator' were) it is only necessary to review the literature.

## The teacher as facilitator

> **facilitate**. To facilitate an action or process means to make it easier for it to happen or be done; a fairly formal word. (*Collins COBUILD English Language Dictionary*)

The ideal of the teacher as a *facilitator* of learning, as a *helper* whose role is to facilitate learning, is perhaps the most commonly used term in discussions of self-directed, self-instructional, individualized and autonomous learning, both in adult learning and language learning contexts. In the field of adult self-directed learning, Knowles (1975) was among the earliest theorists to use and define the term *facilitator*. Later writers who have found the term cogent include Brockett and Hiemstra (1985), Brookfield (1986) and Powell (1988). Tough (1971) used the term *helper* and provided a list of the helper's salient features which were taken up, and expanded upon, by Dickinson (1987) in his work on self-instruction in language learning. The *helper* features prominently in Riley's work on autonomous language learning (1982; 1986) and is implicit in Holec's discussion of the teacher's role in autonomous learning as one of support (1985). The term *helper* is used by Sturtridge in her early chapter on individualization and self-access learning (1982). She also saw the teacher as a facilitator of learning, a view she reiterates in her later work on self-access language learning (1992). The term *facilitator* is likewise used to characterize the teacher's role in self-access by Sheerin (1991) and is used by Hammond and Collins in their work on self-directed learning (1991) though they generally prefer the term *co-ordinator*. Finally, the term has been widely used in communicative language learning (see for example Breen and Candlin, 1980; Littlewood, 1981; Nunan, 1989).

What, then, are the salient features of a facilitator in independent language learning? Sheerin (1991: p.153) points out the 'dauntingly comprehensive' nature of the lists provided by some writers (see for example Holec, 1985; Dickinson, 1987; Little, 1989; Sturtridge, 1992), but an analysis of these lists shows that the facilitator is usually perceived as fulfilling two complementary roles. Holec (1985: pp.184–6) characterizes them as the provision of *psycho-social* support and *technical* support. The psycho-social features listed by these writers include:

- the personal qualities of the facilitator (being caring, supportive, patient, tolerant, empathic, open, non-judgemental);
- a capacity for motivating learners (encouraging commitment, dispersing uncertainty, helping learners to overcome obstacles, being prepared to enter into a dialogue with learners, avoiding manipulating, objectifying or interfering with, in other words, controlling them);
- an ability to raise learners' awareness (to 'decondition' them from preconceptions about learner and teacher roles, to help them perceive the utility of, or necessity for, independent learning).

The list of features associated with technical support is even longer, but is almost wholly consistent with the main characteristics of autonomy drawn up by Boud (1988: p.23). The list includes:

- helping learners to plan and carry out their independent language learning by means of needs analysis (both learning and language needs), objective setting (both short- and longer-term, achievable), work planning, selecting materials, and organizing interactions;
- helping learners evaluate themselves (assessing initial proficiency, monitoring progress, and self- and peer-assessment);
- helping learners to acquire the skills and knowledge needed to implement the above (by raising their awareness of language and learning, by providing learner training to help them identify learning styles and appropriate learning strategies).

But how is this long list of features to be achieved in autonomous learning situations? One way, which I shall return to in greater detail shortly, is through *negotiation*. However, before looking in greater detail at the meaning of negotiation, we need to examine another term that has been widely used to characterize the teacher's role in self-directed and autonomous language learning.

## The teacher as counsellor

> **counsellor**: a person whose job is to give advice to people who need it. **Counsel** is advice to someone which is based on a lot of experience or serious thought. If you **counsel** someone, you give them advice, especially about a problem, as part of your job. **consultant**: a person who gives expert advice to people who need professional help. (*Collins COBUILD English Language Dictionary*)

The ubiquity of the term facilitator should not obscure the fact that there is another way in which the teacher's role has been defined in the literature on autonomous language learning. One could say that although the teacher in autonomous learning situations can be characterized as a facilitator, this is especially so in classroom situations. In more individualized situations, the teacher's role has also been widely defined as a *counselling* one. This characterization of the teacher as *counsellor,* to whom learners turn for consultation and guidance, has been suggested for situations where learning contracts are used, for individualized study programmes and, more commonly, to describe the role of staff in self-access centres.

Knowles (1986) in discussing the use of learner contracts in adult self-directed learning uses the terms counsellor and consultant. Bloor and Bloor (1988) use the terms counsellor and consultation to describe the teacher's role in individualized language study programmes, as do Houghton *et al.* (1988). They, however, equate counselling with dependency: as learners become more self-directed, the counsellor's role will become a more supervisory one. Gremmo and Abé (1985) use the term consultant, allying it with 'expert' to characterize the teacher's role in the CRAPEL self-access system of self-directed and autonomous language learning. Sheerin (1989) also sees the role of self-access centre staff as one of guidance and counselling, as do O'Dell (1992) and Kjisik (1994) while Sturtridge (1992) prefers the term adviser. The term counsellor has also been used in communicative language learning (see Richards and Rodgers, 1986) and is a central concept in Curran's Community Language Learning (Curran, 1976). Finally, Tudor (1993) in discussing teacher roles in the learner-centred classroom,

adopts (unconsciously?) Curran's term 'learning-counsellor' to
describe the role of the teacher in raising students' awareness of
learning and language. But if, as I suggested above, this is part
of the facilitator's role, then it is difficult to see how the use of the
term 'counsellor' in this context can be differentiated from the
term 'facilitator'.

Is there, then, any qualitative difference between a facilitating
role and a counselling role, beyond a broad generalization that the
former is used for a wide range of learning situations ranging from
the classroom to the self-access centre, and the latter for more specifically individualized ones? The answer has to be a qualified negative. The only perceptible difference between the two is in terms
of self-access learning, where the counsellor, in addition to fulfilling all the functions of a facilitator, should be able to provide
information and answer questions about self-access resources and
how best to use them, to both learners and classroom teachers
(see Sheerin, 1989; O'Dell, 1992). However, this informational
role (or at least the guidance part of it) is really also implicit in
the list of features associated with technical support given by the
facilitator. Thus it would appear that the only real difference between counselling and facilitating is in the nature of the interaction: counselling implies a one-to-one interaction. The manner in
which the counsellor interacts with the language learner may well
be very different from the way the facilitator does, as Riley points
out in his chapter in this volume (see also Kelly, 1996, for an overview of the types of interaction, based on a psycho-therapeutic model,
with which the counsellor needs to be familiar), but at this point
in time, little research has been done to determine exactly how
counsellors counsel.

## The teacher as resource

> **resource**: something or someone that you can use or refer to, espe-
> cially when you need information on a particular subject. Someone's
> **resource** is their ability to solve problems and difficulties quickly,
> efficiently, and with initiative. (*Collins COBUILD English Language
> Dictionary*)

The provision of information leads us into the third way in which
the teacher's role in autonomous language learning has been characterized, though surprisingly this role is given less prominence

than the other two, often because it is not clearly differentiated from them. This aspect of the teacher's role has been categorized in terms of expertise (see Gremmo and Abé, 1985), and in terms of the teacher as a *resource* (see Breen and Candlin, 1980; Tumposky, 1982; Banton, 1992). It also appears under the guise of *knower* in Community Language Learning and the learner-centred classroom (Curran, 1976; Tudor, 1993). Finally, Wright (1987) also describes the teacher as a resource (and as a guide). Yet what is meant, precisely, by the term resource? And is there a difference between being a resource and being an expert or knower? Again, it could be argued that the difference in terminology depends on the context in which self-directed learning is to take place: the teacher as expert is more appropriate to classroom or group learning situations, and the teacher as resource is more applicable to self-access situations. Self-access facilities are after all resource centres, containing materials such as books, worksheets, videotapes and audiotapes that help learners to learn a language. Of equal, if not greater, importance are the human resources needed to run such facilities. However, it could also be argued that the difference lies in teachers' views of themselves: there is a great difference between the passive provision of information and the active dissemination of it.

What then is the implication of the teacher as human resource? In one sense, it seems highly desirable: the ability of the self-directed learner to use resources efficiently, skilfully and with initiative should be one of the main proofs of autonomous language learning. But in another sense it is threatening to teachers *qua* teachers. For, if learners have actually reached this autonomous state, then they no longer need teachers. How many teachers could put their hands on their hearts and admit that they would be happy to be nothing more than a talking encyclopedia or a talking catalogue? It is one thing to espouse, in one's role as facilitator or counsellor, that one does not wish to manipulate the learner, but does that mean one is prepared to be used as a mere reference tool by the learner? Defining the resource role in terms of expertise could therefore be construed as a way of maintaining unequal power relations between teachers and learners, because underlying the terms knower and expert is the assumption of unequal expertise, of knowledge to which the teacher is privy and the learner is not.

However, the nature of this knowledge is itself problematic. The implication of the teacher as a resource is that the teacher needs to be knowledgeable about the target language and the materials available for learning it. In this sense, the educated but untrained native speaker would make an excellent resource, once he or she has mastered the instructional material that is to be made available to the learner. This seems to be the premise that underlies the employment of young graduates of any discipline in many language schools around the world, and perhaps explains both experienced teachers' fears of self-access facilities and administrators' promotion of them as a 'cheap' alternative to classroom-based language learning. But, if we see learning as an interpretative process, in other words, if we believe in the social construction of knowledge, then such a narrow view of the teacher's 'resource' becomes insufficient: the teacher will have to have a profound understanding both of the discourse community that the learner aspires to join, and of the discourse community from which learners come, if the teacher is to mediate effectively between them. This raises questions about whether or not the teacher needs to be fluent in both the target language and the learner's language, and about the degree to which the teacher needs to be aware of both the target culture and the learner's culture. The nature of the teacher as resource in autonomous language learning is as yet little explored or understood.

## The issue of power and control

Wright (1987: p.56) states that teachers control the social behaviour of their classes in two ways: directly through classroom management procedures and indirectly through the learning activity. Autonomous learning theory, on the other hand, demands that learners take control of their own learning, that the teacher's power be lessened and the learner's power concomitantly increased. As Higgs (1988: p.55) says 'autonomous learning is inconsistent with the teacher being the principal/sole source of power and control'. In her view, 'the teacher therefore becomes a manager who delegates some or most of the power, responsibility and choice in learning to the student'. However, there are many who would disagree with her analysis, both with its explicit advocation of the theories and practices of personnel management (teaching as capitalist enterprise?) and with its assertion that autonomy is somehow compatible with the 'delegation' of power. How learners can take control of their learning and to what extent learners' should be empowered, are highly contentious issues within the field (see Benson and Pennycook in this volume for detailed discussions of this issue). What is of more concern in the context of this chapter is the nature of the power relationship between teachers and learners and the extent to which this will influence the possibility, and the success, of self-directed and independent language learning.

There is a paradox about the teacher's role in independent language learning; the truly autonomous learner would not need a teacher at all. Equally, autonomy is not a gift that can be handed over by the teacher to the learner, so is autonomy unteachable? Yet much of the literature states that learners need to be *taught* to be autonomous. Brookes and Grundy (1988: p.6) suggest that there are two ways to do this: by learner training and by negotiation. Dickinson (1988: p.48) defines learner training as follows:

> training in processes, strategies and activities which can be used for language learning; instruction designed to heighten awareness of the nature of the target language, and instruction in a descriptive metalanguage; instruction in aspects of the theory of language learning and language acquisition.

Dickinson's (1987: p.69) use of the term *instruction* is interesting. Wright describes the teacher's *instructional* role as 'likely to be goal-oriented, task-dependent and knowledge-based, and underpinned by a set of attitudes and beliefs, not only about knowledge, but also the appropriate instructional strategies to employ'. In the context of independent language learning it again focuses our attention on the importance of our assumptions about language and learning. The problem with learner training is that it runs the risk of merely relocating the language teacher: instead of transmitting a body of facts about the target language, the teacher's role is now to transmit a body of facts about the most efficient ways (according to expert linguists) to learn a language. Indeed, it could be argued that teaching students metalanguage is really not much different from teaching, for example, the tense system – instead of teaching learners how to use the present perfect tense, we teach them how to identify and name it.

Likewise with awareness training. Raising the awareness of language learners is no doubt a good thing, but how to raise that awareness may be problematic. It would be all too easy to design a course that did such things, but was no different in terms of teacher role and function from an old grammatical or functional syllabus. Indeed, there is a real danger of this happening, given that research into teacher behaviour suggests that 'although teachers may be using different methodological approaches and may think they are therefore employing different classroom practices, . . . their actual classroom practices reflect a pool of common instructional behaviors' (Richards, 1990: p.119). Again, this implies that teachers' beliefs about the nature of language and learning are of primary importance, influencing as they do teachers' instructional practices: it is not sufficient, in order to raise learners' awareness, merely to present them with a set of learner-training materials and get them to practice various learning strategies. Unless learners get beyond what Mezirow (1985: p.23) calls 'recipe learning', and by means of critical self-reflection, go through a process of 'meaning transformation', then awareness-raising will become just another technique in the transmission teacher's instructional practices.

## Negotiated approaches to autonomous language learning

> **negotiation**. Discussions that take place between people who have different interests, in order for them to be able to come to an agreement about something, solve a problem, or make arrangements.
> (*Collins COBUILD English Language Dictionary*)

Given that a learner training approach is problematic, is an approach based on negotiation likely to be less so? Brookes and Grundy (1988: pp.5–6) say the following about syllabus negotiation:

> It has . . . important advantages in developing the perceptions both of the tutor and the learner(s), and in helping both to an awareness of . . . cultural variations . . . Thus syllabus negotiation is a major way of extending the awareness of learners as to what is important and worth learning. This type of syllabus negotiation is important not only when deciding on self-access programmes, . . . but more particularly in determining what whole-class programme best suits individual learners, especially when the syllabus is treated as an 'inventory' of objectives.

Yalden (1987: pp.63–4) explicitly links the negotiated syllabus with a self-directed or autonomous approach to language learning. She also notes that 'the teacher becomes part of the total instructional resources available' and points out that it makes the learner, along with the linguist and materials writer, the 'prime actor' in the learning process. This yet again suggests that there is a risk of teachers being marginalized, unless they can apply their expertise as linguists and materials writers, and can assure themselves a central role as syllabus negotiators.

However, it should be stressed that negotiation in autonomous language learning goes beyond the syllabus. It should also inform much of what goes on in the classroom and the self-access centre through teacher–learner, learner–resource and learner–learner interactions. In other words, negotiation encompasses both syllabus and *meaning*. To paraphrase Breen and Candlin (1980: p.100), the teacher, as a participant in the learning-teaching situation, has a role to play as a 'joint negotiator within the group and within the classroom procedures and activities which the group undertakes'. They continue: 'the implication for the learner [and concomitantly for the teacher] is that he should contribute as much as he gains, and thereby learn in an interdependent way'. This notion of *interdependence* is central to the development of autonomy. Boud (1988: p.29) sees interdependence as an essential component of autonomy, as a stage of development that transcends independence for, as he points out, independence implies 'an unavoidable dependence at one level on authorities for information and guidance'. Bruffee (1993: p.63) also stresses the need for interdependence and explicitly relates it to collaborative learning and the kinds of negotiation that occur in the social construction of knowledge: negotiation among peers and negotiation between knowledge communities and those who want to join them. To summarize, the teacher's role in autonomous learning can be characterized essentially as one of negotiation, both with learners and external authorities (representatives of the educational institution, and professionals from the discourse communities to which learners are trying to gain admittance) about the syllabus, and, as a participant in and facilitator of the learning process, with learners in their classroom and self-access learning activities.

How is this role to be put into practice? Boud (1988: pp.25–8) discusses three different approaches to, or more accurately three different models of, autonomous learning: the individual model, the group-centred model and the project-based model. All are based upon a process of negotiation and have as their underlying rationale not simply the attainment of independence but of interdependence. He points out that there is considerable overlap between the three – all three approaches may be appropriate in any given diachronic learning situation. However, it is possible to identify each model as being the prime determinant of the learning process in various reported experiments into autonomous language learning.

The individual model focuses on individual learners and their needs, and teachers and other learners become resources for the attainment of these individually defined needs. It can be identified with learning situations that involve the use of learner contracts and/ or counselling. Reports of experiments in counselling learners can be found in Bloor and Bloor (1988) and Little (1988) who stresses the generally non-therapeutic nature of counselling for language learning. He also points out that counsellor–learner negotiation is insufficient interaction for learners, who ask for group negotiations. Martyn (1994) in her experiment with learner contracts stresses the importance of co-operative learning and teachers' attitudes. This model is also characteristic of learning exchanges where a counsellor arranges one-to-one interactions between native speakers and learners of their language (see Müller *et al.*, 1988; Voller and Pickard, 1996).

The group-centred model is characterized by learning primarily through group interactions and democratic decision taking. Syllabus negotiation is a common theme in such an approach. Bloor and Bloor (1988) discuss the negotiation and conduct of a writing course. Huttunen (1988) describes an experiment in developing autonomy among secondary students involving negotiation about individual and group objectives, activities and evaluation. Porcher (1988) details how a group of French teachers formulated and carried out their own training programme by negotiating with their instructor and professional producers of such materials. Martyn and Husain (1993) describe an English for professional communication course for nurses in Pakistan. The syllabus was negotiated between all interested groups, students, teachers, faculty and professionals, in the process of planning, implementing and evaluating the course.

The project-centred model places the emphasis on a process of working towards an outcome. It usually requires collaboration and negotiation between learners in order to achieve the outcome and can allow negotiation about the project and its outcome. Examples of this approach include Dam's work with children in Denmark, in which they work, in English, on a variety of self-selected projects in the classroom (Dam and Gabrielsen, 1988; Dam, 1994). Results suggest that learners attain greater fluency and lexis than with conventional approaches (Dam and Legenhausen, 1996). Other reports of this model in action include Moulden's self-directed English course for business students at CRAPEL (Moulden, 1988) and Pang's (1994) work on a group-centred, humanistic project-based approach to self-access.

## Self-monitoring: observation and reflection

As I mentioned in the introduction to this chapter, there has often been a tendency to marginalize, or even exclude, the teacher from the learning process. This tendency has already been noted above in Yalden's (1987) description of the negotiated syllabus and in my brief discussion of learner training, where there is a danger that linguists and materials writers will promote it as *the* method that will best prepare learners for self-directed learning. The problem with methods, as Richards points out, is that they 'reflect an essentially negative view of teachers, one which implies that since the quality of teachers cannot be guaranteed, the contribution of the individual teacher should be minimized by designing teacher-proof methods' (1990: p.37). He goes on to observe (p.88) that this has also been true of second language acquisition research which has 'virtually excluded the teacher as a participant in the process of second language teaching'. Indeed, it could be argued that the current emphasis on the learner-centred classroom and on the development of self-access facilities is merely the latest attempt by academics, administrators, and the writers of language learning and learner training materials to marginalize the teacher's role in the learning process. Learners will be given lots of choices, about appropriate learning styles and appropriate learning materials, and teachers will become simply 'tour guides' and 'event organizers'. If teachers want control to be transferred to learners, then they must also have the means to control, or at least mediate, the other *loci* of authority. Negotiation, I have argued, is the key to doing this. In fact, without negotiation it is arguable that autonomy as an approach to language learning will be unsuccessful, will become yet another 'method' that has been tried and found lacking.

There is one further way in which the teacher can help to ensure that an autonomous approach to language learning is effective. Teachers, as Breen and Candlin (1980: p.99) point out, need
also to be researchers and learners. Apart from the fact that this
makes it more difficult for external authorities to arrogate to
themselves the role of 'expert', it will also help teachers to understand better the processes that help language learners to become
self-directed. The ways in which teachers can research themselves
include personal reflection, for instance by means of diary studies, self-reporting, by means of inventories and checklists, and the
recording and systematic analysis of learning events (see Richards,
1990). Self-monitoring, as Richards suggests (1990: p.119) is one
way for teachers to continue their professional development, to
reflect critically on their teaching practices, and to 'narrow the gap
between [their] imagined view of their own teaching and reality'.

Such methods are, of course, not exclusive to an autonomous
approach to language learning. They are, however, perhaps more
crucial to it, given first, the general unfamiliarity of teachers with
their role as facilitator, counsellor and resource and secondly, the
emphasis that the approach places on the reapportionment of
power relations, of control, within educational practice. The often-
cited 'unpreparedness' of learners for greater self-direction (let
alone autonomy) should perhaps be seen more in terms of the
teacher's 'unpreparedness' for it (see O'Dell in this volume for a
fuller discussion of what this entails). Teachers need to reflect critically not only upon how they act during a learning event, but also
upon their underlying attitudes and beliefs about the nature of
language and the nature of learning, and upon the constraints, such
as the educational culture in which they work, that impinge upon
their learning situation. Only if they have a clear and objective view
of these assumptions, practices and constraints will they be able to
negotiate effectively with both learners and external authorities
and thereby empower both their learners and themselves.

## Conclusion

There are a number of ways of 'empowering' ourselves as teachers.
The first and most obvious is to have a clear view of the attitudes
and beliefs that underpin our view of autonomous language learning. Whether we view learner autonomy as a right or as a distant

goal, and the roles of facilitator, counsellor and resource as stages along the road that leads to autonomy, we need to remain faithful to three fundamental assumptions. The first is that language learning is an interpretative process, and that an autonomous approach to learning requires a transfer of control to the learner. The second is to ensure that our teaching practices, within the external constraints imposed upon, reflect these assumptions, by ensuring that they are based on a process of negotiation with learners. The third is to self-monitor our teaching, to observe and reflect upon the teaching strategies we use and the nature of the interactions we set up and participate in.

# 8

# The guru and the conjurer: aspects of counselling for self-access

PHILIP RILEY

## Introduction

Since the early 1970s, the CRAPEL (Centre de Recherches et d'Applications Pédagogiques en Langues) has been running and experimenting with various kinds of *self-directed learning systems*, that is, pedagogical structures whose aim is to help learners to learn to learn as well as to learn a language. Typically, such learner-centred approaches provide learners with two main kinds of support: access to a wide range of materials through some form of self-access system or resource centre and access to a person specialized in the field of independent language learning, often known as a 'counsellor' (Gremmo and Riley, 1995). It is generally agreed that learners working in self-access systems may benefit from 'counselling'. But there are considerable problems involved in saying just what counselling *is* and how it differs from teaching or therapeutic discourse. This has important implications for the ways in which we train learners for independent learning.

Although it is probably unfashionable to say so, teachers and counsellors are intellectuals. That is, their social roles involve the processing, legitimation and distribution of their society's knowledge (Marx and Engels, 1968 *et passim*; De Huszar, 1960; Znaniecki, 1965). In this chapter, I will be looking at differences in the ways those roles are realized in terms of the communicative practices which constitute 'counselling' and 'teaching'. More ambitiously, I will try to show that these differences arise from different appreciations and conceptions both of what knowledge is and of the roles of counsellors and teachers as intellectuals within the overall social knowledge system (Mannheim, 1936; Holzner and Marx, 1979; Riley, 1993). I also hope to show that such considerations, although

114

clearly theoretical, have important implications for the practice of counselling and for training counsellors.

In this introduction, we will be looking at three points. First, we shall consider the term 'counsellor' itself, since there is by no means general agreement that it is completely appropriate. Secondly, a number of ethical issues will be identified which, although rarely discussed, directly influence decisions as to what is and is not 'good' counselling in both ethical and discursive terms. Thirdly, an attempt will be made to characterize counselling as a specific category of communicative situation.

## The term 'counsellor'

Over the past fifty years or so, a number of different terms have been suggested to describe a person working with learners but whose role, behaviour and objectives differ from those of the traditional teacher in a number of important ways: instead of being the sole source of knowledge, responsible for all the decisions involved in designing and implementing a programme of study (e.g. choice of time and place, materials, activities, pace, evaluation procedures, etc.) this person aims at helping learners to take those decisions themselves. The terms which have been suggested include:

- counsellor
- helper
- facilitator
- knower
- mentor
- adviser
- consultant

Whereas the term 'learner' (as opposed to 'client', say, or 'student') has been easily and almost universally accepted, there is no such consensus in this case. Each of the candidates can be shown to emphasize subtly some aspect of the role in question and each has consequently fallen foul of the proponents of other approaches. However, it is certainly not my intention to argue in favour of the adoption of the word 'counsellor' even though that is the term used at the CRAPEL. The point I wish to make is that the lack of agreement over this single item of vocabulary is in fact symptomatic of a far wider problem: we have no *discourse* in which to discuss or 'do' counselling. Our problem with the selection of one or other of these terms is in fact only the tip of the iceberg: we need to frame a new discourse in which it is possible to 'counsel' learners without constant reference to other interactional genres, and other informational economies, in particular, teaching.

## *Ethical issues*

Helping learners in self-access is not just a matter of telling them where they can lay their hands on such-and-such a piece of material; it also necessarily involves some degree of access to *self*. Language and learning are both areas which are closely related to the individual's whole personality, including his or her emotions, beliefs and values – areas which can be covered with very thin ice and where counsellors or teachers have to tread very carefully indeed. In language learning materials, for example, peoples' moral, professional and religious convictions, their social representations and assumptions are easily challenged and engaged.

For many educationists, this is one of the major motivations and justifications for learning a foreign language. But it is also a major problem, since we have no professional code of ethics to guide us. It is not, of course, a problem that is specific to counselling in self-access: *all* language teaching and learning is an attack on the personality, whatever the situation or methodology in question because it implies new forms of expressive behaviour, and questions both the self-image and deeply held values and beliefs of the learner. On the one hand, it can be argued that at least this is a problem which is explicitly recognized in the general field of self-access and self-directed learning. On the other, it can be held that in that direction complacency lies, since the nature and effectiveness of learner-centred approaches makes them even more vulnerable on this count than more traditional approaches. Their very focus on the individual with communicative and affective needs brings personality to the fore.

At the risk of trivializing such complex issues, I would suggest that they can be boiled down to the following two questions:

1. Do we have either the right or the competence to go meddling with matters related to personality and values?

Here, it is the *invasive* nature of counselling which is being questioned.

2. Can we really counsel for language learning in ways which are not in complete contradiction with the avowed principle of respect for the individual's autonomy?

Here, we are asking whether counselling is *feasible*, or whether it will always involve some kind of pressure on the learner because of epistemic or political asymmetries in the social relationship.

Question (a) clearly relates to the fact that the practice of counselling is *invasive*, in two senses: first, as a social phenomenon which has increased over the last twenty years or so. Along with two other forms of discourse – those of advertising and the market economy – the discourse of counselling has come to occupy a major position in social epistemology. As I write, the BBC News informs me that 'the police officers who are excavating the garden of Cromwell Road [where the victims of a serial murderer have been found] are to be offered counselling.' Such a suggestion would have been quite unthinkable only twenty years ago. A new discourse has been legitimated by interested social groups – those which provide counselling, of course, but also those who feel they benefit from it or who were for some reason dissatisfied with the status quo. Since this implies a shift in the locus for decision making, there has been an inevitable redistribution of power and a modification of communicative practices. Inevitable, too, is the proliferation of 'counselling situations': counselling for victims of violence, accidents, traumas and acts of god; counselling for those with interpersonal problems, at home or at work; counselling for dependency on alcohol or drugs; counselling for careers.

Secondly, counselling can be an invasion of *privacy*, not just because it might be carried out in ways which are insufficiently tactful or sensitive, but because it is postulated on the basis of a relationship between discourse and self which can be individually or culturally inappropriate. That is, it assumes that 'people need to talk', especially about certain areas of their life, such as 'problems', 'relationships' – and self. This assumption flies in the face of a considerable body of ethnographic evidence, which shows quite clearly that the constitutive elements of 'self', the boundaries between 'self' and 'other', and the modes and modalities of 'self-expression' are all subject to considerable intercultural variation (Howell, 1988; Iteanu, 1990; Overing, 1988; Scollon and Scollon, 1992; 1993; Tooker, 1992). Indeed, the belief that 'self' is a universal is being increasingly seen as one of the most important characteristics of western ideology, a point which is central to the attacks on humanism by continental discourse analysts such as Foucault, Althusser and Lacan. 'Self' is variable, a social construct: in the process of self-construction, discourse plays a major role, by verbalizing consciousness through interior monologue, expressing, categorizing and constructing emotions and concepts, and by providing a configuration of discourse positions which fix the individual in the social matrix. To put this proposition in its most rudimentary form, not everyone takes easily to the chat show, the confessional or the psychiatrist's couch. Indeed, they may find such situations distasteful or threatening (Scollon and Scollon, 1980; 1993). Should we add counselling to this list – or at least, certain counselling techniques? Not to examine the question would be a serious dereliction of duty since counselling for foreign language learning is necessarily cross-cultural to some degree, so that the chances of a confrontation between different definitions of self are consequently high. This problem may be exacerbated in cases where the counsellor and/or the language used for counselling are also foreign for the learner.

The second ethical issue, raised by question (b) concern the feasibility of counselling. Will it not always tend to be disguised teaching, in the sense that the counsellor will consciously or unconsciously impose his or her will, if only because he or she is seen as 'knowing better'?

Socratic discourse, which is one of the main sources of western pedagogical practice, is 'maieutic', that is, the questioner plays the role of midwife in the presence of a mother in labour, helping her to give birth to the child that is already inside her, to draw it out, to bring it to light. At first glance, it might seem that this metaphor could be extended to the role of the counsellor. (Indeed, it is the appropriateness of doing so which underlies much of the debate concerning the choice of the term in the first place.) However, in the Socratic method, the questioner knows what answer he or she wants and has clear agenda for obtaining it. The skilled help provided is not disinterested, since the aim is to help the recipient to 'understand', 'see the light', 'find the truth', that is, the questioner's truth. The discursive, and in particular argumentative, strategies employed aim at recognition by the learner of the legitimacy and superiority of the questioner's point of view.

When learners perceive, as they soon do, that counselling, instead of being the disinterested, learner-centred, altruistic assistance it is made out to be, is in fact a highly constraining form of social control, they cannot be blamed for finding the situation hypocritical and for preferring 'honest' teaching.

This is obviously a major problem or set of problems for the would-be counsellor who aims at making expertise available without encroaching on the learner's autonomy or even at increasing the learner's degree of autonomy.

To conclude this brief glance at some of the problematic ethical aspects of counselling, it may come as some small consolation to remember that in Greek mythology, Hermes was not only the messenger of the gods and the representation of eloquent communication: he was also a cheat and a thief. Counsellors, along with translators, interpreters and messengers of all kinds are condemned by the ambiguous nature of their role and of language itself to live with the knowledge that the effects of their messages may not always be those that were intended.

## Counselling as a category of communicative situation

Much of the disagreement as to what counselling 'is' (*really* is) is due to the fact that the term is employed as if it referred to a simple, uniform activity, whereas even the most cursory examination shows it to be a complex and variable discourse type which overlaps with a number of other types and situations. For example, the following have been identified as among the potential aims of counselling sessions:

- information
- diagnosis
- evaluation
- negotiation
- help
- consultation

Such topics may provide the main aims of specific sessions or series of sessions or, of course, several may be touched on in the course of a single session. There can therefore be no single definition of counselling: it is not a concept which is amenable to an essentialist approach (cf. Janicki, 1990). What we need is an analytic grid composed of the factors of variation and which would serve as a rigorous, principled and detailed basis for the description of the range of situation types generically known as 'counselling'.

Since the classification of communicative situations is precisely the object of the ethnography of communication as that discipline has been developed by Dell Hymes (1972) and his colleagues, it seems only reasonable to look to them for inspiration. What we find in their work is a systematic list of 'situational features' (participants, roles, setting, channel, norms, acts, etc.) which allows us to describe communicative situations in a flexible and detailed way. Above all, it helps us identify those aspects of a given situation which are specific to it and to study the consequences of variation along the different parameters. To illustrate this point, let us look in more detail at what we have seen to be one of the thorniest issues in this field, that of the counsellor's *role*.

## The counsellor's role

The term 'role' is used to refer to a social construct which confers on the individual concerned the right/duty to perform a certain set of acts. Role is manifested in discourse by the performance of specific categories of illocutionary acts, interactive acts and non-linguistic acts (cf. Gremmo *et al.*, 1985). For example, in the classroom, it is the teacher's role to begin and end a lesson, ask questions, correct and evaluate answers (illocutionary acts); to manage turn-taking by initiating and closing exchanges and nominating addressees (interactive acts). Non-linguistic acts would include a barber cutting hair, a barman pouring a drink and a surgeon removing an appendix. The performance must be competent, in the broadest sense and it must be socially warranted or approved by other participants in the situation. Otherwise there will be confusion and misunderstanding, at the very least, if not outright confrontation and conflict – 'Who do you think you are?', 'What do you think you're doing?', 'Who do you think you're talking to?'.

Roles often have to be negotiated, especially when the situation type is new to one of the participants. This may be the result of a participant's refusing to recognize another's role and rights, but since roles are often mutually defining and complementary (doctor/patient, shop-assistant/customer, etc.) even in cases where there is no resistance to the other's role, it may well be necessary to clarify one's own. This is in fact, one of the most common occurrences in the counselling situation, where a learner may be perfectly willing to go along with the counsellor's definition of the counsellor's own role, but does not realize that it has direct implications for his or her own role, too.

This largely explains why, in almost all forms of counselling, it is found necessary and worthwhile to spell out the roles, in other words to discuss them explicitly as they form a basis for the distribution of acts, rights and duties during the interactions to come. To take a common enough example in the field of counselling for independent language-learning, the learner who comes with a vocabulary problem will find that it is not the counsellor's role to be a walking dictionary. Instead, the counsellor will try to suggest ways in which the learner can solve the problem alone, thereby becoming a more accomplished learner. One of the great advantages of learning contracts of the 'You'll do this and I'll do that' sort is that they provide a clear statement, not just of learning objectives, but of the distribution of roles.

To illustrate the interest and use of this approach, let us compare the *roles* of teacher and counsellor and compare the different sets of speech acts and functions which realize them (Figure 8.1).[1]

With these points in mind, it becomes easier to make some fundamental generalizations about the role of the counsellor: it involves:

1. *Helping the learner to learn:* that is, to become more skilled and autonomous *qua* learner. This implies raising the learner's consciousness about his or her representations, beliefs and attitudes as regards the learning process and, as far as is possible, helping with the identification of personal learning styles and preferences (Willing, 1989; Ellis and Sinclair, 1989; Duda and Riley, 1991)
2. *Helping the learner to learn X:* (English, Swedish, Swahili, etc.) This implies that learners will need to learn how to analyse and identify their language-learning needs and objectives; how to choose appropriate learning activities and techniques and materials; how to organize a realistic and relevant learning programme; and how to monitor and evaluate their progress.
3. *Helping the learner to learn X in self-access:* Clearly, this will include the tasks and aims mentioned under 1 and 2 above, as these are largely analytic distinctions, but it will also mean introducing the learner to the organization and functioning of the self-access centre (equipment and facilities, cataloguing system, counselling service, etc.).

| TEACHING | COUNSELLING |
|---|---|
| 1. Setting objectives | 1. Eliciting information about aims, needs and wishes |
| 2. Determining course content | 2. Why, what for, how, how long: giving information, clarifying |
| 3. Selecting materials | 3. Suggesting materials, suggesting other sources |
| 4. Deciding on time, place, pace | 4. Suggesting organization procedures |
| 5. Deciding on learning tasks | 5. Suggesting methodology |
| 6. Managing classroom interaction, initiating | 6. Listening, responding |
| 7. Monitoring the learning situation | 7. Interpreting information |
| 8. Keeping records, setting homework | 8. Suggesting record-keeping and planning procedures |
| 9. Presenting vocabulary and grammar | 9. Presenting materials |
| 10. Explaining | 10. Analysing techniques |
| 11. Answering questions | 11. Offering alternative procedures |
| 12. Marking, grading | 12. Suggesting self-assessment tools and techniques |
| 13. Testing | 13. Giving feedback on self-assessment |
| 14. Motivating | 14. Being positive |
| 15. Rewarding, punishing | 15. Supporting |

**Figure 8.1**  Roles in teaching and counselling

Figure 8.2 summarizes the complementary role relationship between counsellor and learner in this context. The learner comes to the counselling-for-learning situation with a *learning culture*, a set of representations, beliefs and values related to learning that directly influence his or her learning behaviour. The counsellor comes to the same situation with a set of representations, values and beliefs which include expert knowledge about the language-learning process as well as the operation of the self-access system in question. As in any communicative situation, common ground has to be found and intersubjectivity to be established. However, the asymmetry of knowledge weighs very heavily indeed on the relationship and on the discourse produced. Given most learners' representations and previous experience, given, that is, the western pedagogical tradition and practice, the pressure on the two participants to reproduce the teacher–pupil relationship is immensely

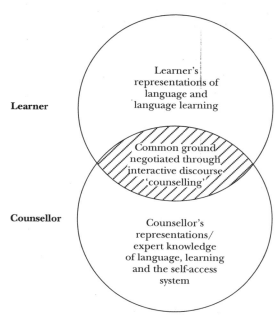

**Figure 8.2**   The complementary role relationship between counsellor and language learner

powerful. It is part of the counsellor's role to see that this does not happen, something which requires both skill and experience.

## Counselling and the social knowledge system

So far, we have been talking about counselling as a category of situation, consisting of complex configurations of identifiable features and parameters. This is a natural enough, commonsense simplification, and a necessary one, too: How could we 'do' counselling or train counsellors if we were unable to identify what counselling is in the first place? However, there are a number of good reasons for trying to situate counselling within a wider conceptual framework, to compare it as a form of knowledge management to other forms of informational economy.

One of the main reasons for doing this is to avoid the logical circularity of arguing for the existence of something we call 'counselling' simply because we have a word for it. However, this epistemological objection will not be pursued here. A second reason, and one which we will concentrate on, is that without any comparative dimension it is in fact impossible to say what the specific characteristics of counselling as knowledge management are. Just as we needed a set of situational features to describe the communicative practices which constitute the practice of counselling, we need a set of epistemic features to describe the role of counselling in the social knowledge system.

## The social knowledge system

Society can be described as a set of structures and functions for the management of knowledge. 'Knowledge' is used here in an anthropological sense to include not just factual information, but beliefs, collective representations and attitudes: near-synonyms are 'socio-cultural knowledge' and 'culture'. All knowledge is socially conditioned, that is, it is established, selected, formulated and transmitted on the basis of social criteria: from this perspective, knowledge, rather than being regarded as immanent, is seen as inseparable from knowers and knowing and from historical and cultural contexts.

However, individual members of a society do not have identical knowledge: all the factors which constitute the individual's social identity (age, sex, occupation, religion, class, place of birth and residence, etc.) are knowledge-related (Riley, 1988b, 1989b). For example, when someone filling in a form states that they are a brain-surgeon, market-gardener or teacher of English, they are identifying themselves on the basis of a body of knowledge.

The specific selection of knowledge acquired by the individual will depend on his or her position in the social matrix. The kinds of knowledge which are available to that person will depend on the nature and the quality of social interaction to which he or she has access. Intellectuals who directly intervene in the operation of the social knowledge system, such as teachers or counsellors (and the traditions and institutions they represent) play roles which determine the characteristics of particular categories of social interaction. Specific sets of communicative practices, such as those realizing the roles of counsellor and teacher which we looked at earlier, but also including doctor–patient interviews and other types of service encounter, bargaining, narration, and the like, are therefore to be seen as the principal mechanisms of the social knowledge system.

They are the ways in which knowledge is used and shared or withheld in particular interactions and in society in general. (For further discussion of discourse in the sociology of knowledge, see Fairclough, 1992a; Riley 1989a.)

The main features of the social knowledge system are:

1. *Knowledge creation.* Society is continuously producing new knowledge, local and scientific, which has to be 'epistemologized' into new domains and bodies. In terms of individual cognition, this corresponds to psychological aspects of the learning process.

2. *Knowledge organization.* Existing knowledge is organized into disciplines and domains with their own objects and principles of relevance. Bodies of knowledge include scientific knowledge, common sense, religious knowledge and magic. In terms of individual cognition, these domains correspond to the cognitive categories members use for the classification of situations, genres, objects, people, knowledge, emotions, and so on. The organization and operation of such criteria may be described as 'personal constructs', 'prototypes' or 'representations'.

3. *Knowledge repositories.* Knowledge is stored in social institutions, such as language, codes of law, oral history, mythology and literature. Modern forms include libraries, data banks, record offices and archives, expert systems, and so on. In terms of individual cognition, this corresponds to memory.

4. *Knowledge distribution.* Knowledge is distributed differentially, creating epistemic communities, that is, social figurations based on common knowledge (a choir, a profession, a teenage gang) with their own discursive roles and positions, and communicative networks and practices. In terms of individual cognition, this can be usefully summarized as social identity, the sum of the social sub-groups of which the individual is a member.

5. *Knowledge legitimation.* Dominant discourses are established through power, interest and ideology. They are justified by rationality, consensus, revelation, magic, pragmatic procedures. In terms of individual cognition, this corresponds to the member's ideology, the set of beliefs representations, values and attitudes which form his/her interpretative repertoire.

6. *Knowledge use.* Sub-groups apply, implement and transfer knowledge (including skills, technology and competencies) for the benefit of the group as a whole or to gain or maintain advantages such as status, power, or money. In terms of individual

cognition, this can be seen as competence, since all appropriate participation in social activities is knowledge-based.

This account of the social knowledge system is highly schematic and has been limited to the functions and structures of the system, on the one hand, and individual cognition on the other. However, in interaction the social world and the world of the individual meet and are negotiated, maintained and learned reflexively. Social categories, roles and orders of discourse, functioning as it were 'top-down', are differentially available to individuals functioning 'bottom-up'. In the circus ring, under the spotlights, a small number of artists perform for a vast, unseen audience. Reconciling individual talents with audience expectations can only be learnt in and through practice. The forms and content of that learning, the ways in which knowledge is made available in terms of roles, discourse and learning situations are variable and it is to this topic that we will now turn.

## Gurus and conjurers

I have argued that the communicative practices realizing and characterizing social roles such as teacher or counsellor are the forms or mechanisms of the underlying social knowledge system. To illustrate this point, I would like to look briefly at two different systems, two 'approaches' to knowledge management in non-western cultures. My example is taken from Frederik Barth's (1990) seminal essay, 'The guru and the conjurer: transactions in knowledge and the shaping of culture in South-East Asia and Melanesia'. Basing his analysis on his anthropological studies in northern Bali and Inner New Guinea, Barth compares the role, practices and statuses of two types of 'intellectual' or 'teacher' (though, of course, the whole point is that such labels belong to other knowledge economies). On the one hand, there is the conjurer or initiator, on the other, the guru. He writes (1990: pp.643–4):

> I am trying to expose the *wellsprings* of two basically different informational economies, by identifying the pressures that direct the intellectual efforts of incumbents of these two very different roles.
> First, the initiator. The elements of an initiation are composed of the key objects and acts of the community's ritual and religion, that is, the essential sacred knowledge of the culture. . . . Using secrecy as their means, [initiators] conjure forth a subtle experience

of mystery; and by manipulating concrete symbols they construct a complex and moving tradition of knowledge. The initiator must command this body of knowledge, and know which step of the initiation he is performing. But his task is to put this knowledge to use and affect the novices by its force, not simply to explicate the knowledge to them ... the novices are supposed to be transformed by the rite itself, not by what has been transmitted to them of the knowledge it contains.

The task of a Guru, on the contrary, is to instruct, clarify and educate ... so that his disciples learn from him in a personal and enduring relationship ... [his] task is done once he has successfully transmitted his message. His first requirement, then, is that he must not run out of materials: a guru only lasts so long as he has more to teach ... Secondly, his different statements must be, or appear to be, consistent. If he contradicts himself, or if his store of knowledge is exhausted, he is quickly eclipsed by rivals or pupils. These pressures should indeed be realities familiar enough to academics.

Unlike the initiator, the Guru strengthens his performance
(a) by the sheer *mass* of knowledge he commands
(b) by replenishing it with more items: borrowing from accessible colleagues, extending his competence to more sections
(c) by creativity: inventing elaborations, involutions or refinements
(d) by subdividing knowledge into increments ...
(e) (employing) strategies of mystifying, complicating and interposing an elaborate ceremonial language of honorific or technical terms ...

Barth argues that these practices are the direct result of the different ways in which knowledge is conceived. The initiator is limited by the idea that sharing knowledge devalues it, so that he will try to withhold it, whereas the guru obtains merit from sharing his knowledge, so that he is motivated above all things to talk and teach. He also notes that guru-managed knowledge

is free to develop into the most extraordinary scholasticism ... characteristic and heavy pressures are placed on pupils and disciples. They are enrolled in the Guru's own project.

We are now in a position to understand better *why* it is that teacher's discourse and counsellor's discourse differ so much in terms of the communicative practices, categories of acts, strategies of which they are composed. They represent different ways of controlling, evaluating and even conceiving of knowledge, different stances towards knowledge as power, as property, as a condition for group membership, as a necessary prerequisite for acting on the environment. In other words, they have different functions within the social knowledge system.

In very general terms, teachers operate in an informational economy where knowledge, which is seen as both valuable and dangerous, has to be handed on in small quantities at a time, so that merit is to be gained by controlling the conditions and modalities of this process of transmission. To exert control, they have to take all the decisions which are constitutive of the learning programme (syllabus, organization, methodology, etc.). So closely identified are 'knowledge' and 'control', that terms such as 'discipline' and 'authority' are completely ambiguous in this respect.

Counsellors, on the other hand, operate in an informational economy where knowledge is acquired, and earn merit by explaining the conditions and modalities of the process of acquisition and by helping learners to achieve self-control.

Despite the caricatural nature of these descriptions, I hope that it is quite clear that I am not suggesting any simple equation of the 'teachers are gurus, counsellors are initiators' type. Barth's ironic comment quoted above that 'these pressures should indeed be realities familiar enough to academics' is fair and insightful, but there are many differences, too. Moreover, it would be easy to find certain teachers – and very many learners indeed – who subscribe to the initiator-like view that all that is required is simple physical presence in the classroom for some kind of mystical transformation to take place, or that understanding is secondary to the formal manipulation of symbolic objects.

## Counsellor training

We have been looking at the differences in discourse types resulting from ways in which roles such as teacher, counsellor, guru and initiator are realized in their various informational economies. One of the main implications of such comparisons is that counselling is a complex skill and that teachers cannot be changed into counsellors overnight. To conclude, then, let us look briefly at some aspects of counsellor-training.

It is convenient to handle the topic of counsellor-training under three broad headings, though in reality there will always be considerable overlap between them.

## Academic

Here we are referring to the acquisition of relevant specialized knowledge in the fields of language and language-learning: phonetics and phonology; morphology; lexis; syntax; semantics; pragmatics; sociolinguistics; psycholinguistics; language acquisition. For purely practical reasons, this knowledge will usually be the fruit of an institutionally-based course leading to a formal qualification in a language or linguistics. It would obviously be helpful if the programme of study provided students with the possibility of relating their knowledge in these fields directly to topics such as self-access and self-directed learning, as is the case at the University of Nancy, where my colleague Marie-José Gremmo runs a course entitled 'Self-access systems' as an optional part of the applied linguistics syllabus.

## Practical

It is clearly essential that the counsellor should be familiar with the particular self-access system in which he or she is to work. The only realistic way in which this kind of knowledge can be acquired is hands-on experience, possibly under the guidance of a more experienced colleague. Besides learning to operate the various types of equipment included in the centre, priority will probably be given to getting to know what materials are available, how they are acquired, processed and catalogued and, where relevant, how they relate to the wider institutional context, including such things as study needs and examination requirements.

## Counselling

The first generation of counsellors for self-access, indeed for self-directed learning in general, naturally had to acquire the necessary skills 'on the job'. This is still very often the case and, of course, there is no real substitute for practical experience. But neither is there any justification for not learning from other peoples' mistakes or for trying to reinvent the wheel, so it makes good sense to reflect on previous experience and to try to systematize what has been acquired, so that it can be transmitted and shared in as clear and efficient way as possible. Here, then, is a brief list of techniques which have been found helpful for training and developing counsellors' skills:

1. *Hospitation.* 'Sitting in' on a more experienced colleague's counselling sessions can be useful and enlightening, although in some cases there may be the danger of 'observer effect'. That is, the trainee's presence may influence the behaviour of either counsellor or learner.

2. *Self-directed learning of a foreign language.* It is essential that counsellors should know what it is like to be a self-directed learner in order to give realistic, relevant and trustworthy help and advice.

3. *Sharing and discussion.* 'Thinking aloud', that is, talking things over, whether with fellow trainees or with more experienced counsellors, seems to be a very necessary part of developing the range of concepts and attitudes, including a modest self-confidence, required of a skilled counsellor.

4. *Critical analysis of recordings.* In our experience at the CRAPEL, this is probably the most useful single technique for counsellor-training. It involves the critical and detailed analysis of sound or video-recordings of counselling sessions. Topics for examination might include the realizations of categories of speech acts closely related to the counselling role, such as *suggesting*, or the learner's development of metalanguage from one session to another. This is a major field for research, of course, and one hopes to see a literature on this topic develop which would be comparable to that on the language of the classroom.

5. *Guidance manuals.* Most busy counsellors, whether experienced or not, find it useful to have a 'checklist' of points to remember and producing and maintaining this document is itself a valuable exercise.

6. *Listening exercises.* Listening, both for content and for empathy, lies at the heart of the counsellor's work. It is not a skill that can be taken for granted, by any means. One of the simplest forms of exercise involves stopping a tape or live discussion and trying to summarize to the satisfaction of the *speaker* just what it was he or she has been trying to say for the past five minutes.

7. *Research.* Self-access is proving to be a rich and complex field of activity, so much so that people caught up in it can sometimes feel overwhelmed and anxious, not knowing where to start. Research projects provide the foci for sustained attention and systematic investigation. They also provide invaluable feedback about the functioning of the system. Obtaining and analysing this feedback and trying to implement any necessary

modifications is in itself a highly formative experience for the individuals concerned.

For reasons which have been discussed above, the whole thrust of a counsellor-training programme of any kind will be to provide conditions in which the trainees will gain and critically reflect on relevant experience. They will need to hammer out their own ideational and transactional discourse positions, their own roles with respect not only to the particular self-access system in which they happen to find themselves, but also to the way in which they conceive of the status and transmission of knowledge.

## Conclusion

Counselling for self-access can only be understood and practised if we develop the conceptual and methodological tools necessary for distinguishing it from other forms of discourse, especially teaching. Comparing the counsellor's and the teacher's roles as they are manifested in the performance of different sets of speech acts throws light on their respective aims and on the characteristic ways in which counsellors and teachers try to manage and share knowledge. Investigations of this kind can provide a useful framework for counsellor training.

## *Note*

1. This list is taken from my colleague Odile Régent's 1993 paper 'Communication, strategy and language learning', where she presents a comparative analysis of classroom discourse and counselling discourse. The paper includes lengthy extracts in French of both types of discourse.

# 9

## Shooting arrows at the sun: perspectives on a pedagogy for autonomy

MICHAEL P. BREEN AND SARAH J. MANN

### Introduction

Our purpose in this chapter is to explore the meaning and experiences of autonomy in the language classroom. We seek to do this from four related perspectives: (i) from that of the learner; (ii) from the perspective of the wider social context in which learners and teachers work; (iii) from the focused perspective of the classroom; and (iv) from the perspective of the teacher.

We aim to raise issues which are directly related to the practical implementation of autonomous language learning and the principles which motivate it. The perspectives we offer and the issues we address derive from our reflection on three areas of experience. First, a long-term involvement with the professional development of primary and secondary teachers of language who have moved towards the introduction of autonomous work with their learners (an account of one of these experiences is offered in Breen *et al.*, 1989). Secondly, our own teaching on two distinct professional postgraduate courses – one in Linguistics for English Language Teaching and one in Management Learning – in which the sharing of responsibility between teachers and students for the content and working procedures of these courses was a key characteristic. The third area of our work which informs this chapter is case study research of students' own experiences of learning.

In beginning with the perspective of the learner, we consider what it means to *be* autonomous. Here we will be concerned with the existential position of individual autonomy virtually regardless of the particular context in which the person is acting.

The second part of the chapter situates autonomy in terms of how the macro-social context may impact upon learners in educational settings and upon ourselves as professionals who are wishing to implement autonomous language learning. Here, the tensions and paradoxes of autonomy become more transparent.

We then focus in on the micro-social context of the classroom and the possible evolution of autonomy within it. Finally, we examine the implications of our discussion for the teacher who engages in a pedagogy for autonomy.   ·

The chapter assumes that the processes and goals of autonomous language learning are desirable, although arguments for their acceptability are not detailed here. Our intention is to examine the concept in terms of its potential for classroom practice. In doing so, we express the argument that the gradual establishment of a pedagogy for autonomy is a complex challenge and not unlike trying to shoot arrows at the sun.

Our metaphor needs explaining. In Pre-Columbian Mexico it is said that there existed people who believed that they could make the sun die by firing arrows at it. As this ritual tended to be performed towards evening, their success rate tended to maintain their faith. If we are trying to develop genuine autonomous learning in our language classes, it is possible that we could be sharing a similar degree of self-delusion. We may well be strongly resisting the likely trivialization and commodification of the concept of autonomous learning which is often the fate, as David Little reminds us, of 'fashionable' innovations in language teaching (Little, 1991). Nevertheless, we may be at risk of reducing the actual complexity of the task, rather like those Mexicans who notionally reduced the distance between themselves and the sun.

However, the story has a positive point also. There can be little doubt that the sunset ritual enabled the people to shoot arrows over a greater distance than most people before or since. The benefits to their other arrow-shooting activities such as hunting were obvious. Our argument is that we may seek to develop the ideals of autonomy in practice but, being alert to their complexities, are better able to struggle with the constraints upon them. The professional energy which we may devote to aiming towards autonomous language learning will almost certainly uncover and achieve an unanticipated range of new possibilities in language pedagogy.

# Being autonomous as a language learner

What does it mean to be an autonomous person in a language learning classroom? In this section we consider eight different qualities that we see as characterizing being autonomous: the person's stance towards the world, their desire for what it is they are learning, their sense of self, their metacognitive capacity, their management of change, their independence from educational processes, their strategic engagement with learning, and their capacity to negotiate.

## The learner's stance

Learners see their relationship to what is to be learnt, to how they will learn and to the resources available as one in which they are in charge or in control. From this perspective autonomy is not a language learning process which can be learnt as if it were a set of rules or strategies. Rather autonomy is seen as a *way of being* in the world; a *position from which to engage* with the world. Unlike Holec, we are proposing that autonomy is not an ability that has to be learnt (Holec, 1988), but a way of being that has to be discovered or rediscovered.

## The desire to learn

Autonomous persons in the language learning classroom are in an authentic relationship to the language they are learning. They have a genuine desire to learn *that* particular language. Since their position is one of 'I really want to do this' rather than 'I do this because I feel I ought to, or because someone requires this of me', their relationship towards what is being learnt is not mediated by the eye of the Other or by their own assumptions about what the Other demands. This desire to learn can be either intrinsic, 'I want to learn this for its own sake' or instrumental 'I want to learn this because it will help me to achieve x'.

## A robust sense of self

The autonomous person has a robust sense of self. Thus autonomous learners' relationship to themselves as learners is one which is unlikely to be undermined by any actual or assumed negative

assessments of themselves or their work by significant others in
the teaching-learning process. Assessment can be used by the autonomous learner as a potentially rich source of feedback or can be
discarded if it is judged to be irrelevant or unhelpful.

## Metacognitive capacity

The autonomous person is able to step back from what they are
doing and reflect upon this in order to make decisions about
what they next need to do and experience. This metacognitive
capacity allows the autonomous person to make decisions about
what to learn, when, how and with what human and material
resources. Furthermore, it allows the autonomous learner the
possibility of making constructive use of any offered feedback.

## Management of change

Metacognitive capacity allows the person to constantly assess the
usefulness and relevance of the changing resources around them
and, at the same time, to change what they do and seek to experience as a result of this monitoring. Autonomous learners are thus
both *alert to change* and *able to change* in an adaptable, resourceful
and opportunistic way.

## Independence

A person who is taking an autonomous position towards learning
a language in a classroom is someone whose capacity to learn and
whose success at learning will be independent of the educational
processes taking place there. Such learners are able to make use
of the resources available to them in that context for their own
learning and to seek others from outside the classroom, whatever
the teacher does. Illich has suggested that schooling teaches people
the need to be taught so that we give up our autonomy and come
to 'demand instruction' (Illich, 1971). For the autonomous learner,
on the other hand, *the locus of responsibility for instruction has shifted
from the teacher to the learner.*

## A strategic engagement with learning

Autonomous learners are able to make use of the environment
they find themselves in in a strategic way. They can assess their

own needs, wants, interests and preferred ways of working in order to identify appropriate goals which can then guide the decisions they make about their next steps. Autonomous learners are able to choose the right thing at the right time for the right reasons against their own evolving criteria. In essence, such learners construct and evolve their own language learning curriculum.

### A capacity to negotiate

The impression given so far of autonomy may be one in which learners are somehow operating in a world in which there are no other people, or in which the needs of others do not intrude on their exercise of their own autonomy. However, learners never work in a social vacuum. In the classroom, they participate in and help establish social routines and procedures with a teacher and other learners. The autonomous learner therefore needs to be able to negotiate between the strategic meeting of their own needs and responding to the needs and desires of other group members. Thus, although autonomous learners and their success at learning may be independent of the context in which they find themselves, they will need to negotiate and collaborate with the other members of the group in order to make *best use* of the potential resources available in the classroom.

We suggest that the above points are a kind of existential characterization of the autonomous learner. Learners interact with their social environment and, not least because of the ways in which they define the situation in which they are located, they may constrain their own potential for autonomy or may perceive constraints upon it.

## Asserting or giving up autonomy as a learner

If we take the view that autonomous learning is a desirable goal in the language classroom, we need to ask why there appear to be few autonomous learners in our classrooms in the first place. The following quotations (reported in Mann, 1987) express the words of two different students describing how they study, and what reading and studying mean to them. The students are both at the same institution, studying the same degree in the same class. In order to be a student in this context they have both been highly successful in the educational system.

When talking about how she reads, Sheila says:

> For the first five to ten minutes I don't absorb much of what I read. It takes a while to get concentrating, at least with set texts, then there comes the middle period where my concentration and absorption is at its greatest, lasting about half an hour, then concentration and interest ebb and I have to do something else for a short while. This cycle is then repeated.
>
> I don't approach it expecting it to be either difficult or easy but I approach it expecting having to concentrate. I know that I'm going to have to think about it. It's not just going to float above my head. I'll have to really get into the text.
>
> At university, you do a lot more thinking for yourself and if you do that then you've got to concentrate more and formulate your own ideas as opposed to just reading things through and having someone tell you what was in it.
>
> It is a protective outer garment that will protect you and look after you while allowing you to be yourself. It may give gentle hints as to the right direction but it is somewhere you can go and be yourself in an intellectual atmosphere, an atmosphere of thought. It's home from home really. It's a comforting place.
>
> My responsibility as a student is to do enough work, be able to contribute and put forward ideas, discuss things and maintain my own personal view while accepting the views of others and the facts behind them.

Sally, another student, describes her approach to reading:

> I probably go into too much detail, into it too thoroughly, and can't see the wood for the trees. I used to take notes but now because it takes so long and I end up not finishing the task and then I'd have to come back to it, and it's rather depressing because it is half finished.
>
> I'm totally lazy, partly because I'm nervous because I put things off. When I know I ought to be doing something I put it off, nearer the time I get panicky and therefore more nervous. It's a vicious circle. I know I do that.
>
> There's pressure on you now. Everything you have to read you have to concentrate more on. Here I don't read much for pleasure as I feel I ought to concentrate on academic work. If there is no pressure to do something with a text then I can read it more and I'm less worried of the consequences of reading it.
>
> I felt a tremendous change because when I wasn't at university it's almost as if you've got nothing to define yourself by.

I couldn't stand it because I was being compared to my brother and because of the difficulties I had at Manchester, and in the sixth form, everyone starts comparing because he went to Cambridge, and he isn't cleverer than me . . . I felt I was being dismissed as the stupid one, 'he's academic and you're not'.

It's a matter for me of establishing a good reputation by getting good marks. I want to be thought of as a good student. Not average. What counts at the end is the mark you are going to get.

As it was my second start I was worried whether I would stick it out. I was conscious of having to prove myself a lot. Before I had taken it for granted I was intelligent, I would go through the system but when I found I had nothing to identify with, no academic status at all, I felt as if I had lost all my brain power.

While there may be many interpretations of Sheila's and Sally's experiences, a crucial variable in the learning experience which Sally reveals is the impact of the eye of the Other upon her sense of self as a learner. Her interpretation of her experiences renders her more vulnerable to viewing learning and particularly its assessment as a disempowering process; as something which appears to happen to her rather than being within her own control.

Sheila and Sally represent that proportion of young people who successfully enter higher education in Britain. More than 75 per cent of their own age group, however, cease participating in the education system at the age of eighteen. Of these, there is little doubt that a fair proportion have asserted their autonomy by 'dropping out'. It is reasonable to suggest, however, that the educational system as it operates in a society like Britain is structured and functions in such a way that it is less and less likely for a person to develop as an autonomous learner because the formal conventions of the system seriously challenge the exercise of authentic autonomy.

Although a range of classroom conventions can be seen to undermine autonomous learning, not least the whole cultural process which maintains particular working relationships in the classroom (Breen, 1985b), a crucial convention which exemplifies the challenge to autonomy is the assessment process as it largely operates within formal education. A student's sense of self *as a learner* is most often constructed against evaluative criteria over which they have no control and through a process in which they have virtually no negotiating rights. As Sally's perceptions reveal, this construction of a false and vulnerable self can occur informally and as an on-going process with which Sally conspires, or formally through the grading system. Of course learners need to know where they stand in relation to a body of knowledge or a range of capabilities which require levels of achievement. However, in mass educational systems, conventional procedures of assessment most often remain mystifying to students and part of this mystification is necessary in order that the learner's autonomous right to challenge the judgement of others will be strongly constrained. The system protects itself. The effect of this process is that a learner's potential robust sense of self is displaced by a publicly judged self. Most young learners, because of their inherent wish to be approved of as a person, discover this explicit construction of themselves from the earliest years in school while the whole experience of schooling tends merely to confirm its seeming inevitability.

The assessment process can be seen as one expression of the inevitable tension between the learner as an individual and both the learner as a member of a classroom group and the learner in relation to the 'code of law' of the wider society which will be internalized as the eye of the Other. As Sheila and Sally illustrate, such 'codes of law' have negative or positive potential. The seeking of approval or the affirmation of self by the Other can breed compliance and dependency or a counter-dependency where a learner rejects how they are being judged *as a learner* and subsequently 'drops out'. Alternatively, the confident affirmation of self through taking responsibility for one's own progress locates the assessment process as a *contributory* element which actually enhances learning and informs the sense of oneself. It appears, therefore, that any pedagogy for autonomy has to critically address formal and informal assessment and evaluative processes operating within the classroom and, by implication, in the educational system wherein that classroom is located. Assessment and the whole activity of judging learners and learning remain a key element in the culture of the language classroom, but a pedagogy for autonomy requires us to consider additional influences upon the teacher who seeks to promote autonomous learning.

## Autonomy in a professional context: confronting paradoxes

In this section, we maintain the wider contextual perspective but move from the perspective of the learner to the influence of context upon ourselves as teachers. Here we raise a number of paradoxes which confront our interest in autonomous language learning. We briefly discuss in turn the possible underlying motives for the innovation and the self-deceptions these may entail; the difficulties in proving that such an innovation is beneficial to language learning; the impact of power relations in the classroom and how learners may perceive these; and, finally, possible limits upon the teacher's responsibilities for autonomy.

The growth of professional interest in autonomous learning warrants explanation. Elsewhere in this volume, two deep influences have been identified: an emerging consciousness of language teaching as political and cultural action and the greater access to information provided by evolving instructional technologies. Explanations must also embrace our own historical, social, and economic circumstances.

A common experience among many teachers in western democratic societies in recent times is the growing sense that the locus of control over their work is shifting away from themselves and their immediate institutions to centralized bureaucracies. This trend is manifest in explicit intrusions upon a teacher's previous work experience in terms of formalized systems of accountability, the introduction of top-down predesigned assessment and curricula frameworks, and employment conditions overlaid with enterprise bargaining which many teachers perceive as entailing greater insecurity and more work for less reward. Might it be possible that the current interest by teachers in the autonomy of learners is an expression of a growing personal uncertainty and a feeling of powerlessness so that many teachers are beginning to question the culture of 'authority' as it manifests itself towards the end of the century, including that which they themselves represent as teachers?

More positively, however, we can see that moments of uncertainty are precisely those when creative and worthwhile innovations can emerge in our search for alternatives. If we are currently trying to achieve the impossible, our energy will nevertheless enable innovations to occur. The question remains as to whether the innovations which emerge are the ones we originally intended. In other words, teachers who are strongly committed to the concept of autonomous learning may be embarking upon a continual struggle with self-deception or false optimism. In these circumstances, it may be important for us to acknowledge and make clear our own *uncertainties* about the future directions in our work because the critical awareness that will result can both refine the innovation and generate reasons and evidence to support the endeavour.

While teachers are being required to honour their accountability to the wider community through bureaucratic procedures, it is important that an educational innovation such as autonomous language learning can be *shown* to be beneficial. In a sense, autonomous language learning entails an even greater concern than usual with evaluating learner progress and a heightened awareness of our classroom pedagogy. However, conventional quasi-experimental or observational studies comparing autonomous language classrooms and their learners' achievements with other kinds of classrooms and other learners bring with them certain risks. This kind of comparison is based on the clearly false assumption that *all* the variables in a teaching approach can be accounted for and controlled. Similarly, to argue in favour of autonomous language learning on the basis of successful *language* learning alone is to disregard and devalue some of the defining processes and goals of autonomous learning. In other words, because of the need to provide evidence to support the innovation, we nevertheless need ways of providing that evidence in addition to more conventional ways of proving one thing is more effective than another. We are very likely to have to struggle for what *we* want to count as evidence for the benefits of what we are trying to do. The onus remains on us, however, to make clear what that evidence may be.

In being committed to autonomous learning, we also need to be alert to the power relations that underlie the culture of the classroom. Learners will generally seek to please me as the teacher. If I ask them to manifest behaviours that they think I perceive as the exercise of autonomy, they will gradually discover what these behaviours are and will subsequently reveal them back to me. Put simply, learners will give up their autonomy to put on the mask of autonomous behaviour. Alternatively, if we acknowledge that lessons are jointly constructed events over which learners have fair control – too often exercised by the most autonomous of learners as disruption or, more gently, changes of direction – then it is plausible that such learners will exercise their autonomy by demanding that I teach them in ways that are anathema to the proponents of 'learner centredness'.

In the light of these power relations, a key issue in the introduction of autonomy as pedagogy is to consider how our learners are themselves defining the classroom situation. Why is it that learners may resist or appear to avoid exercising autonomy? If a number of learners who withdraw or drop out of their language programmes could be seen as those who are certainly exercising their autonomy, perhaps we should be investigating *their* definitions of the situation.

If we seriously seek to work with learners at a deeper level than their outward behaviour in the classroom, the question arises as to the extent of our rights in the socialization of language learners. Should the language teacher be pursuing relatively subtle ways of winning over the 'hearts and minds' of students? Might we be participating in a paradoxical process which ultimately renders our students more vulnerable to compliance than do other pedagogic approaches?

It is often asserted that there must be necessary limits upon autonomy, especially in the classroom context. Is one of our functions as teachers to enable learners to become more critically aware of the limits of the choices and freedoms which society places upon them? Might we be naive to assume that they are not already critically aware of these things? Alternatively, might we be indulging in an even greater self-deception in assuming we *can* work with our learners upon processes of awareness and questioning that may lead ultimately to cultural change? To participate in a genuine cultural transformation unavoidably leads us to question the integrity of the classroom as an institutionalized location for learning and the current definition of what it is to be a teacher. Do we seriously seek to fire our arrows as far as this?

## The dynamics of autonomy in the classroom context

A central paradox for autonomous language learning is the unavoidable tension within any class of learners between the individual and the group. In this, a classroom reveals itself as a microcosm of the wider world in which the self relates to society. We illustrated how this tension can be revealed when discussing how Sheila and Sally relate to the external 'code of law' against which their achievements or otherwise may be judged.

In seeking to promote autonomy in the classroom, a pragmatic awareness of the dynamic involved in its possible evolution highlights particular tensions which can emerge between the individual learner and the classroom group which we here take to include the

| THE LEARNER | CLASSROOM GROUP (including the teacher) |
|---|---|
| *Phase* 1 Dependent or Counter dependent | *Phase* 1 Autocratic |
| *Phase* 2 Independent or Individualistic | *Phase* 2 Anarchic Uncertain and fragmented |
| *Phase* 3 Interdependent | *Phase* 3 Collaborative learning community |

**Figure 9.1**   The evolution of autonomy in the classroom

teacher. Figure 9.1 illustrates the likely evolutionary process towards autonomous learning. This evolution is described in general and rather stereotypical terms, but our purpose is to map in a bold way the possible consequences for the individual and group relationship.

We can trace the evolution of autonomy in the classroom with reference to (i) the learner's own shift from one phase to the next, (ii) the classroom group's shift from one phase to the next, and (iii) possible relationships between the learner and the group in each phase. We will briefly describe each of these in turn.

If we may assume that many learners in the classroom situation have been socialized into a dependent relationship to the teacher in particular and, possibly, to the wider classroom group, a shift towards autonomy by the individual opens up two strategic pathways for the learner: either counter-dependency through 'dropping out' or independence from the group. This might manifest itself in individualistic and non-co-operative or competitive ways of being. This phase, however, may be *a necessary intervening step* towards the fuller realization of autonomy in interdependent relations with the other people in the classroom.

Taking a similarly extreme starting point, the society of many classrooms might be described as autocratic, either because of the particular controlling stance of a teacher or because the group – including the teacher – have jointly conspired to maintain autocracy in its typical ways of working. When a teacher initially expects and encourages autonomous learning, a phase of relative anarchy typi-fied by uncertainty of purposes and responsibilities is very likely to arise. In this phase, roles and responsibilities begin to fragment and either the group reverts to a former phase or becomes more open to the possibilities of genuine collaboration. Autonomous learning is most likely to be expressed through the establishment of agendas and procedures which typify a learning community wherein responsibility for one's own and each other's learning and the shaping of the teaching-learning process is shared.

Finally, it is possible to anticipate likely relationships between the individual learner and other people in the classroom when these phases of evolution occur. An autocratic classroom culture is likely to be perceived by a learner as a potential threat to the self, not least through its judgement of the learner's worth. Hence the individual's tendency to compliance or self-exclusion. The necessary and intervening shift from autocracy to relative anarchy and its attendant loss of former certainties may well push the learner to rely solely on an independent agenda and way of working. However, if the group does not flee backwards from the uncertainties, the learner may come to perceive the value and benefits of collaboration and, thereby, locate themselves as contributing members of a learning community and, through this, help to create and maintain its existence.

Of course, this is rather a simplistic account. There are (at least) three complications to this general picture. First, as has been suggested the process is dynamic and the classroom group or individual learners within it may, at any time, revert to a previous phase, particularly if the phase they are entering appears to demand much more of them than before. The attainment of interdependency and collaboration does not mean immunity from reversion to a previous way of being. It is entirely plausible that a class will constantly fluctuate between phases and that the maintenance of autonomous learning entails a continual and explicit struggle with such fluctuations.

Secondly, while the classroom group can be regarded as more than the sum of its individual members, the teacher and any individual learner in the group might be struggling towards – or from! – different phases at different times and be interpreting these phases in different ways. Finally, a particular source of tension between individual and group is the distinct possibility that their own phases of development *may not so neatly coincide* as the diagram suggests. It is possible, for example, that a learner may be choosing to remain dependent upon the teacher while the group is moving towards developing a collaborative learning community. Similarly, an autocratic teacher or group, while posing a serious threat to an individual's autonomy, might nevertheless contain learners who are gravitating between independence and competitive individualism.

Very few practitioners of autonomy in the language classroom would claim that the process is uncomplicated. But, if we are to explore autonomy through practice, a pragmatic anticipation of the likely dynamics of the social relationships in the classroom and how these may constantly impact upon the learner's opportunities to be autonomous seems to be an essential element in a pedagogy for autonomy.

## Being a teacher of autonomous learners

Building upon the ideas we have so far explored, there appear to be a number of key implications for the teacher who engages in a pedagogy for autonomy. These are, perhaps, most clearly expressed in terms of the attributes and roles of teachers which are integrated within their own professional practice. In what follows, we distinguish between deeper attributes which may describe the teacher of autonomous learners and those explicit roles or forms of classroom action which may create space for learners to exercise their autonomy.

### *Attributes*

Here we deduce three attributes which the teacher can *bring* to their relationship with their learners.

#### Self-awareness

We suggest that an essential precondition for the teacher to be able to foster autonomous learning is an explicit awareness of the teacher's own self *as a learner*. This awareness includes a critical sense of when I am able to act autonomously and when I am not able to; to know what beliefs I hold about teaching and learning, and to know how my own biography as a learner and a teacher has shaped my current assumptions, perceptions and practices in the classroom. It is very likely, for example, that my experiences of learning and, therefore, how I define learning will often be different from that of many of the learners whom I teach.

I need to be able to *reflect* on the decisions and actions I take in the classroom and on how I interact with each learner, and to assess the extent to which these actions contribute to or hinder the learners' exercise of autonomy in terms of what *they* mean by the concept. I need to be able to ask myself the extent to which my own biography as a learner, including significant issues which relate to and characterize my own learning experiences, may impinge on my classroom practice.

### Belief and trust

I need to believe in each learner's capacity to learn and to trust in each learner's capacity to assert their own autonomy. The teacher cannot teach learners to be autonomous, this would be a contradiction in terms. But I can *act* out of the assumption that each learner is able to learn and is fully capable of taking an autonomous stance to their learning.

### Desire

Self-evidently perhaps, I need to *want* to foster the development of learner autonomy in the classroom and be prepared to live through the consequences for my own practice from this position.

We suggest the following practical consequences and express these in terms of questions relating to six ways of acting within the teaching-learning process.

## *Classroom action*

### Being a resource

Can I accept an essentially responsive role in relation to learners' on-going and emerging needs and give this explicit priority while also implicitly maintaining my responsibility for the body of knowledge and range of capabilities which I hope my learners will attain? Can I sustain the appropriate balance between being a resource and guide?

### Decision sharing

If I acknowledge that even a single decision which I unilaterally take deprives the learners of an opportunity to take responsibility, can I give up the feeling of being responsible for most of the things that occur in the classroom? Can I find ways of gradually sharing all classroom decisions with learners so that I am perceived as an equal partner in the process whose greater knowledge and experience relating to language learning are seen as rich resources which enable rather than inhibit their own exercise of autonomy?

## Facilitating collaborative evaluation

How can I release and build upon the *positive* potential of assessment and evaluation in providing feedback that contributes to achievement while also enhancing autonomy? Am I also aware of the informal and spontaneous moments when I make a judgement of a learner's contribution or achievement and how these may add up to the more public construction of the person *as a learner*? How might I reduce some learners' dependence upon my evaluative comments as cues for compliant behaviour or, more deeply, as indicators of their worth as language learners? As an alternative, can I initiate collaborative procedures which enable learners themselves – as individuals and as a group – to exercise responsibility for making clear the criteria for success in learning and for making their own judgements against agreed criteria? As a start, how might I contribute to the learners' emerging and changing criteria for success those criteria implicit in proficient language knowledge and use which I am mediating through an external syllabus or curriculum? And how can I do this without seeming to undervalue or displace the learner's criteria? If I can achieve this, what collaborative procedures can be adopted which also respect and maintain individual autonomy?

## Managing the risks

Am I willing to *mediate* between the individual's preferred learning agenda and ways of working and those which are constructed and routinized by the group? How can I help maintain a balance between the inevitable constraints of the group process and the potential benefits that derive from collaborative endeavour? Crucially, am I willing to go through the disorientating but developmental phase of 'anarchy' in the teaching-learning process during which I and the learners will be uncertain and our purposes and procedures seemingly fragmented? Can I take this risk in the belief that such a phase typically follows from my wish to challenge learner dependency and can reveal to me and the learners possible directions towards interdependency and collaboration?

### Being a patient opportunist

Can I accommodate the dynamic nature of autonomy knowing that different learners will be at different stages between dependency and interdependency as learners? How will I deal with the likelihood that some learners will revert to the easier option of transferring their responsibility either back to me or to the group? Am I willing to stand back during the teaching-learning process and remain alert to those opportunities when the group or the individual can exercise autonomy? Can I make sufficient space for these opportunities to arise and how will I recognize them?

### Getting support

Because a classroom of learners struggling towards or exercising autonomy is a personally demanding environment, not least because it may require that I redefine my roles and responsibilities as a teacher, I need support and continual reminders that my actions are likely to be beneficial to language learning. Also, given the need to confront and assert my own autonomy – and possibly even discover what this is *and* the limits placed upon it – it is more than likely that I will need support particularly at the early stages of introducing autonomous work in the classroom. Put simply, I need the kind of support I would be willing to offer my learners during their own phases of adaptation. Therefore, can I create a situation in which I obtain support of a colleague or colleagues in my institution? Can we undertake a joint venture of mutual benefit, perhaps at least through a small action learning project on how the innovation is taking shape in the classroom?

## Conclusion

The above six ways of acting which may create space for learners to exercise their autonomy in learning seem to entail that, as a teacher, I need to recognize and assert my own autonomy. This implication takes us back to the opening section of this chapter which characterized the state of autonomy. It also raises three key questions. First, can the teacher be alert to and enable opportunities in the classroom process which explicitly foster the attributes of 'Being Autonomous'? Secondly, can teachers exercise these characteristics in their own professional life? The third and final question seems to us to be a central issue. Is it still worth, metaphorically speaking, trying to shoot arrows at the sun and, thereby, attain a positive measure of autonomous learning in the language class while knowing that there will always be necessary and unnecessary limits upon this and upon our own autonomy as teachers? The continual questioning and struggle with these limits are very likely to be an inherent characteristic of any future pedagogy for autonomy.

Put more directly, perhaps, a genuine autonomous language learning context might require us to involve our learners and our teaching colleagues in directly helping us to answer our questions. This process of collaborative enquiry could be seen as *part of* language learning and *part of* on-going professional development.

Finally, do we need some unified theory of autonomy to protect the concept from dilution, trivialization or commodification in the wider language teaching industry? We suggest that the real issue is how different teachers are interpreting the concept in what they actually do in the classroom as an expression of their beliefs. We further suggest that a diversity of interpretations is actually preferable to some consensus definition, even if such were feasible. This diversity allows the innovation in action to reflect variability in cultural interpretations and classroom practices and, thereby, generates a multiplicity of alternative realizations. As a result, the concept of autonomous language learning may itself become enriched and extended.

The teacher's sense of plausibility appears to be the starting point for the introduction of autonomous language learning. We offer this chapter as one contribution to building bridges between some of the essential features of a pedagogy for autonomy and what teachers perceive as plausible in their own working contexts. In doing so, we acknowledge that we are expecting ourselves and our colleagues to risk shooting arrows at the sun.

# 10

## Confidence building for classroom teachers working with self-access resources

FELICITY O'DELL

### Introduction

Self-access resource centres open up a wide ránge of opportunities for both students and teachers. Students can concentrate on their own specific needs and interests and can acquire learning skills which should stand them in good stead whatever they wish to study in the future. Teachers can find satisfaction from being able to meet their students' individual needs more effectively and from providing their classes with potentially life-enhancing skills. Teachers themselves benefit from access to resources which can enrich their own lessons; they can also enjoy the change of focus and pace that conducting a lesson in a self-access centre will bring.

Yet when a self-access resource centre is being set up in an EFL institution, many teachers express some apprehension about having to start helping their students to make use of those resources. There seem to be four main areas of anxiety.

1. *Apprehension about student reaction to learning centre work.* Many teachers maintain that their students will not like class time being spent on activities that 'could just as well be done outside class time'.
2. *Anxiety about own pedagogic skills.* Some teachers feel that exploiting self-access centres requires different pedagogic skills from those which they have been trained in and they are unsure where to begin.
3. *Concerns about getting familiar with the resources available.* Some teachers have more practical than pedagogic worries. They may,

150

for instance, be concerned that they will not have the time to familiarize themselves adequately with the materials in the self-access centre in order to be able to advise their classes in the most effective way; they feel that they will not know what the centre holds or where to start looking for what they think might be there.

4. *Technological worries.* When the centre is being equipped in a technically up-to-date fashion, many teachers are apprehensive about practical aspects of using the equipment.

To what extent are these pedagogic and practical fears reinforced when the centre is opened and the teachers have to use it with their classes? Do the fears quickly disappear with experience? Do teachers with varying degrees of experience share the same anxieties or are they significantly different? One study (Martyn and Voller, 1993) suggests that teachers' views of self-access centres do change over time. The aim of this chapter is to describe a small research project which considered the concerns voiced by teachers in a well-established self-access centre and assessed the extent to which teacher worries with regard to self-access resources are the same for long-term teachers and for those who are new to the institution in question. The chapter will then go on to discuss some methods for building teachers' confidence by combating the various anxieties articulated.

The research project was carried out at Eurocentre, a language school for adults in Cambridge, UK. The Learning Centre at Cambridge Eurocentre is a multimedia learning facility heavily used not only in true self-access mode but also as the basis for class lessons. Learning Centre class lessons usually focus on one theme, such as education, small talk or the future, and provide a choice of tasks using the different media and practising different skills but all relating in some way to the theme. The Learning Centre lesson is then followed up by a classroom activity in which students use or share what they did in the Learning Centre in some way.

Observation of students' behaviour in their own time in the Learning Centre had from the first suggested that the extent to which students made use of the facilities in their out-of-class time depended to no small degree on the enthusiasm of the students' own particular class teacher for the self-access resources and on the use which the teacher made of those facilities with her class. Support for teachers in their Learning Centre work has traditionally included induction materials, learning centre lessons, counselling materials and seminars/workshops (O'Dell, 1992).

Watching students during their independent use of the Learning Centre, it also seemed that they tended to make use of materials which they had been introduced to by their teacher. This observation was supported by a study conducted by an external MSc student into what learners chose to do in their own time in the language laboratory area of our Learning Centre (Macdonald-Smith, 1993). This research showed that students' choices of materials coincided quite closely with teacher recommendations.

These findings served to strengthen our view that teacher training is one of the most important aspects of Learning Centre development work and encouraged us to carry out a small research project focusing attention on how to help all teachers feel confident and enthusiastic about using Learning Centre facilities with their classes.

## The survey: conduct and results

Our first step was to try to pinpoint what teachers find to be their main difficulties in using the Learning Centre. All the teachers at the school were given a questionnaire covering various aspects of Learning Centre use particularly problem areas and training needs. We had become increasingly aware over time that training needs varied for teachers having different lengths of experience within the institution. As a result we were anxious to add another dimension to our investigation by comparing the questionnaire answers for those teachers who had been in the school for some time with those who were relatively new to the school.

The questionnaire had four sections. The first dealt with the problems experienced by teachers. The second asked for an evaluation of different kinds of in-house Learning Centre training possibilities. The third asked teachers to indicate what kind of training they needed most. The fourth simply asked 'What word or expression best sums up for you your feelings about using the Learning Centre?'. Fifteen teachers in all answered the questionnaire. Eleven were long-standing permanent members of staff with at least four years' experience in the organization and four were temporary teachers with 2 to 18 months' experience at Eurocentre.

The first section, that focusing on problem areas, included a list

| Problem | Long-term (teachers n=11) | Short-term (teachers n=4) | All teachers (n=15) |
|---|---|---|---|
| Knowing what there is in the Learning Centre | 7 | 0 | 7 |
| How to find materials | 4 | 2 | 6 |
| How to answer students who ask for advice | 3 | 3 | 6 |
| Making ready-made lessons successful | 3 | 1 | 4 |
| How to use the laboratory | 3 | 3 | 6 |
| How to make students enthusiastic about the Learning Centre | 2 | 2 | 4 |
| What to do in Learning Centre lessons | 2 | 1 | 3 |
| How to use the computers | 1 | 2 | 3 |
| How to use the videos | 0 | 1 | 1 |

**Figure 10.1**  Numbers and percentages of teachers reporting specific problems with regard to Learning Centre use, compared in terms of length of teacher experience

of possible difficulties; teachers were asked to indicate which of these they found to be a problem. They were also encouraged to add any other difficulties not covered by the list.

Figure 10.1 summarizes the results of this first part of the questionnaire.

Two significant points emerge from the figure. First, more experienced teachers perceive the technical problems of using the technology (the laboratory, the computers and the video) as less of a problem than do less experienced staff. Secondly, and more surprisingly, knowing what materials there are in the Learning Centre is not a problem at all for short-term teachers but it is the major issue for long-term members of staff. The numbers are small but the conclusions they suggest bear out the impressions gained by Learning Centre staff over the previous ten years.

Teachers were also asked to indicate other problems which they have with Learning Centre use. The points raised here support the tendencies suggested by the numbers in the figure. Two other areas of difficulty were added by short-term members of staff – both of these related to exploiting the technology, namely the computers and the language laboratory. Long-term teachers' concerns were quite different; they were worried by administrative details relating to booking extra time in the Centre and they expressed uncertainty about whom to inform or get help from if they encountered difficulties. They were also concerned about problems with materials; one teacher specifically mentioned difficulties arising from outdated materials, disappearance of materials, re-located materials and withdrawal of materials. In other words, long-term teachers get particularly worried when things 'go wrong'.

To return to the four areas of concern listed in the introduction, it would seem that concerns about student reactions to the Learning Centre, worries about pedagogical skills (as evidenced by uncertainties expressed over how to give advice, what to do in the Learning Centre and how to make lessons there successful) and about use of the technology diminish – but do not disappear – with experience; concern about familiarization with resources, on the other hand, dramatically increases.

What are the implications of the above results for training needs? Clearly, training in the use of the technology is of great importance for new members of staff. It is self-evident, however, that hands-on experience of using the technology increases teachers' confidence so that they gradually cease to find it much of a problem and it is no longer such an urgent training need – at least until a new bit of technology is introduced.

But why should knowledge about Learning Centre materials be a matter of increasing concern over time and what are the implications of this for training? It would seem that teachers, when new to a self-access system, can cope with not knowing precisely what materials are contained in it. They do not expect to have this knowledge at their fingertips and they can use their general experience of libraries and other self-access systems to help them find something to correspond to their own and their students' needs. They accept that they, like their students, are ignorant about what exactly is to be found in the Learning Centre. However, longer-term members of staff have higher expectations. They feel more pressured into the role of 'knower' about the Learning

Centre and feel disorientated, possibly even threatened, when their knowledge turns out not to be complete, when they cannot, for example, immediately find a piece of material requested by a student or when they recommend an activity which turns out to be unavailable.

It is impossible for teachers to know exactly what is where in a self-access system at any given point. Books are borrowed and, occasionally, stolen. Sometimes they are returned to the wrong location on the shelves. Outdated materials are withdrawn. New materials are purchased which may lead to some re-location of stock. Communication of information about such changes in resources is clearly an extremely important on-going task for Learning Centre staff.

However, communication alone is not enough. The most important point is that teachers need to be helped to have sufficient confidence in their use of the Learning Centre so as not to be fazed when a piece of material they hoped to use is not in its place. They need to be provided with – or encouraged to develop – strategies which will enable them to take such situations in their stride. Long-term teachers need, perhaps, to become closer to short-term staff in their attitudes to themselves as 'knowers'.

The second part of the questionnaire listed a number of teacher training methods which have been used – or, in a couple of cases, have been proposed for use – in the school as part of the Learning Centre development programme. Figure 10.2 summarizes the results of this part of the questionnaire.

What information does Figure 10.2 provide us with? First, there is clearly some agreement about the relevance of certain training methods between the two groups of teachers. Both groups express some preference for informal training methods over formal ones, for informal chats with colleagues and for asking for help when needed. Similarly, information derived from personal experience is rated more highly than that gained through impersonal modes of information dissemination like newsletters or notice boards.

There are probably a number of reasons why this should be the case. First, informal, personal training methods allow teachers the opportunity to concentrate on the aspects of Learning Centre work that are of particular concern to them at the moment; they can ask for colleagues' advice on questions relating to the specific classes they are currently teaching and so ideas gained are more likely to be put into immediate use. Secondly, teachers themselves

| Type of training | Order of importance for long-term staff | Order of importance for short-term staff |
|---|---|---|
| Informal chats with colleagues | 1 | 3 |
| Asking for help when needed | 2 | 2 |
| What's new in the Learning Centre seminar | 3 | 7 |
| Learning Centre lesson development workshop | 3 | 10 |
| Teacher-initiated development group | 5 | 5 |
| Involvement in Learning Centre development work | 5 | 8 |
| Induction file | 7 | 1 |
| Learning Centre handbook for teachers (proposed) | 8 | 6 |
| Problem-sharing workshop | 8 | 8 |
| Introduction to the Learning Centre seminar | 8 | 4 |
| Learning centre noticeboard in staffroom | 11 | 12 |
| Team-teaching session (rarely tried as yet) | 12 | 10 |
| Newsletters providing staff with updating information | 13 | 14 |
| Outside speaker (not yet used for training)) | 14 | 12 |

**Figure 10.2**   Rank order of importance ascribed to possible training methods by long-term and short-term teachers (1 = most important, 14 = least important)

have more independent control over this kind of training; it is not imposed by management and so may for this reason be more acceptable to some teachers. It may also be that there is a kind of privacy in the informal chat with colleagues that is reassuring to teachers lacking in confidence and reluctant to make their own perceived inadequacy public to the staff as a whole.

The reasons why more impersonal training methods like newsletters or noticeboards are not rated highly may be simply because they do not have the immediate personal relevance of the methods discussed above. It may also be that such methods are felt to foster an unwelcome sense of a 'them' and 'us' division between those who are the 'experts' providing the information and those who are expected to make use of it. There is also the point that reading a newsletter or a noticeboard requires an individual investment of time for no guaranteed return in terms of usefulness to the individual teacher. Given most teachers' pressured schedules, that investment may be too much to expect.

As well as the similarities between training preferences of long-term and short-term staff, there are significant rating differences with regard to certain training methods, and these follow on logic-ally from the problems isolated by the two groups of teachers. The induction file – a reference document supplied to all teachers including, among other things, simple instructions on laboratory use – is of far greater value to new teachers in the organization. Similarly and obviously, a seminar introducing the Learning Centre is only of real value to this group of teachers.

Longer-term teachers inevitably ascribe far higher importance to seminars about 'what's new in the Learning Centre' as this helps them to increase their confidence as 'knowers'. Long-term staff also recognize the importance of becoming involved in Learning Centre development work (aimed primarily at producing either lesson ideas or materials) as an effective means of training; such development could take place in a workshop or in a weekly teacher development group or through a specific Learning Centre-related project. Long-term staff's appreciation of involvement in such development work may be because they will have already had experience of it and so will realize how, by allowing themselves time and space to think about Learning Centre use, development work of this type can raise their confidence in their ability to cope with Learning Centre work with their classes.

The third section of the questionnaire asked teachers to answer the question 'What kind of Learning Centre training do you think you personally would most like to have in the next six months (if any)?' Again all the short-term teachers emphasized their need for training in the use of the laboratory and the computers, with just one teacher requesting something more general about Learning Centre use as well.

The requests of the long-term staff were more diverse: nine out of eleven teachers expressed a specific need; the only two who did not state any such need were teachers who are already heavily involved in Learning Centre development work. Curiously enough, given the lack of concern indicated by long-term staff (see Figure 10.1) with regard to technical training, five of the nine teachers made a request for it. This may be because new computer software had recently been introduced and gaining familiarity with it was seen as a particularly immediate need. Those requesting laboratory training were specifically interested in mastering the more complex technical possibilities of the equipment; in order to expand their repertoire of uses for the laboratory. Thus, their request for training was probably based more on technical interest and was qualitatively different from short-term teachers' feelings that they might not be able adequately to handle a class in the laboratory. More consistently with Figure 10.1, three of the nine teachers made a plea for extra time to familiarize themselves with the Centre and with how students and other teachers make use of it. A couple of requests focused on using and developing Learning Centre lesson materials.

## Training implications of the survey's results

What do the results of this survey suggest for staff training with regard to Learning Centre work? For short-term staff the importance of the induction file is crucial. The contents of our induction file was modified to some degree as a result of the comments made by the staff during the investigations described above and it now includes three sections of information that were not there before. First, given short-term teachers' concern with all the technical aspects of Learning Centre use, basic instructions on computer use as well as laboratory use are now contained in the file. Secondly, we have also attempted to forestall some of the worries about administrative matters which longer term members of staff express by adding a document which details precisely what teachers should do if they come across problems related to the administration of the Learning Centre in some way. Thirdly, in response to some comments made in informal chats about Learning Centre use – both long-term and short-term teachers had expressed some uncertainty about what the organization actually expected of them in terms of Learning Centre use and about what the rationale for these expectations is – we included some information about Eurocentres' philosophy of Learning Centres. This focuses particularly on the importance of multimedia in Learning Centres, on their use as a bridge to the 'real' language environment, on the strong links between the Learning Centre and the classroom and on a belief in the pedagogic value of autonomous learning skills. In conjunction with this we added some notes on the implications that this philosophy has for teachers and students within the organization. This section is now used as an introduction to the Learning Centre induction file.

As well as adding new sections, we also updated a number of already existing sections – particularly those which provide recommendations for Learning Centre use for teachers working with one-month and three-month courses – to take account both of additions to the resources of the Centre and of further experience gained since the file was initially produced. It seems that we now have a much more coherent and up-to-date induction file and it is hoped that this will be more effective as a confidence builder for temporary and new teachers.

Another long-standing way of helping new staff is by arranging an introductory seminar as part of their general induction programme. The aim of this has been two fold: to provide both pedagogic guidance on Learning Centre use and also to be an introduction to the use of the equipment in the Learning Centre. In practice, those organizing the sessions have followed new teachers' requests to use the time as hands-on experience of working with the laboratory and the computers. This has been at the expense of more general pedagogic discussions and guidance, which are of greater importance in the long term than technical matters but certainly do not seem so to any new teacher in their first couple of days in the school.

Thanks largely to the questionnaires, but also to informal discussions with new members of staff, it has now been recognized that there is no point in trying to mix these two elements of Learning Centre induction training. There must be a session first of all which is explicitly intended to deal with teachers' concerns about the use of the technology. Only in a rather later session when new teachers are no longer dominated by worries about which buttons to press in the laboratory and about disk manipulation in the computer room, can we begin to discuss pedagogic issues of Learning Centre use.

In any well-stocked Learning Centre it is important to make sure that all the staff, but new teachers in particular, are made specifically aware both of the materials which are likely to be of immediate use and of the relevant experience in using them which teachers have already accumulated. The most successful way we have found of doing this has been by collecting together all the Learning Centre lessons which tie in with the syllabus of each coursebook we use. Thus, we have gathered together, for instance, a '*Headway Intermediate* file', which contains examples of all the intermediate level Learning Centre lessons which correspond in topic or grammar point to areas covered by *Headway Intermediate.*[1] A teacher using this coursebook is given a copy of the file to keep for the duration of the course. Similar files have been made for all the coursebooks we are currently using.

For long-term teachers, the problems of training are, as we have seen, more complex as individuals' needs and interests become more diverse. As was pointed out above, long-term teachers, in particular, need to be helped towards having the strategies to cope when they cannot find the materials they had seen there previously. Communication about new acquisitions and other developments relating to the resources is, of course, important. The findings of our small research project suggest that if circumstances permit, a regular seminar where new materials are actually handled is more effective than merely informing the staff of changes by notice or newsletter. But, on a deeper level, how can long-term teachers be helped towards the confidence which will make them effective and enthusiastic Learning Centre users?

This can be fostered in three main ways:

1. idea and experience sharing
2. team teaching
3. involvement in Learning Centre development

All these methods are marked by the apparently significant characteristic that they involve teachers working together as peers rather than being told what to do by Learning Centre experts.

First, teachers can be encouraged to share their ideas in a staff workshop and three examples of workshops we have held are outlined below. When our Learning Centre originally opened in 1984, a useful session devoted itself to teachers pooling ideas about ways in which the Learning Centre improved life for them as teachers within the institution, thus encouraging positive feelings at a time when there was not inconsiderable insecurity among teachers having to deal with these complex new facilities. Another session where teachers each came with a favourite idea for using the laboratory resulted in a document now included in the induction file and of great benefit to all new teachers. In yet another workshop of a rather different sort teachers worked in pairs on devising a Learning Centre lesson round a topic written on a card which each pair chose at random – the topics were selected as ones where we had no such lessons already prepared and a number focused particularly on the needs of elementary students, a group hitherto rather neglected in Learning Centre development work. A number of useful and original lessons were developed at this workshop; these were later tried out by classes and then modified where necessary and are now part of the bank of Learning Centre lesson materials available for all teachers to use.

A second important method of confidence building is team teaching. This method was not rated particularly highly by teachers (see Figure 10.2) but this was probably due to lack of practical experience of it at the time the survey was conducted. A self-access centre can provide an ideal focus for team teaching as it often has the space to accommodate a couple of classes and their teachers. Lessons which have been tried have focused on the preparation of questionnaires, book reviews or talks by one class to be presented later to the other group. It would seem that there is scope for a great deal of interesting and original work here. Other ideas that could be considered for team taught lessons, for example, might be for students each to write a brief autobiography which they then give to a student from another class who reads it and prepares a set of questions for an interview with that student. The questions prepared, the students interview each other and then, in the follow-up class lesson, introduce their partner to the other students in their class giving as much information as possible about him or her. A third idea might be for students from different classes to talk to each other about their main language problems and then to choose Learning Centre exercises to meet one another's needs.

During such lessons, the two teachers are on hand in the Learning Centre to answer questions, to correct work as requested and to offer guidance to any student in need from either of the two classes. In the feedback sessions, the lesson can either take place with one large group or each teacher can take half of the members of each of the two classes and split off into two classrooms, later to compare notes with the other teacher involved.

Sharing the experience of conducting a Learning Centre lesson and, more importantly perhaps, its feedback session in the classroom, should help teachers both to gain new ideas and to feel more confident about their own performance. Trying out such ideas with two classes rather than just one would benefit not only the teachers who can gain confidence and interest from working with each other;

students would also enjoy the experience of getting to know other students and of sometimes competing with another class.

A third particularly effective way of enhancing teacher confidence in their Learning Centre work is by providing them with the opportunity to get involved in Learning Centre development. This not only helps teachers towards an increased knowledge of the resources available and their potential for exploitation but it also gives them a personal stake in the centre which serves to encourage positive attitudes towards the resources. Certainly, those teachers in our organization who have had some share in the time available for developing resources or for taking occasional pedagogic responsibility for the self-access centre tend to be those who express greatest confidence and flexibility over its use. The centre also benefits from some variety in approaches to development work. One teacher, for example, was particularly interested in working on Learning Centre lessons for a group of Arab beginners and elementary students. These were students who were having considerable difficulties with the lesson ideas used previously by other classes in the school.

I should like to conclude by referring briefly to one point which relates to all teachers working with a self-access centre, be they long-term teachers in their organization or new and temporary teachers. The importance which was ascribed by all staff to informal 'training' such as asking for help when needed and informal chats with colleagues (see Figure 10.2), should not be underrated. Provision of adequate support staff to turn to in time of need and creation of a culture where teachers have the energy and enthusiasm to discuss pedagogical issues in their non-teaching time should, in my opinion, be recognized as significant by any organization that wishes to develop a confident and creative staff, particularly where something as complex as self-access resources are concerned. In other words, it is not enough to spend money on resources; it is at least as important to provide the administrative staff, to organize and maintain those resources effectively, and the pedagogic staff, to provide the support needed to ensure that they are used in an effective and creative way. As the discussion in this chapter would seem to indicate, the work of such pedagogic staff is most likely to be successful if they bear in mind the different training needs of staff with differing lengths of experience and if they do not forget the crucial role of informal training methods.

# Conclusion

A final and very open-ended question in the questionnaire asked teachers to sum up their feelings about using the Learning Centre in one word or expression. As expected, there was a wide variety of responses covering a large number of the themes touched on in some way in this article. One short-term teacher wrote 'lack of confidence', the combating of which has been the focus of this chapter. Some of the long-term teachers, too, expressed at least some degree of anxiety about Learning Centre work; one teacher wrote 'Sceptical'; another said 'Demanding. I feel that Learning Centre lessons should be structured and specifically aimed but I am not familiar enough with the materials and always feel that I have to check in advance that the lessons will work.' Another wrote 'I love it but sometimes I get frustrated when things are not working or are just not there.'

By far the majority of teachers, however, particularly those with the most experience in the school, tended to emphasize the positive aspects of Learning Centre use – 'great' was the comment used by three teachers to summarize their feelings. One teacher put it more expansively: 'Lucky me! A very positive treasury of resources.' Several teachers tried to explain their experience more fully. One wrote: 'Great to break out of the classroom and mingle with students in a more relaxed self-access atmosphere.' Another summed it up particularly well: 'A pleasant, successful learning experience for the students; a frenetic 15 minutes for me followed by quality individual time with students.' The aim of the research project was to help make that initial 15 minutes rather less frenetic without any diminution of the ensuing quality time.

## Note

1. The *Headway* series is written by John and Liz Soars and published by Oxford University Press.

# 11

## Learner training for autonomous language learning

### EDITH M. ESCH

### Introduction

Over the past thirty years, the radicalism of the concept of learner autonomy as promoted by Bertrand Schwartz, Yves Chalon and Henri Holec (1981, 1988), seems to have been gradually emptied of its substance. Practitioners appear to be unable to avoid the 'fossilization' (Little, 1991: p.1) of the concept in attempting to implement it in institutional contexts. The debate about the aims of developing learner autonomy has been forgotten to give way to shorter-term targets, and problems of management and the implementation of organizational principles like self-access and other techniques, have been brought to the fore instead (for example, Harding-Esch, 1977, 1982; Sheerin, 1989; Esch, 1994). Meanwhile, the concept of learner training, which has been closely associated with learner autonomy (Holec, 1980; Ellis and Sinclair, 1989; Dickinson, 1992) seems to have been merged into that of study skills.

This chapter aims to be optimistic. It is a report on an experimental learner training workshop organized by the Language Centre of the University of Cambridge for non-specialist university students (i.e. students who do not read modern languages for their degree). One of the main features of the workshop was that the participants largely determined the content and conduct of the sessions themselves. The experiment suggests that supporting learners' ability to take charge of their own language learning can be done successfully in an institutional setting by means of regular meetings and without compromising the concept of autonomy.

In the first part of the chapter, three requirements for any situation aiming to support the development of learners' autonomy are identified. These are that it should be critical, conversational and collective. The three requirements are derived from an analysis of three misconceptions about the concept of autonomy.

In the second part, the apparent success of the workshop is ascribed to three factors: the students were self-selected; the feedback was essentially given in the course of conversations but always seemed to be to the point because it was a conversational topic shared by the whole group; the syllabus was selected by the members of the group from the second week onwards.

In the third part, the chances of learner-training courses in support of autonomous learning. taking off are evaluated.

## Autonomous learning: three misconceptions to be avoided

There are no 'autonomous language learning skills' to be trained and, indeed, the word 'training', with its connotations of automatic behaviour and its associations with 'drills' – military or otherwise – seems to sit particularly unhappily next to 'autonomous learning'. To raise the question of training students for autonomous language learning, we need to be agreed on what we mean by 'autonomous language learning'. We started by identifying three main misconceptions about autonomous learning which had to be avoided: the first was its reduction to a set of skills, the second was the avoidance of language-learning specific issues and the third the belief that autonomous learning means 'learning in isolation'.

### *Reduction of autonomous learning to a set of skills*

The first misconception concerning the promotion of autonomous learning is to reduce it to a series of techniques to train language learning skills leading to the display of 'autonomous behaviour': in other words, the negation of the radical content of the concept. Not surprisingly, this misconception seems to be increasingly popular at a moment when the range of technical possibilities for accessing information and manipulating data at a distance is increasing. Competing for markets is higher on the agenda than reflecting about educational values.

Confusion about the meaning of autonomy is not new. Indeed, as we were recently reminded (Namenwirth, 1994) the two meanings for 'autonomie' in the *Petit Robert* Dictionary seem to summarize the issue.

(Philo) Droit pour l'individu de déterminer librement les règles auxquelles il se soumet [the right of an individual to determine freely the rules s/he obeys]

(XXe) Distance que peut franchir un véhicule . . . sans être ravitaillé en carburant [Distance a vehicle . . . can run without being refuelled]

The first definition states the radical view and supports the argument for negotiated arrangements about the content and form(s) of the learning situation(s), which, in turn, presupposes that the teacher's contribution and role can be talked about. The second definition, dates back to the time when the capacity of engines started to free humans from constraints of time and space. It is interesting because of the shift of attribution of 'autonomy' or 'freedom' to the machine, while man is the fuel supplier. By analogy, we can read that humans are machines which can be made to work – as learning machines or as teaching machines – on their own for a certain amount of time and require periodic boosters. Alternatively, we can read that thanks to machines and technology, humans can do a lot of language learning without the help of a teacher. The first interpretation presupposes that humans, by their very nature, are not autonomous. The second interpretation is one possible description of what learners can do once they have taken charge of their learning. By placing the learner in the position of agenda setter, it immediately refers us back to the first definition. To support autonomous learning, it is necessary to face the radical aspects of the concept and the question of teacher control versus learner control in particular.

## Avoidance of language-learning specific issues

It is also necessary to consider whether language has specific features which need to be taken into account when we talk about autonomous language learning. Is language learning different from any other learning, say physics or geography? The answer is yes because we use language to describe and talk about our learning experience. In any community, language constitutes a powerful vehicle for culturally transmitted views of language, of learning, and of learning situations (Riley, 1994). This makes it very difficult to get out of the straitjacket and to become autonomous. A clear example is the use of words such as 'rules' and 'grammar' in discourse. Typically, in the West at least, learners who talk about 'rules' restrict the domain of reference to language in its written form only. It is easy to test this with French native-speakers. If you ask them to state how to form the plural in French, they usually talk in terms of 'adding -s, -aux, etc.', thus referring directly to the written form where, say, 'le lit' (the bed) becomes 'les lits' (the beds) but not in terms of 'changing the vowel of the article. My point is that learners typically fail to realize that this use of words acts as a barrier to their learning the rules of the spoken language. In reality, they not only believe but act upon a folk theory that (1) the spoken language does not have rules or grammar, and that (2) the written language – which has rules and grammar – is more valuable.

Our conceptualization of learning a new language is crucially affected by these views but often we are unaware of them. Becoming more autonomous amounts to realizing the extent to which language use constrains and restricts our views about language and language learning. If we want to encourage autonomous learning, we need to provide means to help learners talk and a format where learners' attention is attracted to these phenomena. Moreover, the process whereby learners share their experience is a means of enhancing their language learning awareness. Hence the idea of a workshop in which learners would be invited to reflect on their language learning experience as well as on the way they talked about it.

## Learning in isolation

In higher education, the radically social character of autonomy in language learning has been obscured by two factors in the last decade. One comes from psychological research on individualistic approaches to language learning which stress individual differences between learners and their personal characteristics (for example Skehan, 1989) rather than what learners have in common. Another factor has been the popularization of personal computers which gave independence to a generation brought up to think of Computing Centres and Language Laboratories as buildings where one had to go if one wanted to use a computer and/or practice languages. This new-found 'freedom' has led to confusion with individualization and isolation, neither of which are relevant to autonomous learning. New technologies and possibilities in distance learning have further popularized the misleading idea that being autonomous was 'the same' as being isolated. One example of this 'organizational fallacy' (Little, 1991) is to be found in the section on autonomous learning in the Study Guide of the new *Cadences* (1994) French course of the Open University which begins: 'Autonomous learning is working on one's own.'

Having analysed these three misconceptions about autonomous learning, we decided to run a workshop which would at least seek to avoid them. This meant that we had to work out a format which would meet three requirements: it would be critical, conversational and collective.

## Three determinant ingredients for success

The workshop was organized for learners of French by the Learning Advisory Service of the Language Centre[1] in 1990–91 and was proposed to a group of students who were at intermediate level. All the students involved stayed on throughout the one-term (eight-week) course, which we take as a measure of success. This may seem a superficial measure, but in this case 100 per cent attendance must have been the result of high motivation and sustained interest given that the course had all the usual hallmarks of non-starters: it was not compulsory and did not lead to any certification or 'badge'. Moreover, because students came from a variety of faculties, the classes had to take place over lunch-time. Finally, the course required a lot of work between classes.

The pattern was that every week, for an hour, the students would meet in the Resource Centre when they would try to carry out the activity they had planned collectively the preceding week. However, on arrival, they would usually also discuss and evaluate (in French) the work they had carried out individually between sessions. The role of the adviser was limited to that of observer and recorder of what was said. Fundamentally, the students were sharing their experiences as learners and – apart from moments when they were carrying out tasks for the group, such as going to a shelf to get a dictionary or selecting a videotape – their contribution could be largely defined as participating in conversations with peers.

The three requirements outlined at the end of the last section, once identified, were relatively easy to achieve. The critical aspect was supported mainly in the fact that the 'adviser' helping the group used a non-directive approach, the conversational aspect was achieved because of the focus on language learning and the shared learning experience between the participants. It was often associated with the collective aspect, or the spontaneous product of bringing back together students who had been working independently throughout the week but knew that they could express themselves about their experience and that the whole group had an interest. However, if these three conditions were necessary, they were not sufficient to make the course a success. We think the following three aspects of the implementation of the course were determinant: self-selection of the group, the type and level of feed-back and the self-selected syllabus from week 2.

## *Self-selection*

Self-selection brought together non-specialist students who had in common not so much that they were highly motivated as the fact that they had started to reflect about their own language learning strategies. The group which followed the course was brought together in several stages. The first stage was the identification of a significant number of individuals from a variety of faculties who shared similar difficulties by the Language Learning Advisory Service of the Language Centre. This University-wide service is a 'listening system' which offers individual interviews to students who find it difficult to work out what the actual range of language learning opportunities are in the University context or need help to work out a language learning plan. One of the main objectives of this service, run by an academic, is to support students' efforts in 'learning to learn languages'. Also, from the purely managerial point of view, the early identification of new needs which constitute significant trends and concern the students' population across the board is an advantage. In this case, the Language Learning Adviser had noted that at least two dozen people had come to see her recently to talk about their difficulties in progressing in French at an upper intermediate or advanced level. She had also noted the general quality of the reflection which had motivated these students' visits, whether they came to discuss the availability of appropriate materials in the resource centre or enquired about advanced conversational classes. From there the idea of an experimental workshop was mooted. The term workshop was preferred to the term 'course' on the basis that there was no predetermined syllabus or progression.

At the second stage, self-selection was achieved by means of a letter and a questionnaire. The letter was an offer which stated the aims of the proposed workshop and specified the constraints very clearly. It invited students to express their interest in a workshop 'aiming to help participants to develop their skills as independent language-learners'. No negotiation about time-tabling or frequency was attempted. There would be a weekly one-hour meeting for one term (i.e. eight weeks) and the amount of work quoted pre-supposed strong personal commitment: 'those taking part would be expected to do about three hours of independent work on their French every week'.

The same mailing also contained a short questionnaire. Apart from the usual basic information, there were four questions designed to reveal to the respondents an image of themselves as learners: the kind of motivation they had, the strength of their motivation, their ability to be coherent and consistent in making a learning plan, and lastly their ability to be realistic in terms of time management. The four questions were requests for:

1. a brief description of what they had done to maintain their French since leaving secondary school, i.e. typically five to six years before;
2. a self-assessment of their level in French in comparison with the level they had reached at the end of secondary school, i.e. whether they had progressed, were at a lower level or were about the same;
3. a statement of why they were trying to do something now;
4. a list of the extra-curricular activities planned during the academic term concerned (some, like rowing, are well known to be lethal for language learning activities).

In the end, eighteen students were invited to attend.

The last and third stage of self-selection concerns the bringing together of students especially interested in the lexicon and the development of strategies for storing, memorizing and retrieving vocabulary items. The process whereby the self-selected syllabus was arrived at from the second week was made is reported below. This process of selection, it will be noted, was achieved by means of listening to what the learners had to say, which made it possible to take their actual needs into consideration. This very fact partly explains why the workshop could be a success while supporting students' autonomy, which leads me to my next point.

## Type and level of feedback

Another explanation for the success of the workshop is that group advising with a collective focus ensures that feedback is available and relevant. Advising, as practised in our Centre since the early 1980s is a discourse-based mode of teaching, which until this course had been restricted to one-to-one, face-to-face interviews. The idea is that learners determine their own progression or action plan on the basis of a succession of conversations with an adviser. The main aim of these 'learning conversations' (Harri-Augstein and Thomas, 1991) is to support learners' reflection on their experience since the last session. In comparison with traditional one-to-one teaching, a major difference is that learning is interactionally initiated and led by the learner. Given the systematic organization of conversations, if the learners come first sequentially, they can also control the content of the conversation, in particular because they fill in the first topic slot, which normally counts as 'the reason for calling'. The learners' contributions display their categories and priorities as well as their mood. Quite clearly, the conversation will not focus on the same aspects if one student starts by saying: 'I have succeeded in doing my reading programme systematically but I think the evaluation grid I used is not sufficiently elaborate', and another displays time-management difficulties and despondency by saying: 'I'll never do it. I just couldn't implement my reading programme.' Advising could be described as a systematic exploitation of conversational organization.

In the workshop, there were two significant differences: first, the learners actually carried out language learning activities together, during which time the adviser's role was exclusively to observe. This means that there was a shared collective experience which triggered a lot of talk and constituted the main topic of the conversation. This also means that all students not only participated but felt engaged in the process and concerned with the outcome. The following example comes from the notes I was making, since, as acting adviser, I was observing the group and intervened only if asked specifically to do so. It shows how the discussion is anchored into participants' experience and how much material is encoded in the way we talk about our learning experience.

In the second week of the course, one of the students, Flora, re-ported to the group on the language learning work she had done the preceding week and explained that she had decided to 'learn vocabulary'. The point of the discourse-based approach is that in so doing Flora was not only expounding the way she had been making decisions, but displaying her priorities and the implicit categories and presuppositions she was using when she was talking about 'vocabulary'. My comments are in square brackets:

> Flora had decided to use the press [words exist primarily in their written form]. She had found a weekly magazine in her college and selected it because she thought it would provide a wide enough range of vocabulary items but also provide short enough and not too difficult articles [Flora's principles for selection show she is able to chunk the learning task into manageable bits – she is not a naive learner]. Her technique was to read and whenever she came across a word she did not know [there is no assessment whether she was able to guess what the meaning might be and, if so, how successful she was at guessing, so no reflection on the process of understanding] she would write it down [this means that only the particular meaning relevant in that context is selected out but the context is not noted], look it up in her bilingual dictionary and write the English translation in a column opposite [implicit theory of associated pair learning for memorization of words]. At the end of the week she had a long list of French words with the English equivalent but she could not remember them and she felt very depressed. She felt that what she had learnt was 'that she knew fewer words than she thought she knew at the beginning'!

Flora's experience was taken up by the group in the following way. The group first discussed what 'learn vocabulary' meant and settled on the following definition: 'increase the number of words one knows'. Then the discussion moved to what was meant by 'knowing a word' which raised the problem of written form versus phonological form as well as problems of identification of words in context. From the notion of context, the question of the appropriateness of the technique used by Flora was raised and they concluded that she should start again with the same magazine but try to make guesses and try to remember words in their context and to look for other occurrences of the same words in other contexts. Also, the question of the kind of dictionary to be used was raised with a majority of students in favour of trying to operate with a monolingual dictionary to avoid interference.

Another student, Peter, volunteered at this point that perhaps we had different attitudes towards words in our own language and in a second language. In a second language, we are immediately aware of the fact that we do not know a word, whereas in our own language, simply because it is more familiar generally, we feel we 'know' words and constantly make guesses even though we may not be able to give a definition. The group agreed at the end that a major part of learning a language was to make it familiar and literally 'not foreign'.

This example shows how from one member's experience, the group really progresses and covers a lot of material. What constitute 'appropriate learning situations' and 'acceptable language learning objectives' for the students of the group is brought to the fore and discussed in a non-threatening, conversational mode. As in the example above, the quality of the students' learning experience did count – and this was because they did work between the meetings – but their ability to reflect upon it and to converse about it was also important.

This way of proceeding supports a process view of learning how to learn but requires at least two things: first, that the adviser or helper is effectively non-directive, and secondly, that enough time is given to the group.

## Non-directivity

The main spin-off of a non-directive group approach is that students realize that a number of stumbling blocks and barriers which get in the way of language learning are the direct consequence of social and cultural norms. By the same token, they realize that nothing prevents them from changing these shared in-built constructs if they wish to. In this way, there is a destructuration of long-ingrained habits. At the most basic level of the organization of the class and the allocation of turns at talk for example, one student raised her hand to ask 'Can we start?' at the beginning of the first meeting. This is not superficial as it revealed to the others that they are used to acting as if they needed to be controlled externally to start learning and to considering that an activity is a learning activity only if it is 'ratified' by an authority.

## Time

A practical outcome is that time is needed for a group to take in and digest the experience. 'Intensive' group advising does not work. Meetings separated by periods during which the individuals can engage in new experiences and reflect upon them seem to support the process much better.

## *Self-selected syllabus from week 2*

The first meeting was carefully prepared. The decision was made that we would speak French from the outset, that is language choice in favour of the target language was imposed, in fact, by the advisers. The idea was threefold: first, it gave participants an occasion to practice a range of communicative functions rarely useful in class – expressing their views and describing and talking about their learning experiences in French. Secondly, the workshop would, by itself, become a learning activity through communication. Thirdly, as it was for us an experimental course, we felt this was a kind of guarantee. If the learner training bit did not work, students would at least get something like a 'conversation class' and would not be frustrated.

The first meeting was devoted to the identification of problem areas and led to the group splitting into two: those who wanted to work on 'vocabulary' (with me) and those who wanted to work on 'grammar' (with the other adviser). From that point on, by means of the discursive process illustrated above, there was no difficulty at all in proceeding from topic to topic. The only constraint was for the group to state at the end of each session what they intended to do the following week, and for what reason. This plan was promptly recorded and produced again at the beginning of the following week, as a kind of mirror for the group. It usually served as the starting point to evaluate what the group members had done individually during the week.

# Evaluation: realities for learner training

Ellis and Sinclair (1989: p.1) tell us that 'helping learners take on more responsibility for their own learning can be beneficial' because:

- learning can be more effective when learners take control of their own learning because they learn what they are ready to learn;
- those learners who are responsible for their own learning can carry on learning outside the classroom;
- learners who know about learning can transfer learning strategies to other subjects.

In the case of this workshop, it was clear that the students concerned benefited from the course both individually and as a group.

From the point of view of the development of learner autonomy, the benefits of such ventures are perceived as a function of the care taken in negotiating the objectives of the course with the students and above all of the degree of reflection achieved by the group. Although there is no hard and fast evidence, exemplary attendance does show that students were really interested. After eight weeks, the students were beginning to realize not only how complex the language learning task was but how much we take for granted when we go to a class or buy a language course.

A very interesting consequence was that the students started realizing that the materials catalogued in the private study area of the language centre could be useful. Their tendency, throughout the course, had been to use 'raw' television programmes received by satellite but they concluded that for a number of purposes, using ready-made materials could save them a lot of time. Hence they started looking at the retrieval categories of the catalogue with great interest, which we saw as a very positive outcome of the course. Generally, one can say that the course succeeded in promoting a deep approach to language learning (Gibbs, 1992). One would expect any improvements in the students' study skills to be transferred to other areas of study.

To conclude, the question whether learner training courses can be designed to foster learner autonomy must be raised. At one level, as Ellis and Sinclair (1989) clearly demonstrate, it is possible to organize such courses systematically, and the outcome should be to produce learners who are better aware of the learning process and of the various techniques available for language learning. At the other level, the fostering of autonomy in language learners by means of workshops where learners 'train' one another is more difficult but possible as long as it does not become a routine. Control by the teachers, if it returns through the back door, will produce some short-term language learning gains but will not help learners reap the benefits of taking charge of their own learning.

## Note

1. The workshop was arranged and monitored in cooperation with Dr S. Rybak. The names of participating students have been changed.

# PART III

# Methods and materials

## Introduction

In Parts I and II several contributors raised questions about methods and materials for autonomous learning. It was noted that self-instructional materials are often highly directive, providing the user with explicit instructions on how they should be used and giving feedback in the form of cut and dried answers. In some ways these materials can be less flexible than those designed for classroom use, which often include a measure of flexibility to accommodate their mediation by teachers. It was also noted that self-access methods and materials tend to favour the 'receptive' skills of listening and reading over the 'productive' skills of reading and writing and individual, analytic activities over collaborative, experiential strategies. There is evidently a risk that the kinds of methods and materials commonly used in autonomous learning projects will tend to inhibit rather than promote autonomy unless they are able to accommodate more directive roles for their users. One solution to the problem may be to help learners to develop skills which enable them to cope with methods and materials that are not specifically adapted to the kinds of purposes that they have in mind. Another solution could be to abandon methods and materials altogether. We might also, however, look more closely at the design of methods and materials and try to establish relationships between their design and the promotion of autonomy and independence. The final six chapters in this collection explore in different ways the proposition that autonomous learning implies new methods and materials.

Andrew Littlejohn (Chapter 12) provides an overview of issues in this area, making a powerful case that both the materials used in self-instructional work and the tasks based on them must be considered in terms of the ideologies they convey. Basing his argument on a critical approach to ideological encoding in learning materials, Littlejohn locates the conflict between the ostensible aims of self-instructional materials and their ideological effects in the discourse roles that are conventionally proposed for their users. Typically, he argues, learners are positioned into a limited range of responses and are not invited to engage in learning in a deep sense. They are encouraged to engage in reproductive language use and to respond rather than initiate. He argues that self-instructional materials should be open-ended and encourage creativity, and that ways need to be found for learners themselves to become engaged in the production of their learning tasks and materials.

David Nunan (Chapter 13) follows on by looking at textbook materials as a means to promote autonomy and independence. Nunan argues that it is unreasonable for advocates of autonomy to assume that learners are already autonomous before they engage in a programme of learning. Indeed, the development of autonomy depends upon explicit attention to learning process goals in the course of the programme. These goals, he suggests, can best be achieved when they are integrated with language learning goals. Nunan also argues that learning process materials corresponding to growing levels of independence can be introduced progressively as a course develops, illustrating the point with examples from his own published materials. However, unless there is a direct relationship between levels of language proficiency and levels of independence, it may be difficult for textbook writers to know how to match up the two in a particular set of materials. Nunan's suggestion that teachers can modify materials to include process goals at appropriate levels for their own students is, therefore, a useful one. It is also interesting to observe that as we move towards the higher levels of independence in Nunan's schema, we also appear to move away from teacher-produced materials towards learner-produced materials and tasks that break down the barriers between the classroom and the world beyond.

In Chapter 14, Guy Aston takes up the issues of open-endedness and learner design in the context of negotiated self-access work with electronic text corpora. Aston describes an experimental course at the University of Bologna where learners and teachers collaborated to develop ways of using corpora in self-access mode. His account illustrates an approach to the use of materials in autonomous learning which differs radically from those conventionally used in self-access. Rather than pick and choose from a wide selection of pre-constructed materials, learners use a particular tool (the computer) to immerse themselves in an environment of authentic language (the corpora), and autonomy is developed as the learners experiment with their own methods of organizing and using the resources available to them. Aston's proposal can be described as a 'method' in as much as there is a prescribed set of materials and a specific sequence of actions on the part of learners and teachers. But it is a method which allows for a good deal of creativity and initiation on the part of the learners. In this sense, it appears to be a good example of Littlejohn's criteria of open-endedness and learner design.

As students of translation in an Italian university, the participants in Aston's course were both highly proficient and highly motivated and we may speculate how much this contributed to the reported success of the activity. By contrast, the participants in Stephen Ryan's (Chapter 15) experimental course, final year engineering students in a Japanese university, were ostensibly less proficient and less motivated. Ryan suggests that one way to help such students develop greater independence is to encourage them to make use of language learning resources outside the classroom. In the course described, participants follow a procedure in which there is constant interaction between the classroom and the world beyond. The course also includes a component in which students are encouraged to develop methods of working with authentic resources that allow them to self-assess outcomes. Ryan's course is highly-structured, but again leaves room for students' creativity and initiative. It also illustrates that successful autonomous learning is not necessarily' dependent on high proficiency or initial motivation.

David Little (Chapter 16) is known in the field of autonomous learning for his emphasis on the importance of authentic materials. In this chapter he confronts the problem of how authentic materials can retain their authenticity when they are removed from their natural contexts and used in self-instructional facilities. His answer to the problem is to suggest that authenticity of response does not necessarily mean replication of the original context of use. He argues that the most important factor is whether the tasks that learners are asked to perform allow them to respond both as users and as learners of the target language. It is the capacity of authentic texts to draw language learners into the communicative world of the target language community and to facilitate the interaction between learning and use that constitutes their importance for the development of autonomy.

The role of new technologies in autonomous learning is an issue in need of considerable debate. Language learning technologies have long been subject to the same kinds of criticisms that Littlejohn makes of methods and materials in general, namely that they tend to offer a limited range of responses to the user. Little concludes his chapter on a positive note, suggesting that new computer technologies, the Internet especially, hold the potential to create 'virtual target language communities' for communicatively isolated students. John Milton's concluding contribution to this collection (Chapter 17) offers a similarly positive view on uses of writing technologies for autonomous learning. Milton is critical of the notion that the computer can be a 'teacher'. In contrast to the position taken by many advocates of computer-assisted language learning, Milton argues that in order for the computer to be instrumental in developing learners' autonomy as writers, it must remain a tool under the control of its users. He goes on to illustrate this point by describing ongoing work at the Hong Kong University of Science and Technology to create computer-assisted writing environments in which student writers can obtain appropriate help while they are writing. Milton's project is particularly interesting for the fact that it does not simply claim to promote autonomy on the grounds that the computer replaces the teacher. On the contrary, it is centrally concerned with the ways in which technological components can be arranged in such fashion that student writers are enabled to explore and develop their writing skills on their own, in Little's words, as both users and learners of language.

# 12

## Self-access work and curriculum · ideologies

### ANDREW LITTLEJOHN

### Introduction

In recent years, self-access work has become closely linked with promotion of autonomy in language learning. Self-access work is often seen as providing the opportunities for learners to make decisions over what they would like or need to study, exercise control over the rate at which they are working and assume greater responsibility for their own language development. While it is undoubtedly true that self-access work may contribute in this regard, I want in this chapter to suggest that we need to reflect further on the nature of self-access opportunities which are provided and the significance these may have in terms of curriculum ideology. I will be using the term 'curriculum ideology' in a broad sense to refer to the ideas implicit within the organization of the curriculum, in particular, the values and priorities upon which it is based and which it promotes, and the roles it allots to teachers, learners and educational administrators. I will suggest that much self-access work places learners in a reactive, disempowered position by virtue of the tasks which they typically do. I will also offer some brief suggestions on ways in which self-access work may be redefined such that it engages learners in a wider range of responses and draws them more into decisions affecting their own work. I will begin, however, by outlining some of the links which may exist between language pedagogy and curriculum ideology.

### Classroom pedagogy and ideological encoding

In the literature on classroom pedagogy, one of the most interesting and revealing areas of debate has been the focus on the relationship between classroom practice and ideological encoding, that is, the way in which classroom practice may carry or reflect a particular ideology. A number of writers in this area have suggested that there exists within much classroom practice a 'hidden curriculum' which promotes ideological messages that may not be immediately apparent to those involved. These messages emerge 'experientially', that is, they emerge through the learners' experience of the manner in which teaching and learning is organized, rather than through its overt content. Many of these writers adopt a position within critical theory, relating the practices of education to the social structure at large and seeing class-based ideas (values, goals and definitions of knowledge) and vested interests in the status quo reflected in the predominant modes of education (see, for example, Althusser, 1971; Bowles and Gintis, 1976; Giroux, 1988).

Michael Apple (1985, 1988, 1989) has similarly applied critical theory to a detailed analysis of classroom procedures. In a fascinating account of the use of prepackaged boxed materials for the teaching and learning of science, Apple suggests that a process of social control is represented in the manner in which these materials provide detailed instructions to the teacher, specify the actual words to be used, and include all the material resources required (1985: pp.143–8). In utilizing the package as indicated, teachers, argues Apple, are *deskilled* in relation to curriculum decisions (in relation, for example, to decisions over what is to be learnt, how, with whom, when and so on) and *reskilled* in terms of techniques for managing pupils and shaping their behaviour to fulfil the goals set out by the materials. The impact of the materials is not, however, limited to the manner in which it deskills and reskills teachers. Much of the classroom work proposed by these types of materials is 'individualized' in the sense that it involves pupils working alone through the various levels or stages within the package. Knowledge and abilities are specified in the materials as discrete targets or 'skills' which pupils are to master or, more accurately, accumulate. Drawing on Gramsci's (1938/1971) work on the relationship between social practice, ideological encoding and consciousness, Apple sees this process of knowledge accumulation as reproducing a psychology at the heart of capitalist economies: that of the possessive individual (1988: p.153). In the curriculum packages which he describes, Apple sees this psychology reflected in the manner in which knowledge and abilities are subdivided into atomistic 'bits' that are transformed into commodities for the pupil to amass.

The particular significance of the work of these theorists is that they suggest – in contrast to the popular notion of 'ideology' – that ideological encodings are present not only in *content* (semantic meanings) but more importantly in the manner in which teaching and learning is organized and the classroom *methodology* utilized. As I have argued at length elsewhere (Littlejohn and Windeatt, 1989; Littlejohn, 1992 and 1995), these encodings may be equally present in the organization of practices within language teaching. In fact, given the emphasis which the profession places on a developed 'methodology', one may argue that ideological encodings will be even more pervasive and more significant. The organization of language teaching, I have argued, may have direct implications for 'non-language learning' outcomes, in terms of classroom and social role relations which students learn, an experienced definition of what 'learning' is and how it is achieved and what constitutes 'knowledge' itself (Littlejohn and Windeatt, 1989: pp.159–68; Benson, 1994). By being positioned into particular relationships with teachers, for example, learners come to see what their role in the educational process is intended to be and in relation to other hierarchies of power, their rights and responsibilities. With the organization of language *learning* predominantly determined by those engaged with *teaching*, learners are additionally shown what constitute legitimate and valid ways of learning. As an integral part of this, a view of 'knowledge' is experienced by learners. Language, for example, may be broken down into 'bits' (grammar items, vocabulary lists, lists of functions, and so on) which the learners are to acquire as 'thing-like entities' with the human mind largely being viewed as an empty bucket. The learners are consequently placed in a passive or reactive role as they endeavour to accumulate these 'bits' of language knowledge presented to them in the processes of teaching.

With the potential for strong ideological messages within language pedagogy, an engagement with self-access work may be seen as having an important role in defining learners as more active agents in their own education. As the analysis by Apple and others has suggested, however, the decision to undertake self-access work is likely to be only part of the equation. What is probably of more importance is precisely what learners *do* in self-access work.

## Self-access work and ideological encodings

While acknowledging that there is considerable diversity in the nature of self-access practices worldwide, I would like in this section to focus on what personal experience suggests is the predominant approach to the organization of self-access work. Readers may well find that this approach reflects their own experience of self-access.

Students may come to a self-access centre by a variety of means. They may be directed to go as a part of their course, perhaps earning credit for self-access attendance. They may be advised to attend (perhaps in the face of an examination), or they may choose to go themselves in order to improve their language skills in particular areas. The centre may be staffed by an 'adviser' of some kind who helps the student find and choose relevant materials to work on. In the centre itself, students are typically offered various 'banks' of exercises and tasks. These may be subdivided into various categories such as 'grammar', 'listening', 'speaking', 'learning to learn', 'business', 'topic' and so on, with indications of the language level required for each task. There may also be additional resources for extensive language work – such as video, literature, CD-ROM, and audio recordings. Typically, however, and especially at lower levels of competence in the foreign language, it is the exercises and tasks provided which form the main work which students do in the centre. These generally come from one of two sources: published materials (which are often cut up and pasted onto cards) and in-house materials, which result from the labours of particular teachers or materials producers.

In working with the provided materials, students may have the services of an adviser available. However, given a general shortage in counsellor time, the typical solution to helping students determine their learning needs and then plan accordingly, is to have answer keys available, such that the students may see for themselves the areas in which they need further language practice. Thus, there is a pressure on the designers and administrators of self-access centres to identify, particularly at lower language levels, exercise and task types which can easily be corrected by a student working alone. This in turn is likely to lead to the selection of 'closed', rather than 'open' task types. Given the predominant nature of much published materials, this is perhaps not surprising in those self-access centres which draw mainly on such materials. A similar situation is likely to

| Input | Skill | Level | Exercise/activity |
|-------|-------|-------|-------------------|
| Source material (e.g. text, picture, tape, etc.) | Listening<br>Speaking<br>Reading<br>Writing<br>Grammar<br>Pronunciation<br>(others) | Elementary<br>Intermediate<br>Advanced | 1. multiple choice<br>2. true/false<br>3. yes/no<br>4. gap-filling<br>5. matching<br>6. listing<br>7. sound discrimination<br>8. shadow reading<br>9. sequencing<br>10. cloze exercises<br>11. completion exercises<br>12. parallel writing<br>13. letter writing<br>14. report writing<br>15. composition writing<br>16. simplification<br>17. transformation exercises<br>18. summary<br>19. communicative activity<br>20. open-ended questions<br>(others) |

**Figure 12.1** 'Ways of exploiting source material' (Lum and Brown, 1994: p.151)

exist, however, in those self-access centres which utilize in-house materials. Lum and Brown (1994), for example, in giving practical advice for the production of in-house self-access exercises and activities to exploit authentic materials, offer a system which eliminates 'pencil-chewing time' on the part of the materials writers through reference to a table summarizing possible exercise types (see Figure 12.1).

There is, of course, nothing extraordinary in the selection of tasks and activities listed in the figure. They reflect the most widespread task and activity-types used in language teaching – certainly among those found predominantly in published materials. Their reappearance in the context of self-access work is, nevertheless, significant since it gives us an indication of what students are likely to be called upon to *do* when working independently. Figure 12.1, then, deserves closer examination. I should stress that my intention here is not to be critical of Lum and Brown's work. I merely wish to draw on the figure as an indicator of what self-access centres may typically contain.

In analysing language learning tasks, I frequently make use of three key questions that aim to reveal the underlying – ideological – subject position which is proposed for the student. These are related to the two areas of content and methodology. They are:

1. What role in the discourse is proposed for the learner: initiate, respond or none?
2. What mental operation is to be engaged?
3. Where does the content for the task come from? From within the task itself, from the teacher or from the students?

I will take each of the questions in turn and briefly comment on what I see as some significant points which emerge from an examination of Lum and Brown's table (Figure 12.1).

## What role in the discourse is proposed for the learner?

In my analysis of tasks, I find it useful to draw on three basic categories in relation to discourse role: *initiate, respond* and *none.* 'None' relates to a situation where the learners are not expected to enter into the structuring of the discourse – simply to attend to what is being presented to them, as, for example, in the presentation of a grammar rule. 'Respond' I use in a particular sense to refer to a situation in which learners are expected to express themselves using language which has been pre-defined (such as in guided writing tasks). 'Initiate' refers to a situation which contains no such constraints or supports – where learners can say what they wish to say without any kind of underlying 'script'. 'Respond' and 'initiate' thus lie at end points on a scale of learner contribution, where at one end the learners have no control over what they are to say and, at the other, they have full control. Tasks can therefore be analysed as being more towards the 'respond' role or more towards the 'initiate' role.

As inspection of Figure 12.1 shows, the listed exercise and activity types generally appear to place the learner more towards a 'respond' position. Multiple choice, true/false, gap-filling, matching, sequencing, completion exercises, parallel writing and so on require students simply to respond and to do so within the specified confines of the task. A notable exception to this is 'open-ended questions' (item 20), and possibly 'communicative activity' (item 19) (though this may imply a scripted information-gap type activity).

## What mental operation is to be engaged?

Inspection of Figure 12.1 once again suggests certain conclusions. True/false tasks, gap-filling, matching, parallel writing, transformation exercises and many other items in the figure are likely to involve the students in a fairly narrow range of mental operations – principally what one may term 'low level' operations of memory retrieval, decoding semantic meaning, repeating, and applying patterned rules which require relatively little cognitive effort. While such mental operations are an essential ingredient in second language learning, it is apparent that the more demanding 'high level' mental operations such as speculating, analysing, hypothesizing, critiquing, and reflecting, appear to be absent, as are any which call upon the affective side of the learner – imagining, reacting, philosophizing, appreciating, and other expressive responses. The learner is thus positioned into a fairly limited range of response, and not invited – or required – to engage in learning in a deep sense.

## Where does the content come from: the task, the teacher or the students?

Figure 12.1 is suggestive of particular content sources. Task and activity types such as multiple choice, true/false, yes/no, gap-filling, matching, and so on suggest that the learner will be called upon to work with content supplied in the context of the task. This is in turn likely to signify that the learners are to engage in essentially *reproductive* rather than creative language use. They will be required to reproduce the language which is contained (or hidden) within the task. They will thus be predominantly engaged in finding predetermined answers, rather than unique ones. Tasks which require students to supply their own content – to work *creatively* with language – appear less frequently. Items 19 and 20 appear, in this regard, as exceptions, as potentially do items 13 'letter writing', 14 'report writing' and 15 'composition writing'.

The key concepts that come through very strongly in looking at Figure 12.1 and the list of task and activity types are the notions of 'scripting' of the language to be used by the learners, a demand for 'low level' cognitive work which is affectively neutral and an emphasis on 'reproductive' language work. The potential for *self*-expression, *self*- development and for the development of autonomy in language *use* is thus under-exploited. In ideological terms, there is, thus, a clear tension apparent here in the ostensible aim in the provision of self-access facilities and its realization in practice. The notions of personally appropriate language work, of personal control, and self-direction *may* be involved at the level of the decision to enter into self-access work, but once this decision is taken the role which the learner then goes on to take is strongly suggested by the closed nature of the tasks which are provided and the existence of 'correct answers'. Thus, an intention on the part of many teachers for self-access work to 'liberate' the learner, is accommodated into social reproduction, a process in which the student now becomes *individually* and, more immediately, engaged.

The resulting challenge for those engaged in organizing self-access work is substantial. A considerable amount of careful discussion and creative imagination will be needed to identify ways in which self-access work can place students in a more determining position in learning, and engage and develop the *individual* rather than the mass anonymous learner. In the last part of this chapter, I would like to offer some general indications of the kind of changes in the organization of self-access work which I feel would move in this direction.

## Redefining self-access work

Part of the origin of the dilemma for self-access work which I have identified lies in the extension of conventional ideological relationships encoded in language teaching practices to the development of self-access centres. The intention in providing self-access work is most usually seen in language pedagogic terms – that is, to get more language learnt more efficiently. Thus, as Benson (1994) points out, much of the existing literature on self-access focuses on *how* self-access can be organized (evidenced by the Lum and Brown extract above) – what he terms 'practical self-access' – without much detailed consideration of the underlying philosophies involved or a macro-sociological view of educational processes. It is as if the notion of self-access work has no significance beyond the walls of the language teaching institution or in other areas of the learners lives.

Language teaching – like any area of education – is, however, a highly political activity. It is political in many aspects: in the status and impact of the language it promotes, in the culture it carries and – as I have been endeavouring to show in this chapter – in the manner in which it positions learners in their relations with learning, teaching, and themselves. It is this latter aspect which I believe needs to be thought through more carefully such that the subject positions ascribed to learners in self-access work complement the ostensible aim. My discussion of the task and activity types frequently offered in self-access work, and the manner in which the learner is viewed as a discrete 'learning entity' will, perhaps, have suggested a number of avenues for development. I would like here to briefly draw some of these together in terms of practical implications.

## From 'reproductive' work to 'creative' work, from 'respond' roles to 'initiate' roles

I have argued in this chapter that one of the determining factors in the role allotted to students in self-access work is the nature of the tasks on which they work. In attempting to open up opportunities for autonomy in language use and self-direction in learning, one of the most important elements will therefore be a reorientation in task and activity types from a predominantly 'respond' learner role and 'reproductive' work towards an 'initiate' role and 'creative' work. This suggests the provision of open-ended (rather than closed) task and activity types, which call upon the unique experiences, imagination and ideas of the learner and which utilize these as content for tasks. At lower levels of ability in the foreign language, this will clearly call for a reconsideration of the extent to which opportunities for language learning need, in any case, to involve tightly controlled exposure to the language and controlled practice. At all levels of language ability, however, it raises for consideration how far direct, explicit feedback needs to be given to students in self-access mode by the teaching institution, or whether the provision of *example* answers to a task (in contrast to the conventional 'correct answers') and the possibility of peer feedback is a viable alternative.

## *Learner feedback: evaluating self-access work*

Much of the nature of self-access work is partly dependent on the fact that it is often seen as an extension of classroom work and thus carries many of the ideological encodings of conventional classroom relationships. In terms of altering the balance of decision-making and power in self-access work, we can thus look to some recent innovations in bases for course design. One of the most interesting of these has been the work in the area of process syllabuses proposed by writers such as Breen (1984, 1987). Process syllabuses focus on negotiation between teachers and learners as a means of establishing what will be done in the classroom and how. To facilitate joint decision making, Breen (1984) suggests an 'index' or 'bank' of alternative activities and tasks. There are clear parallels between this 'bank' and the provision of self-access work but the significant point in process syllabuses is that the nature of the tasks and activities, as well as the choices that are made, are subject to on-going review and evaluation by the participants themselves (Breen, 1989). In some self-access centres, this principle has already been applied with the establishment of procedures for collecting reactions from users of the centre. Evaluation and response forms attached to worksheets and task/activity packs enable greater account to be taken of users' experiences, suggestions and difficulties. There would seem to be much one could do in this respect, however, by involving centre users in not only feeding back on what is provided, but also in planning what the centre offers and how it is organized. Such moves would help to transform learners from the role of *consumers* to the role of producers, exercising some level of control and influence over the centre facilities.

## *Learner feedback: producing self-access resources*

The notion of a transformation of learner role from *consumer* to *producer* is also applicable to the production of materials in the centre. As Lum and Brown's table (Figure 12.1) shows, the production of tasks and activities for self-access work can be accomplished relatively simply through reference to a list of task/activity types. In recent years, I have experimented, particularly with adolescents, in engaging learners in devising their own practice exercises or devising exercises for others to do. In addition to the strong applied linguistic arguments in support of this (exercise production engages learners in a deeper understanding of the language, can raise motivation and diversifies learning strategies), there are powerful arguments related to the construction of the learner as an *active* agent in the learner process, not simply the recipient of teaching. Such an approach could also be applied relatively easily to the production of self-access tasks and activities with which learners could be involved (and which could use content supplied by the learners – for example, texts they write, magazine articles, video and audio recordings either pre-produced or produced by groups of learners). There are obviously practical considerations here (related to checking materials produced, organizing and indexing tasks and activities) but the benefits in terms of a redefinition of the role of centre users would appear to be substantial.

## Conclusion

In this chapter I have endeavoured to show how the role which is allotted to those engaged in self-access work can be seen as fundamentally *ideological* in nature. As I have argued, typically learners using self-access centres are placed in a role in which their language production is scripted and in which they are required to focus on reproducing language supplied to them. I have suggested that there may be a direct conflict here between the ostensible aims of self-access and its realization in practice. The nature of this conflict and its resolution raises a number of issues both for the debate on learner independence and self-access and for the debate on language teaching procedures as a whole.

# 13

## Designing and adapting materials to encourage learner autonomy

DAVID NUNAN

### Introduction

The problem that this chapter sets out to explore is how learning materials can be designed or adapted in ways that encourage learners to develop autonomy.[1] A basic assumption underlying the chapter is that few individuals come to the task of language learning as autonomous learners. Other related assumptions include the belief that developing some degree of autonomy is essential if learners are to become effective language users, and that the ability to direct one's own learning can be developed through pedagogical procedures of one sort or another. A final belief is that autonomy is not an all-or-nothing concept, that there are degrees of autonomy, and that the extent to which autonomy can be developed will be constrained by the psychological and cognitive make-up of the learner as well as the cultural, social and educational context in which the learning takes place.

### Defining terms

Dickinson (1987) draws a distinction between self-instruction, self-direction and autonomy. According to Dickinson, self-instruction is a neutral term for situations in which learners are working without the direct control of a teacher. Self-instructional learning may also be closely controlled by a teacher who may, without being physically present, make all of the key decisions about what will be learned, how it will be learned, and how it will be assessed. Self-direction, on the other hand, describes 'a particular attitude to the learning task, where the learner accepts responsibility for all the decisions concerned with his [sic] learning but does not necessarily undertake the implementation of those decisions' (p.11). Autonomy describes a situation in which the learner is not only responsible for all of the decisions concerned with learning, but also for the implementation of those decisions. The fully autonomous learner, therefore operates independently of classroom, teacher or textbook. It may well be that the fully autonomous learner is an ideal, rather than a reality. In this chapter, I shall focus on the learner who is not autonomous, but who is in a situation in which independent learning is either necessary or desirable.

Holec (1981: p.3) defines 'autonomy' as the ability to take charge of one's own learning. This is elaborated as follows:

> To take charge of one's own learning is to have, and to hold, the responsibility for all the decisions concerning all aspects of this learning, i.e.:
>     determining the objectives;
>     defining the contents and progressions;
>     selecting methods and techniques to be used;
>     monitoring the procedure of acquisition properly speaking (rhythm, time, place, etc.);
>     evaluating what has been acquired.

I would argue that autonomy, is not an absolute concept. There are degrees of autonomy, and the extent to which it is feasible or desirable for learners to embrace autonomy will depend on a range of factors to do with the personality of the learner, the goals in undertaking the study of another language, the philosophy of the institution (if any) providing the instruction, and the cultural context within which the learning takes place (Nunan, 1988). In the next section, a scheme is outlined which illustrates different levels at which learner autonomy can be worked towards, from relatively superficial awareness raising through to complete autonomy where learners transcend the classroom and take complete charge of their own learning.

In this chapter I emphasize the importance of the teacher in fostering self-direction and autonomy because of the claim which is often made that proponents of learner-centredness, self-direction and autonomy hold naive views about skills which learners bring to the learning situation (see, for example, O'Neill, 1991). Thus, Johnston (1985: p.192) writes:

> While I see a fairly clear relationship between learner-centred pedagogy and learner-centred research, from my point of view as

a second language acquisition researcher the relationship between learner-centred research and self-directed learning is in some ways problematic. . . . For me, the worrying aspect of self-directed learning is the following: there is a very powerful assumption in this approach to learning that the learner knows what is best.

In fact, in this chapter, I would argue that most learners, at the beginning of the learning process, do *not* know what is best. It is the function of the materials augmentation that I shall describe below to develop skills and knowledge in learners which ultimately will leave them in a position where they do know what is best.

## Levels of implementing learner autonomy

In this section I shall outline a scheme for gradually increasing the degree of autonomy exercised by learners in a programme of learning. I shall describe these levels of autonomy in terms of two key curricular domains, the experiential content domain, and the learning process domain. The experiential content domain has to do with the topics, themes, language functions, and so on that, along with the linguistic content domain, make up the syllabus. The learning process domain relates to methodology, and is concerned with the selection, creation, modification and adaptation of learning tasks and procedures. Broadly speaking, addressing questions to do with *what* students will learn take us into the content domain, while issues to do with *how* students will learn take us into the process domain (for discussion of these levels, see Nunan, 1995a; Nunan and Lamb, 1995).

The scheme set out in Figure 13.1 proposes five levels for encouraging learner autonomy. Some of these are more readily incorporated into teaching materials than others. The initial level simply attempts to make learners aware of goals, content and strategies underlying the materials they are using. It is a first step towards encouraging learner autonomy. At a slightly deeper level, learners move from awareness to active involvement in their own learning by making choices from a range of content and procedural options. The next step is to encourage them to intervene in the learning by modifying and adapting goals, content and tasks. At the next level, learners will set their own goals, develop their own content, and create their own learning tasks. Finally, the fully autonomous learner will move beyond the formal learning arrange-

| Level | Learner action | Content | Process |
|-------|----------------|---------|---------|
| 1 | Awareness | Learners are made aware of the pedagogical goals and content of the materials they are using. | Learners identify strategy implications of pedagogical tasks and identify their own preferred learning styles/strategies. |
| 2 | Involvement | Learners are involved in selecting their own goals from a range of alternatives on offer. | Learners make choices among a range of options. |
| 3 | Intervention | Learners are involved in modifying and adapting the goals and content of the learning programme. | Learners modify/adapt tasks. |
| 4 | Creation | Learners create their own goals and objectives. | Learners create their own tasks. |
| 5 | Transcendence | Learners go beyond the classroom and make links between the content of classroom learning and the world beyond. | Learners become teachers and researchers. |

**Figure 13.1** Autonomy: levels of implementation

ment, whether this be a classroom, self-access centre or one-to-one tutorial, continuing to create their own learning materials from the resources that exist in the community without the support that a learning arrangement involves.

It needs to be pointed out here that these levels involve considerable overlap, and that, in practice, learners will move back and forth between levels. Even at relatively early stages, some learners are able to modify materials, and make links back and forth between the classroom and the world beyond the classroom.

In addition, when the levels are incorporated into practical pedagogical materials, there will be instances where tasks at a higher level may be less challenging and even less 'autonomous' than those at a lower level. However, I do not believe that this takes anything away from the general principles underlying the scheme.

In the next section of this chapter, I should like to look at ways in which learning process skills for enhancing self-directed learning can be incorporated into pedagogical materials. Before doing so, however, I should like to emphasize that any educational decision, including the decision to encourage self-directed learning (in languages, or any other area) is a highly political one. Any learning endeavour will be carried out within a particular socio-political and educational content in which certain rules and procedures will be in force. The most important of these will be implicit. They will not be found in statements of educational policy or curriculum frameworks. However, they will reveal themselves to the sensitive observer through the actions of the participants in the educational drama. The hidden culture of an educational system or institution will manifest itself as much by what does not happen as what does happen. The culturally aware observer will ask: Why is there no group work in these classrooms? Why do students never ask questions? How is it that the teacher only asks lower order factual questions?

This is not to say that seeds of self-direction, cast out in cultural contexts antithetical to the notion, will fall on barren ground. Precisely because of the interconnectedness of systems and institutions, efforts to develop self-direction in a single classroom may well have a ripple effect outward from that classroom to the rest of the institution and beyond. In fact, it may well be that the only effective, long-term change is that which moves from the bottom up rather than the top down.

## Exemplification

How might some of the principles set out in the preceding section be incorporated into pedagogical materials? In this section, I shall attempt to provide some ideas. These ideas are illustrative rather than exhaustive, but they should serve to show that self-direction and learning materials are not mutually incompatible. I shall organize this section by following the levels set out in Figure 13.1.

### Level 1: awareness

At the most superficial level, learners are made aware of the pedagogical goals and content of the programme and encouraged to identify the learning strategies implicit in the tasks making up the methodological component of the curriculum. While the desirability of making goals and content transparent to learners might seem obvious, it is surprising how infrequently it is done, either by teachers or materials writers. It is also a good idea to remind learners of instructional goals at regular intervals during a course. Samples 1 and 2 demonstrate one way of making pedagogical goals explicit and reminding students of them. (Sample 1 would appear at the beginning of a unit of work, Sample 2 at the end.)

**Sample 1**

> In this unit you will:
> Report what someone says
>   'The police said that I was lucky to get out of the accident alive.'
> Say what people have been doing
>   'They've been working on the project for months.'

**Sample 2**

> Below, look at the language you practised in this unit.
> Can you . . . ?
> Report what someone says:            yes    a little    not yet
>   Find/give an example: ..........................................................
> Say what people have been doing:    yes    a little    not yet
>   Find/give an example: ..........................................................

These first two examples focus on the content domain. In relation to learning tasks and procedures, learners can also be involved in awareness-raising activities of one sort or another. At its most basic, learners will be involved in identifying the strategy implications of pedagogical tasks, and in identifying their own preferred learning styles and strategies. Sample 3 illustrates one way in which learners can be made aware of the strategy implications of pedagogical tasks.

**Sample 3**

> Learning Strategy: Reflecting = thinking about ways you learn best
> (a)  Listen. You will hear four people answering the question: 'How did you learn another language?'
> Make a note of the strategies you hear.

| | | | |
|---|---|---|---|
| 1. _____ [ ] | 6. _____ [ ] |
| 2. _____ [ ] | 7. _____ [ ] |
| 3. _____ [ ] | 8. _____ [ ] . |
| 4. _____ [ ] | 9. _____ [ ] |
| 5. _____ [ ] | 10. _____ [ ] |

(b) Put a check mark [ ✔ ] next to those strategies you agree with.
(c) Listen and identify the speaker who is most like you.
(d) Listen again and identify the speaker who is least like you.


## Level 2: involvement

The second level on the continuum I have labelled 'involvement', for want of a better rubric. This is an intermediate stage between simple awareness and a subsequent stage in which learners become involved in modifying materials. Here learners will be involved in making choices from a range of goals, a selection of content and a variety of tasks. In sample 4, which relates to the content domain, learners are offered a choice of two parallel tasks, and they can choose one or the other according to their own particular interests. In developing attitudes of self-direction and autonomy, the actual task itself is less important than the act of choosing.


**Sample 4**

You choose: Do A or B.

**A**

(a) **Pairwork**. Brainstorm, and decide on ten items to put in a time capsule to give people 300 years from now an idea of what life was like in our times.

(b) Work with another pair. Combine both lists and reduce the twenty items (your ten and the other pair's ten) to a single list of ten items.

(c) Compare your list with another group.

**Example**: '*Well, we'd include a TV remote control, pocket cellular phone, disposable camera, jeans, rollerblades, fax machine, post-it notes, pocket computer, Gameboy and CDs.*'

**B**

(a) **Pairwork**. Brainstorm, and decide on the ten most useful every-day inventions of this century.

(b) Work with another pair. Combine both lists and reduce the

twenty items (your ten and the other pair's ten) to a composite list
of ten items.

(c) Compare you list with another group.

**Example**: '*Well, we think the most important everyday items are the ball-point pen, disposable razor, zip fastener, contact lenses, post-it notes, paper towels, quartz watch, paper-back book, Velcro, and cash-machine cards.*'

## *Level 3: intervention*

The next level is what I have called intervention. Here learners
are involved in modifying and adapting goals, content and learn-ing tasks. As with the two earlier levels, commercial materials can
be readily adapted to encourage intervention by the addition of
follow-up tasks to ones presented in a book.

**Sample 5**

[The following instructions are appended to a textbook or worksheet
task.]

Review the task you have just completed. Make a note of (a) the
goals of the task, (b) the language you needed to complete the
task.

How relevant was the task to your needs?

Modify the task so that it is more relevant to your needs.

## *Level 4: creation*

The penultimate stage is one in which learners create their own
goals, content and learning tasks. It is possible to identify stages
within each of the levels outlined in this chapter. In the case of cre-ation, a step along the road towards tasks and materials which are
totally student-generated, would be tasks which have been partly
developed by the student. For example, students could be provided
with aural or written texts and asked to write a set of comprehen-sion questions to accompany these. In order to produce such ques-tions, students, preferably working in groups, would need to work
intensively on the texts to master the content. Having developed
their questions, they could then exchange these, answer the other
groups questions, and then take part in a larger group discussion

of the text. At a higher stage of autonomy, students could generate tasks and materials based on models.

## Sample 6

Create a questionnaire on a topic of your choice following the model provided.
Interview five native speakers using the questionnaire as a guide.
Audio or video-record the interviews.
Create a worksheet based on the recording for use by other students in the self-access centre. The worksheet should contain the questionnaire, and should ask the viewer to identify the responses given by each of the speakers.

## *Level 5: transcendence*

At the final level, learners transcend the classroom, making links between the content of the classroom and the world beyond the classroom. At this level, learners begin to become truly autonomous by utilizing in everyday life what they have learned in formal learning contexts.

## Sample 7

Record a conversation or an interview from TV or the radio. Listen/ watch for feedback from the listener to the speaker and write down any examples you hear. Think about listener feedback. How would people feel if you didn't give them any feedback? (Try this experiment in your next conversation. Don't give any feedback while the other person is speaking and see what happens.) Write down what you find out about listener feedback.
Think about the techniques you learned while doing task 1. Which might be useful when you are trying to follow other people's conversation (for example, when chatting with other people in a coffee bar)?
During your next conversation, try out a technique that you feel might be useful.
Make a note of your experiences and report back to the next class. Are listening techniques useful in real-life conversation?

In this section I have tried to illustrate ways in which materials might be modified in order to help learners develop the skills they will need for greater autonomy. The examples are illustrative only, as there is no limit to the number of ways in which commercial texts (or indeed, teacher-developed texts) might be modified. Hopefully, the examples show that there is nothing mysterious or esoteric in these 'add-on' features. They also illustrate the important point that developing autonomy can be a normal, everyday dimension to regular instruction. How far one goes, or wants to go, in encouraging learner autonomy will be dictated by the contexts and environments in which the teaching and learning takes place.

## Fostering learner autonomy in the classroom

I took as my point of departure for this chapter the notion that there are degrees of learner autonomy, that it is not an absolute concept. I also made the point that, in my experience, most learners do not come into the learning situation with the knowledge and skills to determine content and learning processes which will enable them to reach their objectives in learning another language. This is an important point because, as I also indicated at the beginning of the chapter, there are those who believe that advocates of learner-centredness, self-direction, and autonomy assume that learners do make false assumptions about the state of knowledge of the learner.

In this final section, I should like to emphasize the point that fully autonomous learners are a rarity, and that encouraging learners to move towards autonomy is best done inside the language classroom. This can be done by incorporating two sets of complementary goals into language programmes. The first set of goals will be language content goals. The second will be learning process goals. I believe it important for both sets of goals to be incorporated into the curriculum in harmonious ways. I do not believe that it is particularly effective to have separate lessons developed to learner strategy training; in fact, it may well be counter-productive.

In the preceding section, I illustrated and exemplified ways in which a strategy dimension could be added to conventional pedagogical materials. These 'value added' features include making goals and strategies explicit, involving learners in making choices, showing learners how to modify and adapt goals, content and tasks to their own emerging needs, creating situations in which learners are involved in developing their own goals, content and learning procedures, and helping learners move beyond the classroom to develop themselves as truly autonomous learners.

The final issue which needs to be dealt with is who should be responsible for these 'value added' features? There is evidence that producers of commercial materials are becoming increasingly sensitive to the need to incorporate these features into materials from the beginning (see, for example, Oxford and Scarcella, 1993; Nunan, 1995a). However, there is nothing to prevent teachers, self-access consultants, teacher educators and others from also adding value to the materials used by their learners, even if these materials are highly conventional in their published form. All language programmes and pedagogical materials have goals, however implicit, and everything that is done in the classroom is underpinned by strategies of one sort or another. Therefore, the modifications suggested in the body of the chapter can be added by those implementing programmes and using materials regardless of how conventional these are. The nature and extent of these modifications, and the distance one's learners are prepared to travel towards full autonomy will depend on a whole host of contextual factors stemming from the learners themselves, the classrooms in which they are receiving their instruction, the constraints imposed by the institution, and the societal and cultural milieu within which the learning takes place. Regardless of these constraints, some degree of autonomy is, I believe, a fact of life, for in the final analysis, if any learning is to take place, the learners must do it for themselves.

## Conclusion

The central point of this chapter is that most commercial materials can be modified and adapted in ways which are likely to enhance learner autonomy. The chapter is based on the following assumptions:

- few individuals come to the task of language learning as autonomous learners;
- developing some degree of autonomy is essential if learners are to become effective language users;

- the ability to direct one's own learning can be developed through pedagogical intervention;
- there are degrees of autonomy;
- the extent to which autonomy can be developed will be constrained by a broad range of personal, interpersonal, institutional and cultural factors.

The body of the chapter is devoted to describing and illustrating ways in which materials can be modified in terms of their experiential content and learning procedures so that they might foster the development of autonomy. There are, in fact, encouraging signs that commercially available materials are also beginning to incorporate some of these ideas (see, for example, O'Malley and Chamot, 1990; Oxford, 1990; Oxford and Scarcella, 1993; NCELTR, 1994; Nunan, 1995b). Hopefully the diffusion of these ideas will lead even more materials writers to consider incorporating them into the design of their materials.

## *Note*

1. The examples in this chapter have been taken from Nunan (1995b) *ATLAS: Learning-centred Communication*. Boston: Heinle and Heinle/ International Thomson Publishing.

# 14

## Involving learners in developing learning methods: exploiting text corpora in self-access

GUY ASTON

## Introduction

The introduction of new types of resources for independent use by language learners presupposes research to develop methodologies for their use. In this chapter I argue that it can be beneficial for institution and learners alike if the latter participate as active partners in this research process. While self-access can of course simply be a way to force-feed learners, who are told what materials should meet their particular needs, and precisely how they should use them, it has more generally been argued that learners should be free to choose from a 'large and varied diet' of opportunities to use the language (Little, 1989: p.33), drawing on a collection of materials which can be individually exploited in different ways, thereby encouraging autonomy (Holec, 1988; Miller and Rogerson-Revell, 1993). This 'open-ended' approach effectively assigns learners the role of methodological researchers, exploring resources and evaluating their potential for learning.

Where such an approach is adopted, it may be productive for learners, teachers and the institution to collaborate in research, in that their interests may overlap. Learners need to reflect critically on their use of self-access resources in order to develop more effective learning strategies. Classroom teachers need to evaluate its implications for classroom content and methodology, both in terms of preparing learners for self-access work and of exploiting its outcomes. The institution needs to monitor learners' use of resources both in order to provide support to individuals, and to evaluate the resources and the guidance provided, which may need refining and clarifying on the basis of experience. And teachers and learners may share the institution's concern to improve the quality of the self-access service itself, whether out of self-interest or social commitment. The convergence of interests seems particularly strong where new technologies are involved. Here there may be little or no consolidated methodological tradition to draw on, underlining McCafferty's paradox (undated: p.26):

> Ideally, everything in the self-access system would have been put there on the basis of its usefulness to learners. But before you have any learners you have no real evidence as to what a particular individual or group will find useful.

This chapter discusses an experiment where learners and teachers worked together to develop methods for the use of a new type of self-access resource, computerized text corpora.

## Corpora and their uses

I use the word *corpus* to mean any computer-readable collection of texts or transcripts which can be accessed and interrogated selectively using text-retrieval or concordancing software. Over recent years the use of very large corpora of texts has become increasingly common in lexicogrammatical description of the language as a whole or of particular registers and styles (Altenberg, 1991). In the ELT field there has been a growing use of smaller, homemade corpora to determine the linguistic content of syllabuses, especially for ESP (English for Specific Purposes) (Flowerdew, 1993), and to create classroom materials and exercises for 'data-driven learning' (Johns, 1988; Tribble and Jones, 1990; Johns and King, 1991). While most proposed pedagogic uses involve mediation by the teacher or course designer, who selects and if necessary edits materials derived from a corpus before giving them to learners to analyse, there seems no a priori reason why learners should not be given direct access to corpora for independent use. Large amounts of computer-readable text are now commercially available, either on disc or CD-ROM, which can be used with simple text-retrieval and concordancing software designed with language learning in mind, such as the *Longman Mini-Concordancer* (Chandler, 1989) and *MicroConcord* (Scott and Johns, 1993), in order to select either a number of *texts*, or a number of brief *contexts* matching specified search criteria. Such procedures can provide various kinds of information

about the language and the culture concerned. They include the
following:

### Lexicogrammatical

Concordances from large corpora have been widely used in linguistic research as a means of finding out how words are used
in context, focusing on collocational and connotative regularities
(Sinclair, 1991). Johns (1991) and Jordan (1993) illustrate how
learners can use smaller corpora to obtain similar information
about relatively frequent lexemes, comparing, for instance, the
contexts of *for* and *since*, or of *convince* and *persuade.*

### Textual

By retrieving groups of texts which share common features, corpora
can be used to study text-types, focusing on recurrent patterns of
information structure, rhetorical organization and speech-act realization (Mparutsa *et al.*, 1991). For instance a collection of 'hard
news' articles from a newspaper corpus allows learners to compare headlines with lead sentences, analysing the nominalizations,
ellipses and tense shifts of the former with respect to the latter.

### Encyclopedic or cultural

The retrieval of groups of texts from a particular domain can also
constitute a rich source of non-linguistic information: most text
CD-ROMs are in fact designed to enable users to recover and read
those texts which deal with particular topics. Concordancing too can
be used to discover such information; for instance the contexts of
references to a specific individual or entity will provide many details
about that individual/entity, and may even include a definition.

   As well as constituting sources of specific information of these
kinds, corpora offer a wide range of opportunities for extensive
reading of texts. This variety of potential gives them the characteristic of open-ended resources for learning purposes.

## Approaches to self-access corpus use

In view of the range of opportunities they offer, corpora would
seem to be powerful learning resources for a user who is able to

exploit them effectively. In making a number of corpora available for self-access use at the Bologna University School for Interpreters and Translators, the key question was to design appropriate methodologies and train learners in their use, bearing in mind the need to develop their control of their own learning in a perspective of increasing autonomy. We decided explicitly to involve groups of learners in this process, exploiting the fact that they were attending regular courses where they could discuss ideas and problems collectively with teachers, while having access to the school's computer room in their spare time.

The corpora available included CD-ROM versions of *The Independent* and *The Daily Telegraph* for 1992 (containing around 75,000 articles each), the collections of newspaper and of academic texts provided with *MicroConcord*; a collection of articles from *New Scientist*; and a collection of simplified readers. A collection of medical research articles was developed in the course of the experiment (see below, p.211). The CD-ROM retrieval software allowed users to select articles corresponding to specified search criteria and to construct specialized subcorpora, while *MicroConcord* could be used to generate concordances for specified keywords or phrases and to examine their contexts.

Initial work with a trial group of learners suggested that these resources could be approached in two ways. On the one hand, a corpus could be treated as a reference tool, which could be looked up to provide examples and thereby clarify doubts on particular problems which had arisen in other tasks. On the other hand, using a corpus could be an activity in itself where, rather than being guided by a specific external goal, learners adopted a 'browsing' mode, moving from one text or concordance to another on a step-by-step basis.

The usefulness of a corpus as a reference tool was readily perceived. One student writing an essay wanted to know the appropriate verb to use with *solution*, and generated a concordance for *solution* which showed that *furnish* and *provide* occurred as collocates. Another student, preparing for a piece of interpreting practice dealing with heart problems, retrieved a selection of texts including the term *heart attack*, from which she deduced that a number of things can *lead* to a heart attack or make you likely to *have* one, while others *reduce the risk* of them; and that a heart attack may be *suffered, died of,* or, if *mild, recovered from*. Their general satisfaction notwithstanding, it was striking that these learners seemed to have made relatively little use of the output from their searches, simply scanning it to find examples which matched the reference problem involved. Much relevant information was overlooked in the process. Hanks (1987: pp.121–2) points out that 'a foreign learner who is struggling to encode English naturally and idiomatically needs guidance precisely on what is typical rather than what is possible' yet these learners appeared to have paid little attention to regularities in the output, unless similar instances happened to be grouped via a default concordance sort. They used the corpus to discover that expression A and context B *could* co-occur, not that they *usually* co-occurred. This was in striking contrast to the uses made of corpora in descriptive linguistics, and in the 'data-driven learning' model of Johns (1988, 1991), both of which stress the value of the corpus in revealing recurrent patterns.

A similar tendency to overlook regularities, though for different reasons, was evident where a browsing approach was adopted. For instance, when examining corpus data and coming across a word of whose uses they were uncertain, some learners generated a concordance and tried to infer a generalized rule from the examples provided. However they found it difficult to formulate rules which would account for all the data adequately. The learner who discovered that a collocate of *solution* was *furnish* had subsequently gone on to see what else *furnish* collocated with. He found *credit, details, a commentary, accompaniment* – a motley (and limited) assortment from which he failed to draw a general conclusion. In trying to find a global rule, however, he arguably overlooked a partial regularity: that *details, a commentary*, and *accompaniment* have semantic features in common, relating to addition.

## Towards principled corpus browsing

The main concern of the trial group in using the corpora had been to obtain information about English language in use; from this perspective, the results seemed limited by their tendency to ignore regularities in the data. Since experience with grammars and dictionaries suggested it would be difficult to dissuade learners from employing maximally economical strategies in solving reference problems, we decided to focus on methods of browsing as a means of stimulating their attention to such regularities.

It was clearly pedagogically inadequate just to tell learners to look for regularities while browsing, without any basis for deciding what regularities to look for, and without any clear motivation for doing so. Most learners' objectives are to be able to *use* the language, and finding out *about* the language is often only of interest when its relevance to potential communicative concerns is apparent. In reference use, learners' searches for information in the corpus generally had such motivation: they were attempting to solve an actual problem of communication encountered elsewhere. In browsing, on the other hand, their decisions as to what to look at in the corpus, and what to look for next, seemed essentially arbitrary, precisely because they lacked such a communicative context.

Traditional communicative methodology teaches that the way to provide a communicative context for language use in the classroom is to assign learners non-linguistic goals (Widdowson, 1978; Johnson, 1982). This principle seems applicable also to corpus browsing; the newspaper CD-ROMs with which these learners were working could be used to find out about particular countries and their problems, to provide evidence and arguments on such controversial issues as nuclear waste or women priests, or even as a source of entertainment (for instance, by retrieving texts including the word *joke*). These uses call for the selection and relatively close reading of a limited number of relevant texts; and they may motivate analyses of linguistic and discursive features in these texts, inasmuch as this can cast light on the realization of current communicative goals (Brumfit, 1984; McCarthy and Carter, 1993).

But even within such a communicative context, learners may still be reluctant or unable to analyse recurrences. One of the difficulties encountered by the trial group seemed due to their attempt to infer maximally generalized rules from the corpus data, which they felt to be of greater value than mere partial regularities. However language use depends on schematic as well as systematic knowledge (Widdowson, 1984). In addition to a traditionally conceived dictionary and grammar, users draw on a very large number of ready-made 'lexicalized chunks' associated with particular context-types, employing relatively simple methods to instantiate and adjust them to specific circumstances (Bolinger, 1975; Pawley and Syder, 1983). To acquire such schemata learners need to focus on regularities at levels which are not merely ones of maximum generality. Faced, for instance, with a concordance of *since* and *for*, then rather than using it to test the rule that *since* is associated with points in past time, *for* with durations, it may be equally useful for learners to identify recurrent patterns such as *since then; since its inception/launch; ever since; for the first time since; has/have long since.* These larger schemata may be associated with particular context-types (for instance *since then* frequently acts as a sentence-initial linker).

In the belief that learners needed to become aware of the importance of such regularities, we spent a significant amount of classroom time discussing the notion of schematic knowledge and its role in language use and learning with a new student group, and looking at different types of regularity in discourse – syntagmatic (collocation, colligation and rhetorical patternings) and paradigmatic (idioms, routine formulae, register associations). It was noted that many of these regularities were associated with particular topics and genres, and that they were of particular importance to native-like production and understanding, since they could be invoked, or heard as absent, in creative and deviant uses (Louw, 1993). In this way we hoped to sensitize this next group to such regularities prior to embarking on experimental self-access use. To develop methodologies collectively is hardly possible without a common theory of how language is used and learned.

## Experimentation

In presenting the self-access resources to this new group, the principles for browsing outlined in the last section were explained: learners should approach the corpus with non-linguistic goals so as to isolate a subcorpus of texts with some common theme, and look for regularities in the way discourse effects are obtained in this subcorpus. Learners were asked to treat these principles as a basis for self-access use and to report on their experiences. They worked in small groups, using the available corpora to obtain sub-corpora dealing with their chosen topics, or in one case typing in their own transcripts. Each group held weekly discussion sessions with a teacher, and prepared a final report which was circulated for discussion by the whole class. The main findings were as follows:

1. Learners felt they had 'got to know' their selected topic, and ways in which that topic was handled discursively in terms of re-current vocabulary, collocations, and discourse patternings. They cited such features as the use of opening and closing metaphors

taken from the same semantic field in a subcorpus of comment articles dealing with third-world nuclear weaponry; that participants in murder trial reports tended to be introduced as representatives of a social category (a policeman, a housewife) prior to being named; that use of the term 'membership' in news broadcast items dealing with Eastern European applications to join NATO recurred in the collocations *full membership, membership of NATO, apply for membership*. In many cases they had turned to a wider or different corpus to see if the same regularity was repeated in other contexts, but this search for generalization had only occurred after they had identified the regularity in the subcorpus.

2. They claimed to have become much more aware of the extent of recurrent patterning in language, and of its importance to 'native-like' performance. Most had made attempts to use their new knowledge in some way, for instance by trying to produce similar discourses in their groups, and then comparing these with those of their subcorpus.

3. There was general agreement that they had developed procedures for acquiring both encyclopedic and linguistic information by browsing through small collections of similar texts. There was, however, uncertainty as to the relative value of the different kinds of regularities noted by different groups, and as to whether potentially more useful information had not been overlooked in some cases.

In order to clarify these latter issues, we recycled the procedure, this time asking the same learners to all work on the same subcorpus, so that they would be more readily able to compare and evaluate their findings. To maximize their independence in this process, and to highlight the potential of browsing as a means of investigating new fields, the chosen topic was one of which the teachers too were largely ignorant. Twelve recent articles were selected from international medical research journals with the help of an expert, all dealing with hepatitis C infection following blood transfusion. As a first approach one article was read and discussed in class, paying particular attention to ways in which its content and organization into sections (Introduction, Method, Results, Discussion) reflected the concerns of scientific research. The remaining articles were divided up, each student being asked to read one, noting similarities in content and form with that read in class, and to type up part of it on a wordprocessor. Their 48 files (1 per section, totalling 35,000 words) were pooled as a corpus in the computer room.

Following discussion of their observations, each student listed three things they felt would increase their understanding of discourse in this field (relating to content or to language), and that they thought could be investigated using the corpus. After exchanging and refining these questions, they worked on them on the computer, and followed up any other issues they found of interest. They then recounted their results and discussed their implications for a browsing methodology, both in terms of what to look for and how to set about it.

They had found it useful to look for regularities involving:

1. 'generic content' terms relating to medicine and its research methods, e.g. *disease, patients, diagnos\*,*[1] *blood, test\**. This had provided basic information about the topic, and a key to its main semantic fields.

2. 'everyday' terms which had specialized uses in this context, highlighting its concerns: *study/studies* (typically a noun, and premodified by *recent/previous/this/our*); *significant/significantly* (collocating with *difference/increase/decrease* and *differ/greater/higher/lower* respectively); *perform* (*tests/biopsies*).

3. grammatical words which might be associated with specialized functions. For instance, *may* occurred overwhelmingly in discussion sections, to formulate conclusions.

4. technical terms and abbreviations, which a concordance would frequently explain by providing definitional instances, e.g. *ELISA* (enzyme linked immunosorbent assay); *ALT* (analine aminotransferase).

5. apparent synonyms. *Serological* and *serologic* appeared to be stylistic variants, some articles using the one, some the other, but never both. On the other hand, *assay* and *test* appeared not to be synonymous, the former being used only to refer to specific biomedical tests.

Discussion of the procedures employed to obtain this information led to the formulation of the following list of tactics:

- *Read first.* Become familiar with at least one text before working on the full subcorpus.
- *Work together.* It is more productive to work in twos or threes

than singly, as you are more likely to notice different regularities and to reach an understanding of individual instances.

- *Focus initially on generic rather than on topic-specific expressions.* The
  latter are more readily interpretable once a general framework
  for understanding the corpus has been established.
- *Cross-check.* If, when examining A, it emerges that B is a recurrent collocate, then examine B for its collocates. For instance, .
  on finding that *study/ies* is regularly preceded by *recent*, investigate the collocates of the latter (*reports, history*).
- *Use different sorting and text-loading orders.* Sorting a concordance
  by the first word to the right highlights, for instance, recurrent
  *of* following the keyword *study/ies*; sorting by the first word to
  the left instead highlights the recurrence of the premodifiers
  *recent/previous/earlier/this/our.* Loading the files by section (first
  all the introductions, then all the methods, etc.), highlights
  recurrences within specific section-types, whereas by loading the
  files by article, stylistic peculiarities of particular texts become
  apparent.

## Conclusions

While in no way pretending that the suggestions listed add up
to a fully principled and evaluated self-access methodology for
browsing computer corpora, some progress seems to have been
made in that direction. While similar proposals might equally well
have been produced and improved on by a sensitive teacher or
team of teachers without the help of learners, there appear to be
advantages – for both learners and the institution – in involving
learners in the development of methods through interaction rather
than simply handing them down from authority. Insofar as learners
participate in their design, they may understand the rationale of
these methods, assume responsibility for them, and feel able to
apply them with confidence. Their critical capacity to evaluate their
use of learning resources in general may improve. To the extent
that they learn to devise ways of exploiting available resources
effectively, they acquire keys to future learning outside the institutional context.

Besides the benefit to their own learning, such learners are well
placed to explain such methods and the ideas which underlie them
to others. Learners not infrequently have greater credibility for their

colleagues than do teachers or the institution, and may be able to provide quantitatively greater assistance and encouragement. Economic pressures limit the institution's ability to research new technologies and provide training for users: involving groups of learners in these processes can reduce costs, while at the same time allowing learners to take greater control over the institutional context in which their learning takes place (Aston, 1993).

There would also appear to be benefits for the classroom. First, feedback concerning self-access learning experience can have implications for taught course content: the work described here highlighted the need for learners to reflect on the relationship between communicative use and the acquisition of competence, and the role of linguistic and discursive regularities in these processes. Secondly, by lessening the institution's monopoly of pedagogic credibility and increasing confidence in their ability to manage their own learning, the involvement of learners may foster more critical participation in the negotiation of classroom content and procedures, as well as in self-access activity.

## Note

1. Most concordancing programmes use an asterisk symbol to mean 'any number of consecutive characters (including none)'. Thus *test** means any of *test, tests, testing, tester,* and so on.

# 15

# Preparing learners for independence: resources beyond the classroom

STEPHEN M. RYAN

## Introduction

Although Kelly (1976), in his famously titled book, outlines 25 centuries of language teaching, he makes it clear that language *learning* has a much longer history. People were learning languages long before there were materials specifically designed for language learning or teachers to give instruction in their use, and certainly before there were self-access or independent learning centres.

As autonomous learners throughout history have known, with the right approach any text in the target language can become a source of information about the structure and usage of that language. Until recently, proximity to a target language community was a good predictor of the availability of such texts. However, with the globalization of trade and communications, texts (both spoken and written) in foreign languages are readily available throughout the world and, in many advanced countries, form an integral part of the social and cultural environment.

This chapter addresses the problem of how to empower foreign language students to make effective use of the potential language-learning materials that exist around them, especially when their need for the target language seems rather remote to them and they thus have relatively low immediate motivation to learn. It first considers the kinds of resources available to foreign (as distinct from second) language learners and outlines procedures for bringing these resources to their attention. It then shows how students can be trained to make use of these materials for language learning, using techniques that they can perform and check without any support from a teacher. Finally, strategies for bringing students to an awareness of the language learning principles which underlie both the selection of materials and the techniques used with them are presented. The combination of achievable techniques and an understanding of language learning principles is the key to preparing such students for independence.

The chapter is based on experience in Japan, teaching engineering students in their final year of formal English instruction. The goal of the course was to enable the students to pursue their English studies, without the aid of a teacher, at any point in the future when it became necessary or desirable for them to do so. Although the students were studying engineering, the English involved was of a general nature, as the most likely situation envisaged for its use was for non-technical purposes on an extended posting abroad.

## Resources available

Discussions of the foreign language/second language distinction often note that while ESL environments are rich in target-language resources, such resources are much harder to find in EFL situations (e.g. Stern, 1983: pp.15–18). While this remains true, the gap between the two is narrowing. Advances in communications technology and global mobility have increased the availability of foreign-language resources throughout the world, especially when the target language is English.

The following discussion explores the kind of resources that are available to the student of English in Japan. Japan may be considered an extreme case, both in terms of the advanced technology it possesses and the intensity of its current passion for the English language. However, many of the resources mentioned here are available in other countries, too.

Materials available in Japan that can be used as English-learning resources fall into two main categories: those that were specifically designed for English language instruction and those that were primarily intended to inform or entertain native speakers of the language.

The first category will be the more familiar to language teachers throughout the world and will therefore receive less attention here. In Japan, the usual range of 'four skills' textbooks, graded readers, listening courses with cassette tapes, phrase books and dictionaries is available. Local broadcasting media provide both TV and radio courses in English at several levels and for various purposes (tourism, business, etc.). A selection of magazines and 'newspapers' for (and sometimes by) learners of English is also available, both from domestic and foreign sources. Advertisements for 'homestays', 'study abroad' programmes and English conversation schools abound. Computer-based genres now commercially available to learners include not only disguised language drills but also word-based games in which players interact with the machine in graded English to participate in some kind of adventure. Presumably increasing interest in interactive multimedia technology will ensure that this area of the market expands in years to come.

Resources in the second category are intended for the English-speakers in Japan's resident foreign community (although many Japanese speakers of English also make use of them). This community is serviced by four locally produced daily newspapers, a wide selection of newspapers from abroad (often available on the day of publication), magazines from abroad and several produced domestically to give entertainment listings, information about Japan or instruction in the Japanese language. Most sizeable bookshops (and there are very many of these) have corners offering books in English, fiction and non-fiction, and can order many other titles for delivery within a week.

Broadcasting media include rock radio stations with American DJs, American Armed Forces' Radio, the usual array of short-wave stations, satellite TV from various countries and a multiplex system that allows viewers of foreign movies on TV to select either the original English soundtrack or a Japanese one. The same system is also used to broadcast an English translation of each day's main TV news show. Cinemas and video rental shops always provide foreign movies with their original soundtracks and Japanese subtitles.

E-mail gives access to bulletin boards on a variety of topics. As well as accessing bulletin boards in English-speaking countries, subscribers will find several domestic services using English.

The resident foreign community itself is a resource for learners eager to converse in English. If approached sensitively, native speakers will often offer casual conversation, language exchange (English for Japanese), correspondence, friendship and more.

A note of caution needs to be sounded about some potential resources. The advertising and design industries make extensive use of words and phrases, giving English high visibility in most aspects of daily life. However, the use of English in these sectors is impressionistic rather than accurate and students need to be warned to mistrust English that appears on T-shirts, posters and fashion accessories. The same goes for the loanwords that make up an estimated 10 per cent of daily Japanese (Neustupny, 1987: pp.84–5). Many of these originate in English but are so nativized by their passage into Japanese that they cannot be directly transferred back (for example, Japanese *manshon* – from English *mansion* – is a type of apartment or apartment block). Some of the loan words are borrowed from other languages, although many learners believe that they are English in origin. Both 'fashion English' and loan words can be used as rich resources for English teaching (Harris, 1994) and the consideration of cultural issues (Prodromou, 1988). However, they need careful handling (the presence of a teacher or a series of well-structured exercises in a self-access centre) if they are not to confuse the student.

## Preparing students to use resources

Despite the richness of their environment in terms of resources for learning English, many learners in Japan are unaware of the possibilities of using them beyond the obvious step of enrolling in a language class.

The aim of the course described here is to awaken learners to the resources in their environment and to the possibilities for their use. The course consists of a series of modules, taking between one and three hours of class-time. Each module is based on a particular kind of resource (newspapers, videos, native speakers you happen to see). Within each module the following steps are followed:

1. consciousness-raising discussion of available resources
2. presenting and practising techniques to exploit resources
3. introduction to the theoretical constructs of language acquisition underlying the selection of resources and techniques.

### Consciousness raising

The first step is to make students aware of the resources that are available. An informal survey at the beginning of the course revealed that very few students had given serious thought to how they might study English without a teacher so it is not surprising to find that they are unaware of the resources available for doing this.

| Title | Price | Pages | Where from? · | When? |
|-------|-------|-------|----------------|-------|
|       |       |       |                |       |
|       |       |       |                |       |
|       |       |       |                |       |
|       |       |       |                |       |

**Figure 15.1**   Table for recording information on newspapers

In the first part of each module information is collected on the following:

1. what resources exist
2. where to find them
3. how to gain access to them.

Where possible this information is elicited from the students: they may not have thought of studying English from movies but most of them know that any video shop in the country stocks foreign movies with Japanese subtitles.

Sometimes the collection of information is assigned as an out-of-class task, such as collecting publicity material from companies offering study-abroad programmes. Completion of such a task requires students to think for themselves about exactly where in their environment information in and about English can be found.

Often some or all of the information is provided by the teacher. In such cases, students are asked to tabulate and record the information in some way that requires them to process it at a deeper level than simply listening to the teacher. In the module on using English-language newspapers, for example, the students are given a table (Figure 15.1) to fill in. Any information they can provide about the title, price, number of pages, place of sale and time of availability of English-language newspapers is entered and students are asked to gather information to fill the remaining cells before the next lesson. After students share the information they have been able to collect, the teacher provides any that is still missing. This activity leads naturally into a comparison of the newspapers in terms of value-for-money, ease of availability and topicality (*USA Today* may be cheap if sent by surface-mail but will be several weeks old when it arrives).

Other typical activities engaged in at this stage of a module include drawing a rough floor plan of a bookshop to show where English books are displayed, inspecting video packaging to make sure that the soundtrack is indeed in English and tuning a short-wave radio. Such practical minutiae are included to show the students that the resources being discussed are indeed accessible to them.

## Presenting and practising techniques

The next stage focuses on techniques which students can use in order to exploit the resources to improve their English. Several techniques are usually presented for each kind of resource, beginning with those that are easiest to carry out.

Each technique is presented as a series of instructions from the teacher. Students carry out the instructions in the classroom in order to practise the technique. This allows the teacher to check that the technique has been understood and the students to gain confidence in carrying it out.

The techniques presented will be familiar to most language teachers. They include: making predictions while watching a video with the sound off; scanning headlines for familiar names; listening for gist; writing First language subtitles for a target language video (or vice versa); using a First language newspaper report to build background knowledge for a target language radio news report and writing letters to pen-friends.

Since the goal is for the learner to carry out these activities autonomously, great care is taken when selecting the techniques to ensure that they do not require the cooperation of somebody more fluent in English than the learner. Comprehension exercises that require somebody with a superior knowledge of the text both to set questions and check answers are not used. Instead, techniques that allow learners to check their own comprehension (e.g. by reference to readily available First language sources) are presented and practised.

An exercise in summarizing a scene from a video, for example, is checked not by the teacher but by reference to the First language subtitles that have been temporarily covered while the exercise was performed. A particularly difficult scene encountered while viewing a movie for pleasure is explained not by the teacher but by careful study of the equivalent chapter in the novel the film was based on.

As students are talked through these activities, their attention is repeatedly drawn to the fact that they are engaged in learning activities that do not require the presence or cooperation of the teacher.

To return to the module on newspapers, it includes the following techniques:

1. gathering from the newspaper useful information available in a readily understandable form (e.g. weather forecast, TV schedule);
2. using photos and names in headlines to predict the contents of articles;
3. reading an article from a Japanese-language newspaper to make predictions about vocabulary that will be encountered in an account of the same story in the English-language newspaper;
4. using a Japanese-language article to check understanding of a story originally read in English;
5. studying the Japanese original together with the English translation of a newspaper column to observe the finer points of the translation.

The range, number and difficulty of the techniques presented here are typical of those covered by other modules.

## Language acquisition theory

The purpose of the third stage of each module is to introduce to the learners some of the basic theoretical principles that underlie the selection of resources and the construction of techniques for exploiting them. Without a grasp of these principles, learners will simply repeat the limited series of techniques presented and practised in class until boredom sets in. In other words, they would not be truly autonomous but, through the techniques learnt, dependent on a teacher who was no longer present.

However, since the students have no background, or even professed interest in TESOL, the principles presented need to be broad, simple and firmly rooted in the students' practical experience. This is the main reason for presenting the techniques before offering any kind of rationale for them: once the students have carried out the techniques they are in a better position to understand the principles behind them.

The explanation offered always begins with a review of the techniques that have been practised and suggestions for simple variations on them. Mention may also be made of similar techniques that have been introduced for using other resources in previous modules.

In the case of the newspaper module, students are given a hand-out which outlines the steps to go through to perform each of the techniques described above. They are also reminded that one of these is similar to a technique they have used in a previous module: reading a newspaper account of a story before watching a TV news report about it.

Students are encouraged to reflect on how the techniques can help them to learn and what makes them achievable. The teacher introduces some of the principles involved, illustrating each point with examples from the students' experience, referring especially to the techniques just presented and practised.

The main principle demonstrated in the newspaper module is that prediction of the contents of a text is a great help in understanding it. It is suggested to the students that reading a Japanese version of a news story (not a translation but an account of the same basic events written in Japanese by another reporter) before tackling the English version is a good way to predict not only the vocabulary but also the contents of the article.

How much of the news story in English would they have understood if they had not read the Japanese version first? How much more could they understand thanks to the Japanese text? Why did it help? At first the answer seems obvious: it was the same story so they already knew it before they read the English version. This is not exactly true, however: some details were reported differently in the English version and students were able to notice this and mention it (such is almost always the case). How, then, was the Japanese text able to help them to understand parts of the English text which contradicted the Japanese version?

Gradually, the teacher brings the students to the perception that the Japanese text has alerted them to the kind of information to expect in the English version and thus made it easier for them to understand the English. What other things, apart from a Japanese newspaper report, could they have used to alert them to what to expect? Radio news reports, TV news reports, previous interest in the story, a few moments of reflection on the topic.

Finally, students are asked to suggest further techniques for the exploitation of materials in the module, based on the principles outlined. Students are encouraged to think of other situations where 'being alert to the topic' (prediction) might help them to understand. Soon the students are designing their own techniques, some connected with newspapers, others not. This is clearly the most difficult stage of the module and not all students are capable of doing it at first. However, careful explanations of why a particular technique is good (or bad) can be helpful in bringing each student towards autonomy.

It seems most effective to concentrate on explaining only one or two principles in each module so that the students' understanding of basic principles accumulates from module to module.

Basic principles covered by the course include:

1. enjoyment and interest are important criteria in selecting resources
2. when dealing with graded material, an 80 per cent mastery of one level is sufficient cause to move to the next level
3. with ungraded material, completion of the task rather than full comprehension of the text should be the measure of success
4. when dealing with a text that uses difficult language to deal with a difficult topic, find a way to acquaint yourself with either the topic or the language before tackling the text
5. prediction is an essential part of the reading/listening process
6. being understood when writing/speaking is usually more important than being formally correct

Again, none of these principles will come as a surprise to the trained language teacher. The important point is that, equipped with these and similar principles the learner is ready to learn without the support of a teacher.

## Results

Since the course was designed to prepare students for a hypothetical posting abroad that may not occur for another 10 or 15 years in the future, it is difficult to measure its effects in any direct way.

The students' level of involvement in the course and many of their anonymous, written comments at the end of it show that there is interest in the course itself and the approach it takes to language learning:

'I was glad to study "How to Study English" because I can do many things to study for no money.'

'Before I thought I must do only what teacher says but now I think maybe I can study with no teacher.'

'This is the first time the teacher says to me "Study what you like."
It is very interesting idea to me.'

They are certainly no longer as naive about the existence of language learning resources in their environment as their responses showed them to be when the course started. Several of them have even begun to apply the principles outlined in the course in their daily lives:

'I ordered *The Japan Times* and it comes every day. I read it – sometimes!'

'My father got angry because I stuck paper on the TV like you told us [to cover Japanese subtitles]. Now I want to buy my own TV.'

I am very shy. Last week there was a foreigner on the train. I wanted to speak to him. I studied the words you gave me and then I said 'Excuse me' to him. He was very surprised but we talked in English. His name is Chris and he came from Canada to study *karate*. I want to meet him again.

This is a pleasant surprise as it was not envisaged that students would have the time or inclination to do this until circumstances, in the form of an imminent posting abroad, forced them to do so.

## Reflections

This course was originally designed for a particular group with a specific problem. However, the principles involved, and perhaps some of the techniques for imparting them, would seem to apply wherever learners have access to target-language resources and a need to become autonomous.

By leading students through a series of achievable language learning techniques to an understanding of some of the principles that underlie them, the course prepares students both psychologically and practically for independence. Students leave the course armed with knowledge about the learning resources around them, confidence to approach these materials and a basic understanding of how to select and make use of them. Thus prepared, students are ready to study a language independently whenever the need arises.

# 16

# Responding authentically to authentic texts: a problem for self-access language learning?

DAVID LITTLE

## Introduction

The terms *authentic* and *authenticity* have been much discussed in relation to the texts used in language teaching, the language learner's response to those texts, the tasks that the language learner is asked to perform, and the social situation in which language learning takes place (see, e.g., Coste, 1970; Widdowson, 1978; Egin, 1982; Breen, 1985a). In this chapter, I am particularly concerned with authentic texts, the ways in which learners respond to authentic texts, and the use that can be made of authentic texts in self-access learning environments.

I use the term 'authentic text' to mean (i) the record of any communicative act in speech or writing that was originally performed in fulfilment of some personal or social function, and not in order to provide illustrative material for language teaching, and – by extension – (ii) any communicative event that can easily become such a record, for example, radio and television broadcasts and certain forms of electronic communication. Thus defined, authentic texts have the capacity to draw language learners into the communicative world of the target language community. This capacity appears to support the communicative purpose of language teaching and is responsible, at least in part, for the widely held belief that it is important to enable learners to respond authentically to authentic texts.

But what exactly is an authentic response to an authentic text? This chapter seeks to answer that question, with particular reference to the use of authentic texts in self-access language learning.

I begin by exploring the role of authentic texts in second and foreign language learning generally, in terms of the relation between language learning and language use. I argue against two widespread assumptions: that authentic texts can only benefit learners who have already achieved a relatively advanced level of competence in the target language; and that the ways in which we exploit authentic texts should always correspond closely to their original communicative purpose and context. I then go on to consider the role of authentic texts in fostering learner autonomy, again in terms of the relation between language learning and language use. The last part of the chapter is concerned with the implications of my argument for the use of authentic texts in self-access language learning.

## Two views of the role of authentic texts in language learning

The role that we assign to authentic texts in language learning is largely determined, I believe, by the way we conceptualize second language use and the view we take of the relation between language use and language learning. One very common view is that language learning is one thing and language use another: that what happens in the language classroom (language learning – the gradual development of a communicative repertoire) is a preparation for what may in due course happen outside the classroom (language use – the deployment of that repertoire in communication with native speakers of the target language). According to this view, authentic texts are one of the means by which we can prepare learners to make the transition from learning to use. As Nunan (1988: p.100) reminds us, 'comprehending and manipulating scripted dialogues does not readily transfer to comprehending and using language in real communicative situations': we cannot expect learners to cope with target language communication in the world outside the classroom if we do not prepare them by bringing examples of that communication into the classroom.

The view that language learning is a preparation for language use tends to have two important consequences. First, it encourages us to see authentic texts and our learners' response to them almost exclusively in terms of their original communicative purpose. This means that we shall be chiefly concerned to ensure that our learners can understand the authentic texts to which we decide they should be exposed – newspaper reports and articles, perhaps the odd novel or short story, recordings of radio and television broadcasts, and so on. The better their understanding, the more likely they are to be able to respond to the authentic text authentically – that is, as though they were encountering it in the 'real world'. At some advanced levels, we may want our learners to use a limited range of authentic texts as models they should imitate in their own productive language use. But this is likely always to be a minority case, since relatively few second or foreign language learners are called upon to produce extended texts in any medium.

The second likely consequence of this view is that we shall postpone introducing our learners to authentic texts until they are nearing the time when they must leave the protective environment of the classroom. After all, if language teaching is a preparation for involvement in the communicative world of the target language community, it seems reasonable not to confuse matters prematurely by introducing elements of that world into the classroom before our learners are fully ready for them. When we contemplate the richness of their lexis and the complexity of their structure, it is immediately clear that authentic texts are linguistically difficult. It surely follows, then, that only more advanced learners can be expected to cope with them; if we impose them on less advanced learners we shall only cause frustration and demotivation. This seems to be the view of a very large number of teachers, and it is a view that corresponds to the intuitions, or at any rate the pedagogical conditioning, of an even larger number of learners: 'most learners and teachers remain convinced that didactic materials, especially textbooks, are the only possible sort which can be used by anyone who has not already learnt the language perfectly' (Riley, 1985: p.283).

The view that I wish to promote in this chapter is very different from the one we have been considering so far. This second view holds that because language learning and language use employ the same psycholinguistic mechanisms, they are essentially inseparable and often indistinguishable. According to this view, analytic and reflective activities designed to facilitate second language learning inevitably involve language use, however deficient; and more often than not, target language use brings issues of learning into the learner-user's conscious awareness. Hence it is misleading to distinguish between the classroom as the place where language is learnt and practised and the world outside as the place where language is used. No doubt language learners cross a succession of thresholds as their target language competence develops, but in psycholinguistic terms it is impossible to identify any one threshold as marking the point at which a shift in status takes place from language learner to language user. On the contrary: all language users, native as well as non-native speakers, remain language learners for as long as they are involved with the language in question. Psychologically, the difference between native and non-native speakers is that the latter are inevitably conscious of their learner status, not only when their attention is focused on learning but also when they are engaged in communicative activity.

This second view of the relation between language learning and language use has very different pedagogical consequences from the first. If we do not believe in the existence of some threshold of competence below which language can be learnt and practised but not, properly speaking, used, we shall have no good reason for postponing the introduction of authentic texts. On the contrary, if language learning depends on language use, we shall want to embed the language learning process from the very beginning in a framework of communicative language use, and one indispensable part of this framework will be an appropriate corpus of authentic texts. We shall also want to develop pedagogical procedures that both explicitly and implicitly exploit the interdependence of learning and use.

At first glance it may seem preposterous to propose that beginning learners should be exposed to authentic texts: how can they possibly understand them? But text linguistics has taught us that meaning is not a property of texts but the product of interaction between text-presented knowledge and the text receiver's stored knowledge (see, for example, de Beaugrande and Dressler, 1981). It has also taught us that our understanding of texts depends not only on our knowledge of the language system but on our knowledge of text-types and our knowledge of the world. This means that second language learners can often compensate for deficiencies in their linguistic knowledge by drawing on their knowledge of text types and, more importantly, appropriate world knowledge (Devitt, 1986). This applies very obviously when a language is being learned for some specific purpose associated with an expertise that the learner already possesses: 'A welder just beginning English knows precious little about the language, but an awful lot about welding, and it is this which enables him to understand technical documents which, for the teacher who is not a welder and who applies purely linguistic criteria, are "difficult" ' (Riley, 1985: p.283). But the same consideration also applies to general language learning provided we use authentic texts that take account of our learners' interests, learning purposes and world knowledge.

According to schema theory, our knowledge of the world is organized in complex structures that reflect our experience and thus facilitate processing and recall (for an introduction to schema theory from the perspective of reading, see Anderson and Pearson, 1988). Devitt (1986) has shown that it is possible to give even beginning learners access to a well-chosen authentic printed text by processes of deliberate schema-activation and schema-creation (see Little, 1989; Little and Singleton, 1992; Little, 1994a). One well tried method consists of three steps. First, the learners are given (say) two dozen words and phrases that are central to the meaning of the text they are preparing to encounter: their task is to establish the meaning of each individual word and phrase. Secondly, they sort the words and phrases into broad semantic categories such as PERSON, PLACE, EVENT. Thirdly, they use this categorization to build a schema, or story outline. In some cases they will arrive at a story outline that corresponds closely to the authentic text; but even when their outline is very different, these procedures give them a collective and individual 'framework' within which to fit the text.

Once learners have derived some meaning, however slight, from their encounter with the authentic text, it can be used as an object of linguistic exploration and a quarry from which learners can borrow words and phrases in order to construct meanings of their own. Although we may have few learners who aspire to write newspaper articles – or any other kind of extended text – we should not ignore the fact that it is possible to reshape, reuse or recycle authentic written texts in a great variety of different ways. The exploratory processes that activities of this kind entail may have little in common with our learners' target repertoire, but they can greatly enrich their learning, promoting the internalization of vocabulary, phonology, morphology and syntax. But again it is worth stressing the interdependence of language learning and language use as psychological phenomena. Pedagogical experiments reported by Little and Singleton (1992) and Little (1994a) showed that when small groups of three or four learners worked together on the schema-activation tasks described above, their focus shifted rapidly back and forth between communication and analysis, use and learning; often, indeed, the two focuses seemed to overlap almost entirely.

## Authentic texts and learner autonomy

The essence of learner autonomy is acceptance of responsibility for one's own learning (Holec, 1981: p.3). This entails establishing a personal agenda for learning, taking at least some of the initiatives that shape the learning process, and developing a capacity to evaluate the extent and success of one's learning (for elaboration of this point, see Little, 1994b). In the development of learner autonomy, learning goes hand in hand with learning how to learn.

The general educational argument in favour of learner autonomy is partly affective, having to do with positive motivation, and partly cognitive, having to do with improved access to the content and process of learning. For the autonomous learner there are no barriers between 'school knowledge', or what is learnt in formal educational contexts, and 'action knowledge', or what is learnt informally and experientially (Barnes, 1976). Language learners, of course, have a special interest in overcoming barriers between 'school knowledge' and 'action knowledge', for it is only thus that they can hope to use their target language for communicative purposes outside the classroom. But my claim that language learning and language use are essentially inseparable entails the further claim that there is a two-way relation between autonomy in language learning and autonomy in language use. We do not seek to develop autonomy in language learners in the hope that at some time in the future they will make the transition to autonomy as language users. Rather, learner autonomy properly understood embraces the domains of language learning and language use in constant interaction with one another.

The concept of learner autonomy naturally tends to highlight the learner's individuality. It is thus important to emphasize that all learning proceeds via interaction, so that the freedoms by which we recognize learner autonomy are always constrained by the learner's dependence on the support and cooperation of others. Not surprisingly, the mode of interaction most apt to promote learner autonomy is collaboration (see, for example, Dam, 1990;

Nunan, 1992), since the interdependence on which successful collaboration depends arises from a balanced interaction between freedom and dependence.

Authentic texts are directly relevant to the development of learner autonomy in two ways. First, on the affective level, learners who from the beginning have been exposed to authentic texts rapidly develop confidence in the face of the target language. In particular, they quickly cease to worry that their comprehension may be incomplete, since they know that much can be achieved on the basis of partial comprehension. Secondly, on the psychological level, authentic texts accommodate the two-way relation between language learning and language use, encouraging the development of techniques of language learning that entail language use and techniques of language use that entail language learning. Let me give an example. Explicit treatment of target language grammar is usually discussed in terms of the extent to which it facilitates those processes of internalization and automatization on which fluent spontaneous language use depends. But this is not the only reason for focusing on matters of linguistic form. Only one kind of communication – reciprocal oral communication – requires language learners to produce an immediate response to (frequently) unpredictable stimuli. All other kinds – non-reciprocal oral and all written communication – allow learners time to plan, monitor, edit and revise their message. Now, the tools that learners need in order to plan, monitor, edit and revise will be developed partly by practice in the production of non-reciprocal texts, but partly also by focusing on matters of linguistic form. Traditionally, this means giving particular attention to morpho-syntax. I intend an altogether wider focus – one that embraces the structural features of texts, sentences and phrases, word-formation patterns, collocational possibilities, and issues of register and style (see West, 1992–4). Authentic texts provide learners at all levels with the means to explore linguistic form communicatively, and the communicative stimulus to produce new meanings that are situated in a genuine communicative context.

## Authentic texts in self-access

If we believe that authentic texts properly belong in the 'real world' of target language communication, we are likely (as I have argued) to judge our learners' response to them in terms of the texts' original communicative purposes. According to this view, an authentic response to an authentic text is essentially the response that it would have received in its original context of use. Such a view may be difficult to align with the exploitation of authentic texts in self-access learning centres, since these belong within the domain of the classroom and language learning rather than that of the target language community and target language use. But if we believe that language learning and language use are interdependent, and that their interdependence is inescapable at all levels of competence, authentic texts present themselves as an indispensable resource for all language learning. By extension, they pose no special problem for the self-access centre. That is not to say, however, that we do not need to give careful thought to the ways in which we use authentic texts in self-access. The last part of this chapter seeks to sketch an approach based on the principle of the indivisibility of language learning and language use. This approach has two principal constraining factors: the environment in which the self-access centre is situated, and the range of authentic texts that it can make available to learners.

The environmental constraint operates on two quite distinct levels. The first has to do with the role that the self-access centre plays in the overall language learning process. In essence there seem to be three possibilities, though each is capable of almost infinite variation. First, the self-access centre may play a subordinate role, supporting a learning process which is mostly shaped and pursued in the classroom; secondly, it may stand in a more or less equal role to the classroom; and thirdly, it may be the principal or only language learning environment. The first role is the one most often encountered in schools, whereas the second and third are more likely to be found in tertiary and adult education.

Whichever role the self-access centre plays, I assume (following my earlier argument) that it will be organized to assist learners' development towards autonomy, which entails the steady growth of a critical awareness of themselves both as learners and as users of the target language. In our first two cases the initial impetus towards autonomy will come from the interactive processes of negotiation that are the foundation of good classroom practice. In the third case the self-access centre will itself have to provide the impetus, perhaps through a combination of induction courses and regular counselling, whether of individuals or groups of learners.

In order that learners derive maximum benefit from their use of the self-access centre, it is essential that they come to it with a sense of the interdependence of language learning and language use; but equally essential that they know when to give greater conscious attention to one or the other focus.

The second level on which the environmental factor operates has to do with the situation of the self-access centre in relation to the target language community. Specifically, is it within or adjacent to the target language community, or at a distance from it? Or does it perhaps straddle these two positions, catering equally for second and foreign languages (in the sociolinguistic sense)? When the self-access centre does cater for a language which is in regular and widespread use in the surrounding community, there will be many kinds of authentic text that learners encounter in their daily lives outside the language learning environment. This does not mean that such texts have no place in the self-access centre; but it may indicate that we should encourage learners to approach such texts more from the learner than from the user perspective. Conversely, when the self-access centre caters for foreign languages, it may offer learners their best chance of certain kinds of language use – those entailed, for example, in comprehension of radio and television broadcasts that are not otherwise available to them. This brings us to the second constraining factor, the range of authentic texts that the self-access centre can make available to learners.

The precise range of authentic texts that any particular self-access centre can offer will depend on the language(s) and learning purposes it supports and the resources at its disposal – accommodation, technical installations, and funds with which to purchase printed materials, video and audio recordings, and software. Each environment makes its own demands and imposes its own constraints. But in principle, self-access centres can provide learners with authentic written and spoken texts in various media. Written texts may be printed – books, newspapers, magazines, brochures, etc.; or they may be stored in digital form. Spoken texts may be stored on magnetic tape; or they may be available 'off air' as live television or radio broadcasts. It is no doubt important that our learners work intensively on small amounts of authentic text; but it is equally important that we encourage them to browse through large quantities of text as a regular part of learning and using the target language.

A self-access centre needs to offer a wide range of authentic texts, many of which will have a short shelf-life and thus will need to be replaced on a regular basis. This means in turn that we can never hope to provide a set of fully worked exercises for every authentic text in the self-access centre. This does not matter. On the contrary, we should make a virtue of necessity: when learners want to approach authentic texts more from the learner perspective than from the user perspective, we should encourage them to generate their own exercises and learning activities by applying a range of simple analytical procedures to the authentic texts they encounter – procedures calculated to promote vocabulary learning, for example, or a greater sensitivity to morphosyntactic structure (for suggestions, see Little, 1989; Little and Devitt, 1991). In the case of digitally stored texts, concordancing software furnishes a powerful tool for exploring a wide range of linguistic features (cf. Johns, 1994). Audio and video recordings are easier to work with if a written transcript is available, while live television and radio broadcasts are more easily approached from the user than from the learner perspective – though techniques of self-preparation associated with learning may well lead to more effective use. For example, before watching a television news bulletin a learner might attempt to predict what the main items will be, making a conscious effort to recall the personalities, institutions, actions, events and concepts associated with them. Even when the prediction is entirely wrong, the additional focus that this activity achieves can aid comprehension (for further suggestions, again see Little and Devitt, 1991).

I referred above to pedagogical experiments in which small groups of learners shifted their focus rapidly back and forth between language learning and language use. I believe that the explicit language learning focus that evolved as they performed their schema-activation and schema-creation tasks should be attributed in large measure to the fact that they were working in small groups rather than individually. In order to achieve the level of mutual comprehension necessary for successful collaboration they were forced to try to make explicit what in individual performance of the tasks in question might easily have remained implicit, or at any rate unexamined. Since explicit analysis and conscious awareness are at once fundamental to what I have called the learner perspective and essential for the development of learner autonomy, the question arises whether we should encourage group work in the use of authentic texts in self-access. Experiments carried out in

Trinity College, Dublin, using the *Autotutor*, an interactive video-cassette system developed by the Centre for Language and Communication Studies, suggest that we should. The experiments used learning modules comprising small amounts of authentic video material embedded in a simple interactive programme that offered learners a range of pre-, while- and post-viewing activities calculated to encourage group interaction. Over the past three years several modules have been developed and used with small groups of volunteer learners, all of whom have been video-recorded working on their own with the programme. The video recordings provide strong evidence that programmes of this kind can act as a powerful stimulus to the interaction of learner and user perspectives which I have argued is fundamental to the authentic reception of authentic texts by language learners. (For a fuller account of this work, see Little, 1994c.)

## Conclusion

I began this chapter by suggesting that the role we assign to authentic texts in second and foreign language learning will depend on how we conceptualize second and foreign language use and what view we take of the relation between learning and use. I argued that because they use the same psycholinguistic mechanisms language learning and language use are essentially inseparable, so that it is logically impossible to define a threshold of target language competence that learners must achieve before they are exposed to authentic texts: authentic texts should play a central role in language learning at all levels. I went on to argue that authentic texts can help to foster learner autonomy because that too depends on the conscious interaction of learner and user perspectives. Finally, I considered the general implications of these arguments for the provision of authentic texts in self-access language learning centres. The issues I have raised are, I believe, particularly urgent in view of the current rapid expansion of electronic communication and the Internet. Already language learners in many parts of the world have access, at least in principle, to a mixture of live and recorded written and spoken communication in an infinity of new combinations. Already it is possible to think of a 'virtual' target language community, available to language learners anywhere in the world. If we can have a 'virtual' target language community, however, we can also have a 'virtual' self-access centre. That offers exciting possibilities for second and foreign language learner-users. But they will be able to benefit from those possibilities only if they are critically aware of their learner-user status and have been given the tools that enable them to use that awareness as the basis for continuing personal enrichment.

# 17

## Providing computerized self-access opportunities for the development of writing skills

JOHN MILTON

## Introduction

The problem of developing self-access methodologies that help learners acquire *productive* language skills is a key one for computer assisted language learning (CALL). The way that computers are used in language learning has failed to address this issue: they can provide an information-rich environment, but so far have offered only text manipulation to learners, with their role restricted to one of programmed instruction and testing. This chapter will outline how the use of computers needs to be rethought in CALL. The concept of autonomy provides a way out: computers need to become learners' tools rather than expert tutors, and three new technologies are very promising for allowing CALL to develop in a more autonomous direction. These technologies are networking, concordancing and wordprocessing. The final part of this chapter will show how these technologies can be integrated to improve learners' access to both language and to information about language, and also to provide electronic composing tools for writers of various ability levels.

## Writing, independent learning and CALL

Many EFL learners have not had much experience or training in writing in their native language; those who have frequently find the conventions of English writing very different from those of their first language. At any rate, the processes of learning how to write and learning how to write in a second language are often intimately related and EFL learners usually require both information about composing skills and comprehensible access to specific types of linguistic knowledge. However, critical examination (see Silva, 1990) of the practices which have been used to teach EFL writing (e.g. controlled composition, the process approach and English for academic purposes) question the adequacy of these strategies for the effective instruction or learning of writing. The lack of demonstrable success by conventional instruction has been a justification for the exploration of independent learning strategies to improve writing skills among these learners.

One of the premises for the promotion of independent learning in education is that instruction, by its very nature, often presents extended solutions to problems learners may not have experienced or may never experience: that instruction alone cannot provide information in as timely, consistent or individualized a manner as students require. Given the varied needs of EFL writers and the importance of addressing those needs at the moment they arise, the development of writing skills would seem to be at least partly served by modes of learning which allow the student a high degree of independence. However, as Littlewood and Littlejohn have argued in this volume, self-access methodologies have, to date, shown themselves to be weakest in the area of productive language skills, which call for creativity on the part of the learner. It appears that neither traditional classroom instruction nor self-access strategies have satisfactorily addressed the needs of EFL writers.

This failure is related, at least in part, to the difficulty of getting information to the learner when it is most needed and of providing effective feedback. Learners require more than a priori instruction and post hoc correction to become effective writers. The great strength of computers is that they make it possible to put large amounts of information at the control of the user, but this facility has not been adequately exploited in the design of applications for autonomous language learning. Technological potential is often not followed by productive applications. The means used to deliver information, from chalk-and-talk to scripted, interactive, multimedia programs, have often failed to encourage or even allow learners to take control of their own development as language users. An effective application of technology needs to do both.

CALL courseware (often most familiar as grammar-based,

multiple-choice and gap-filling exercises) has rarely moved beyond text manipulation exercises which attempt to address localized problems of grammar and lexis. These programs generally place the computer in the role of a programmed instructor which tests students and provides more-or-less accurate feedback in the form of 'correct' answers to problems it poses itself. Although much of this software is authorable, it typically attempts to mimic a kind of decontextualized instruction which may or may not be relevant to the immediate needs of the learner. These techniques may be adequate for very limited drill and practice, but cannot be a basis on which to design tutorials for language production. Software which relies solely on prescribed rules and scripts (i.e. attempts to predict each step every user will take through the program) pretends to the role of a tutor without being able to respond as effectively as a human expert (criticisms of this approach to educational software design have been voiced for at least a decade (cf. Self, 1985). Not only is this poor technical design, since it fails to make much use of the most obvious advantage of the machine (that of information storage and retrieval) but it is also bad pedagogy in light of what we know of the communicative conditions under which people acquire and use language.

The current state of technology does not enable us to create a reliable artificial language expert. However, advances in both computer hardware and software are making possible new ways to make the machine a provider of conceptual information and appropriate writing tools. The distinction between perceiving the machine as a tool rather than the common attempt to model it as an expert tutor lies not only in accepting the current limits of technology but also in embracing concepts of autonomy, which propose that learning is more effective when students have direct access to information and timely advice on its use rather than having to rely solely on an expert (human or programmed).

Although current educational expertise maintains that no learning takes place without the full cognitive participation of learners, courseware design still often allows learners to make only the simplest decisions (usually outside the context of any communicative activity). Most CALL applications, including the so-called 'expert' language systems (so far widely represented only by computerized grammar checkers), fail to provide language learners with any but the most trivial facilities to improve their language production. Of growing interest for EFL professionals is the application of three technologies to language learning which offer more robust opportunities for assistance with language production than current 'intelligent' tutoring systems. These are computer-mediated communication; text-retrieval techniques, which EFL teachers know best as concordancing programs; and wordprocessing applications.

## Promising technologies

### *Networking*

One of the most compelling ways the computer is being used as a facilitator of collaborative writing is in computer mediated communication (CMC). Electronic mail, sometimes used as a vehicle for international simulation projects, offers opportunities for foreign language learning that takes place at a distance from the target language community. Anyone who has worked with EFL students who use e-mail will probably be aware of the potential that it has for the development of 'higher order' writing skills (see Hawisher and LeBlanc, 1992, for several discussions of this). This opportunity would appear to be of eminent value for students of English in Southeast Asia, who often live in monolingual societies where authoritarian teaching and rote learning practices are the norm. If nothing else, it gives such students a reason to put the communication of ideas and information ahead of the stilted and formulaic expressions they often acquire.

Like any other learning activity, electronic conferencing is most effective as a sustained language-learning activity when it is integrated into a coherent program where learners are able to get some degree of support and encouragement from a teacher. If e-mail continues to develop as an international communication system beyond the confines of educational and professional circles and carries English along as its primary language, we can expect it to provide EFL learners with a vehicle for English practice and, more importantly, a motivation to sustain a lifelong interest in the language.

The medium that has recently emerged as the apparent sine qua non of electronic information resources is 'the Web'. Graphical browsers such as Mosaic and Netscape have made the world-wide web a vital research base for those with access to the Internet. The promise of this technology as at least a one-way vehicle for communication, and for lifelong learning, is undeniable. The chief characteristic that sets this technology apart from printed materials is that an enormous quantity of information can be accessed by electronic searches; its hypertext features give it a degree of interaction that is difficult to reproduce in print form (however, the opportunity to be able to read information on screen offers no advantages beyond environmental ones, compelling as this may be for some). While the application of graphic and iconographic skills certainly enhance design, text is the most cost-effective way of conveying and understanding the information, at least as long as bandwidth remains relatively expensive, and the only way of interpreting information until audio throughput is much better. There are, however, a number of economic, technical and political/social impediments that may limit access to the technology: the cost of Internet connection (a fast machine, a modem, and usually connection fees) will probably decrease; the reliability of connection, navigation and ease of operation will also probably improve, but the degree to which information will be free in either a political or commercial sense is far less certain.

This technology provides great opportunities for the concept of data-driven learning discussed by Johns (1994). Language learners can, for example, use various search engines to look at particular lexical expressions and grammatical structures to see how they are used in authentic contexts. Most language learners nevertheless require some means of identifying, narrowing and filtering the large amount of text and information made available by this technology: searches result in all sorts of text types, which vary widely in level, quality, and so on. Hopefully, information retrieval technologies will improve in directions that make it possible for non-native speakers using this medium to find and interpret information. To some degree these needs are being met by on-line language resources which are developing as freely accessible dictionaries, thesauri and grammars, and resources by subscription. However, on-line information and language resources are no different than that provided in any other medium in their differences in usefulness, accuracy and appropriacy. There are plenty of teaching opportunities for us in introducing this resource to learners and in encouraging and guiding them in its meaning and application (I am not suggesting that we limit access, though many will suggest it: there will probably always be a yen for tabloid information and a corresponding method of supplying it).

## Text retrieval

Text retrieval has become associated in the area of second language acquisition with the concept of data-driven learning (Johns, 1994). This technology has suggested powerful new methodologies for autonomous language learning by giving the EFL learner access to large amounts of language in free-text format (i.e. corpora). It has delivered concordancers (programs that extract target words and their contexts) which give students opportunities to study the way specific vocabulary – both as single words and as collocational units – behaves in authentic language. These are potentially ideal tools for the autonomous learner. By making it possible for language students to focus on authentic usage in particular text genres, these techniques allow them to acquire knowledge of how specific words and expressions behave (and often behave differently) in the written language of various text types, registers, and so on.

## Wordprocessing

Wordprocessing is becoming an increasingly common composing instrument for EFL students, although it is still more frequently used to produce final copies of assigned work that have been drafted by hand. Despite mixed early reviews of the effectiveness of computers in improving writing, there is currently general (though not universal) agreement that wordprocessors assist the writing process (see Hawisher and LeBlanc, 1992). At any rate, the argument has become largely irrelevant given the ubiquity of the technology, at least in business and at the tertiary level. As with most arguments over the benefits of technology, the real issue is not whether we should use it, but rather how it can best be used.

## Limitations of current technologies

However, each of these three technologies has limitations when considered as a means for the autonomous development of EFL writing skills. For example, while CMC gives learners a wider audience and possibly increased feedback on their writing, it does little to relieve their impoverishment for information about words and the idiomatic nature of language. While text-retrieval technology provides details of how words behave in authentic text, this information can be overwhelming for all but the most advanced learners. Also, it has yet to be integrated into programs that provide lexical, syntactic or semantic information to students in the context of such language activities as reading or writing. Wordprocessors would appear to be the ideal environment in which to provide assistance to the writer through electronic spellcheckers, thesauri and grammar-checking programs. However, because these programs currently make no allowance for second or foreign language learners and are of limited assistance with the demands of academic writing (see Pennington, 1991, for an analysis of the shortcomings of grammar-checkers), they are more often a hazard than a help to EFL learners.

In the remainder of this chapter I will outline our strategies to exploit these technologies so as to deliver relevant information about language and the composing process to EFL writers.

## The application of technologies

I believe that much of the futility, and possible active harm to students of language correction (and its drudgery for teachers), could be avoided if learners had greater access to linguistic information from within their immediate writing environment. One dilemma of correction is that although we know that errors are a productive aspect of language learning, learners often seek to avoid problematic language structures and consequently fail to learn difficult, but essential, linguistic patterns. In the heat of composition students also often fail to apply teachers' comments and corrections (we assume of course that the teachers' advice is always helpful). It seems a valid hypothesis that these issues are best addressed by making information about language available to learners as they compose.

The electronic tools I outline in this chapter are meant to address lexical, grammatical and organizational problems documented from thousands of papers written by school-leaving and first-year tertiary students studying English in Hong Kong (see Milton and Chowdury, 1994 for a description of how this corpus was collected and annotated). A prototype application is now being implemented; the next stage will be extensive testing (for a more detailed technical description of this application, see Milton *et al.*, 1996). The need to develop new electronic tools is occasioned because our students have shown themselves disinclined to consult paper-based references (dictionaries, grammars, etc.) possibly because they are often not at hand, because they distract from the process of writing or because they may not give the information students need in the way and at the point they need it. The program uses various electronic information storage and retrieval strategies to address this situation and exploits the 'multi-tasking' interfaces of popular operating systems (e.g. MSWindows) to allow users to consult electronic resources while writing and to retrieve text directly into their documents.

### *Networking: structured input, collaborative writing and revision*

As mentioned earlier in this chapter, networks permit students, teachers and others to work together in ways that address many of the shortcomings of current educational practice. International networks (e.g. the Internet) also make possible access to, literally, a world of information. One immediate way of facilitating students' access to the relevant rhetorical and language demands of their academic community is by assisting and encouraging instructors of all courses at The Hong Kong University of Science and Technology to provide particular information about their writing assignments on the university's local area network so that it is available to the students at the moment they need it from within their word-processor. This may address the common complaint of instructors that students are unable to anticipate the language and rhetorical demands of academic writing, and that of students who often complain of the lack of explicit instruction from their lecturers. This information can be gathered through an electronic form which allows instructors to choose from set defaults for particular assignments or text types, specify preferred citation formats, stipulate the grading criteria which will be used, and so on. This information can then be reported directly to the students within their writing environment. This appears a popular self-access feature for those instructors who admit to not having had much training in the teaching of writing skills and who have difficulty articulating the criteria of their writing assignments. The availability of an on-line reference of the type described here should enhance the use of local area networks in promoting collaborative writing between students. While collaboration may result in fuller, more expressive and possibly even more accurate writing, EFL writers require third-party reference such as that which the program described here provides.

## Text retrieval: structured and free text searches

Because programs can be dynamically linked to each other in a graphical operating system, it is possible to make such techniques as text-retrieval facilities available to users within an interactive writing environment in ways that are responsive to the text type that the student is currently writing. The intention is to provide access to a richer set of resources about the language for the EFL writer than those provided by current on-line dictionaries and thesauri. These include:

- Functionally indexed databases of language 'chunks' (e.g. collocations, fixed expressions, sentence frames, etc.) that users can refer to as they write, e.g. expressions that are typically used for description, instruction, explanation, and so on.
- A text-lookup facility that provides manageable access to relevant corpora that students can use freely to explore word forms, collocational behaviour, and so on.
- Information about the frequency of structures in particular contexts that enables students to make richer and better-informed language choices and to develop an understanding of various text types (e.g. how the language of academic essays differs from that of sales letters or laboratory reports).

This program provides students with access to text structures which they have shown difficulty using in both indexed databases and authentic context. Text retrieval tools are made available to the students within their wordprocessor to give them a way of comparing their language with that of other, more polished, writers. The program, in prototype form, already appears popular among students because of the information it provides about the collocational properties of target vocabulary in corpora of polished English. The program so far relies on limited grammar-checking techniques to flag fixed lexical structures. Morphological patterns which have been shown to be frequently associated with error are highlighted and the student can then choose to investigate the use of these structures in NS (Native Speaker) corpora. These features are incorporated in the student's wordprocessing program and can be accessed by intuitive icons and pull-down menus. With manageable access to real language it is expected that students will be more inclined to experiment with language, self-correct and use these tools to evaluate their results.

## Wordprocessing: reshaping the writing instrument

In addition to providing students with resources from outside the wordprocessor, I am also modifying and reprogramming the word-processor itself. Providing students with guided access to vocabulary and grammar used in authentic contexts will not necessarily in itself make them better writers. Many language teachers have come to subscribe to the view that linguistic competence and composing competence are not necessarily directly related and that effective composing strategies are possibly more important than linguistic competence in producing proficient writing (see Krapels, 1990, for a review of studies supporting this view). Extending the facilities of the students' wordprocessors gives them greater control over the composing process. The programmability of modern wordprocessors provides opportunities to allow learners to explore various composing strategies, including how to formulate purpose, generate and develop ideas, refer to others' ideas, analyse audience, organize ideas and revise.

Rather than acting as just a blank writing space (which a sheet of paper offers just as well), the document screen can be made to interact with the student writer and provide help to meet the specific composition and revision needs that the teacher's preparation and response alone cannot meet. There are many aspects of composing skills that instructors currently spend time preteaching and subsequently correcting that can be put directly under the control of learners themselves in the context of their own writing environment. The challenge is to encourage students to exercise this control and take an approach to their writing which is both structured and personal. Among the features of our program which the student can access are:

- Style templates of essay and report formats that obviate the common practice of our students to overemphasize mechanical details (e.g. they often concentrate on graphical design at the expense of organization and content).
- Idea generation tools that students use to formulate relevant questions about their purpose, methods, and so on, appropriate to specific text types.

- A toggle function that allows the users to transform their ideas and the relationships between the ideas into graphic form (e.g. 'mind maps').
- Organizing tools that use the outlining feature of the wordprocessor to help novice writers see relationships among their ideas and decide on the nature of these relationships, experiment with the positioning of ideas in the document, understand the implicit organization of a text, and so on.
- Referencing tools that automatically format quoted materials, in-paper citations and bibliographies and encourage users to make their purposes for using secondary sources explicit, thereby reducing the likelihood of inadvertent plagiarism.

Some of these features are already separately available in commercial software programs, but the purpose of this design is to present an integrated suite of composing tools relevant to the needs of EFL students. In addition to providing information about language at the word and sentence level, this program makes it possible for inexperienced writers to attend to the rhetorical organization of their texts and target specific communication goals in ways which neither current electronic nor paper-based references do.

## Conclusion

The purpose of this chapter has been to suggest one method of using computer technologies now available to serve the aims of the autonomous development of writing skills. The premise is that it is technically and pedagogically more effective to provide learners with writing tools than to present them with a computer program that models a human tutor. I have illustrated how several applications (local area networks, text-retrieval programs and wordprocessors) can be married and enhanced so as to provide a 'user-friendly' environment for novice EFL writers, give them access to descriptive and, possibly, prescriptive information and thereby free them and their instructors from some of the wasted effort of decontextualized instruction.

Many of the facilities described in this chapter require specialist skills and time beyond the resources of most educators (e.g. programming and design, research into learners' needs and the compilation of text corpora). However, there are already editing features implemented in released wordprocessors which are of potentially great value to teachers for the enhancement of autonomous, peer and instructor editing and evaluation (e.g. outlining and annotation features). The development and exploitation of these various tools can significantly contribute to the development of writing skills by giving students greater access to the target language and greater control of the writing process than has been previously possible.

# References

ALLWRIGHT, D. (1988) 'Autonomy and individualization in whole-class instruction'. In A. Brookes and P. Grundy (eds) *Individualization and Autonomy in Language Learning.* ELT Documents, 131. London: Modern English Publications and the British Council, pp.35–44.

ALTENBERG, B. (1991) 'A bibliography of publications relating to English computer corpora'. In S. Johansson and A-B Stenstrom (eds) *English Computer Corpora: Selected Papers and Research Guide.* Berlin: Mouton de Gruyter, pp.355–96.

ALTHUSSER, L. (1971) *Lenin and Philosophy and Other Essays.* London: New Left Books.

ANDERSON, R.C. and PEARSON, P.D. (1988) 'A schema-theoretic view of basic processes in reading comprehension'. In P. Carrell, J. Devine and D. Eskey (eds) *Interactive Approaches to Second Language Reading.* Cambridge: Cambridge University Press, pp.37–55.

APPLE, M. (1985) *Education and Power.* London: Ark.

APPLE, M. (1988) *Texts and Teachers.* London: Routledge and Kegan Paul.

APPLE, M. (1989) 'The politics of common sense: schooling, populism and the New Right'. In H.A. Giroux and P. McLaren (eds) *Theories and Resistance in Education.* London: Heinemann Educational Books, pp.32–49.

ASTON, G. (1993) 'The learner's contribution to the self-access centre', *ELT Journal,* 47, pp.219–27.

AUERBACH, E.R. (1986) 'Competency-based ESL: one step forward or two steps back?', *TESOL Quarterly,* 20:3, pp.411–29.

BANTON, A. (1992) 'Successful self access through learner development'. *Independence, the newsletter of the IATEFL learner SIG,* 8, pp.20–2.

BARASCH, R.M. and JAMES, C.V. (eds) (1994) *Beyond the Monitor Model: Comments on Theory and Practice in Second Language Acquisition.* Boston: Heinle and Heinle.

BARNES, D. (1976) *From Communication to Curriculum.* Harmondsworth: Penguin.

BARTH, F. (1990) 'The guru and the conjurer: transactions in knowledge and the shaping of culture in South-East Asia and Melanesia', *Man,* 25:4, pp.640–53.

BENESCH, S. (1993) 'ESL, ideology and the politics of pragmatism', *TESOL Quarterly,* 27:4, pp.705–16.

BENSON, P. (1994) 'Self-access systems as information systems: questions of ideology and control'. In D. Gardner and L. Miller (eds) *Directions in Self-access Language Learning,* Hong Kong: Hong Kong University Press, pp.3–12.

BENSON, P. (1995) 'A critical view of learner training', *Learning Learning,* 2:2, pp.2–6.

BENSON, P. (1996) 'Concepts of autonomy in language learning'. In R. Pemberton *et al.* (eds) *Taking Control: Autonomy in Language Learning.* Hong Kong: Hong Kong University Press, pp.27–34.

BLOOR, M. and BLOOR, T. (1988) 'Syllabus negotiation: the basis of learner autonomy'. In A. Brookes and P. Grundy (eds) *Individualization and Autonomy in Language Learning.* ELT Documents 131. London: Modern English Publications/British Council, pp.62–74.

BOLINGER, D. (1975) 'Meaning and memory', *Forum linguisticum,* 1, pp.1–14.

BOUD, D. (1988) 'Moving towards autonomy'. In D. Boud (ed.) *Developing Student Autonomy in Learning,* 2nd edn. London: Kogan Page, pp.17–39.

BOWLES, S. and GINTIS, H. (1976) *Schooling in Capitalist America.* New York: Basic Books.

BREEN, M.P. (1984) 'Process syllabuses in language teaching'. In C.J. Brumfit (ed.) *General English Syllabus Design.* Oxford: Pergamon/Modern English Publications, pp.47–60.

BREEN, M.P. (1985a) 'Authenticity in the language classroom', *Applied Linguistics,* 6:1, pp.60–70.

BREEN, M.P. (1985b) 'The social context for language learning: a neglected situation?', *Studies in Second Language Acquisition,* 7:2, pp.135–58.

BREEN, M.P. (1987) 'Contemporary paradigms in syllabus design'. Parts 1 and 2, *Language Teaching,* 20:1/2, pp.81–92, 157–74.

BREEN, M.P. (1989) 'The evaluation cycle for language learning tasks'. In R.K. Johnson (ed.) *The Second Language Curriculum.* Cambridge: Cambridge University Press, pp.187–206.

BREEN, M.P. and CANDLIN, C. (1980) 'The essentials of a communicative curriculum in language teaching', *Applied Linguistics,* 1:2, pp.89–112.

BREEN, M.P., CANDLIN, C.N., DAM, L. and GABRIELSEN, G. (1989) 'The evolution of a teacher training pogramme'. In R.K. Johnson (ed.)

*The Second Language Curriculum*. Cambridge: Cambridge University Press. pp.111–35.

BROCKETT, R.G. and HIEMSTRA, R. (1985) 'Bridging the theory-practice gap in self-directed learning'. In S. Brookfield (ed.) *Self-directed Learning: From Theory to Practice*. San Francisco: Jossey-Bass, pp.31–40.

BROOKES, A. and GRUNDY, P. (eds) (1988) *Individualisation and Autonomy in Language Learning*. ELT Documents 131. London: Modern English Publications in association with the British Council (Macmillan).

BROOKFIELD, S. (1985) 'Self-directed learning: a critical review of research'. In S. Brookfield (ed.) *Self-directed Learning: From Theory to Practice*, New Directions for Continuing Education, No. 25. San Francisco: Jossey-Bass, pp.5–16.

BROOKFIELD, S. (1986) *Understanding and Facilitating Adult Learning*. San Francisco: Jossey-Bass.

BROOKFIELD, S. (1993) 'Self-directed learning, political clarity, and the critical practice of adult education', *Adult Education Quarterly*, 43:4, pp.227–42.

BROOKS, N. (1964) *Language and Language Learning*. New York: Harcourt Brace.

BRUFFEE, K.A. (1993) *Collaborative Learning: Higher Education, Interdependence and the Authority of Knowledge*. Baltimore: The Johns Hopkins University Press.

BRUMFIT, C. (1984) *Communicative Methodology in Language Teaching*. Cambridge: Cambridge University Press.

*Cadences Study Guide* (1994) Milton Keynes: Open University, Centre for Modern Languages.

CAMPBELL, C. and KRYSZEWSKA, H. (1992) *Learner-based Teaching*. Oxford: Oxford University Press.

CANDY, P.C. (1988) 'On the attainment of subject-matter autonomy'. In D. Boud (ed.) *Developing Student Autonomy in Learning*. London: Kogan Page, pp.59–76.

CANDY, P.C. (1989) 'Constructivism and the study of self-direction in adult learning', *Studies in the Education of Adults*, 21, pp.95–116.

CARVER, D. and DICKINSON, L. (1982) 'Learning to be self-directed'. In M. Geddes and G. Sturtridge (eds) *Individualisation*. London: Modern English Publications Ltd (Macmillan), pp.15–21.

CASTORIADIS, C. (1991) *Philosophy, Politics, Autonomy: Essays in Political Philosophy* (edited by D.A. Curtis). New York: Oxford University Press.

CHANDLER, B. (1989) *Longman Mini-concordancer*. London: Longman.

CLARKE, J. (1987) *Curriculum Renewal in School Foreign Language Learning*. Oxford: Oxford University Press.

CLIGNET, R. (1978) 'Damned if you do, damned if you don't: the dilemmas of colonizer-colonized relations'. In P.G. Altbach and G.P. Kelly (eds). *Education and Colonialism*. London: Longman, pp.122–45.

*Collins COBUILD English Language Dictionary* (1987) J. Sinclair (ed.). London: Collins.

COSER, R.L. (1991) *In Defense of Modernity. Role Complexity and Individual Autonomy.* Stanford: Stanford University Press.

COSTE, D. (1970) 'Textes et documents authentiques au niveau 2'. *Le Français dans le Monde* 73.

CURRAN, C.A. (1976) *Counselling-learning in Second Languages.* Apple River, Illinois: Apple River Press.

DAKIN, J. (1973) *The Language Laboratory and Language Learning.* London: Longman.

DAM, L. (1990) 'Developing awareness of learning in an autonomous language learning context'. In R. Duda and P. Riley (eds) *Learning Styles.* Nancy: Presses Universitaires de Nancy, pp.189–97.

DAM, L. (1994) 'Developing learner autonomy in a school context – what about the teacher?' Paper presented at the *Autonomy in Language Learning* International Conference, University of Science and Technology and Chinese University, Hong Kong, June 1994.

DAM, L. (1995) *Learner Autonomy 3: From Theory to Classroom Practice.* Dublin: Authentik.

DAM, L. and GABRIELSEN, G. (1988) 'Developing learner autonomy in a school context – a six-year experiment beginning in the learners' first year of English'. In H. Holec (ed.) *Autonomy and Self-directed Learning: Fields of Application.* Strasbourg: Council of Europe, pp.19–30.

DAM, L. and LEGENHAUSEN, L. (1996) 'The acquisition of vocabulary in an autonomous learning environment: the first months of beginning English'. In R. Pemberton *et al.* (eds) *Taking Control: Autonomy in Language Learning.* Hong Kong: Hong Kong University Press, pp.265–80.

DE BEAUGRANDE, R. and DRESSLER, W. (1981) *Introduction to Text Linguistics.* London and New York: Longman.

DE HUSZAR, G.B. (ed) (1960) *The Intellectuals.* London: Allen and Unwin.

DEVITT, S.M. (1986) *Learning a Foreign Language through the Media.* CLCS Occasional Paper No. 18. Dublin: Trinity College, Centre for Language and Communication Studies.

DICKINSON, L. (1987) *Self-instruction in Language Learning.* Cambridge: Cambridge University Press.

DICKINSON, L. (1988) 'Learner training'. In A. Brookes and P. Grundy (eds) *Individualization and Autonomy in Language Learning.* ELT Documents 131. London: Modern English Publications/British Council, pp.45–53.

DICKINSON, L. (1992) *Learner Autonomy 2: Learner Training for Language Learning,* Dublin: Authentik.

DICKINSON, L. and WENDEN, A. (eds) (1995) 'Special issue on autonomy', *System,* 23:2.

DUDA, R. and RILEY, P. (1991) *Learning Styles.* Nancy: Presses Universitaires de Nancy.

EGIN, G. (1982) 'Documents authentiques: réflexion essai de définition', *Bulletin de l'ACLA*, 4:1, pp.53–63.

ELLIS, G. and SINCLAIR, B. (1989) *Learning to Learn English: a Course in Learner Training.* Cambridge: Cambridge University Press.

ESCH, E.M. (ed.) (1994) *Self Access and the Adult Learner.* London: CILT.

FAIRCLOUGH, N. (1992a) *Discourse and Social Change.* Cambridge: Polity Press.

FAIRCLOUGH, N. (ed.) (1992b) *Critical Language Awareness.* London: Longman.

FERRIS, D., NORTH, B., SUTER, B., MAXWELL-HYSLOP, H., SHAW, K. and DAWSON, S. (1988) 'Promoting learner autonomy through fluency activities'. In H. Holec (ed.) *Autonomy and self-directed learning: present fields of application.* Strasbourg: Council of Europe Project No. 12, pp.93–116.

FLOWERDEW, J. (1993) 'Concordancing as a tool in course design', *System*, 21, pp.231–44.

FOUCAULT, M. (1970) *The Order of Things: An Archeology of the Human Sciences.* New York: Vintage Books.

FREIRE, P. (1970) *Pedagogy of the Oppressed.* New York: Herder and Herder.

GARDNER, D. and MILLER, L. (eds) (1994) *Directions in Self-access.* Hong Kong: Hong Kong University Press.

GEDDES, M. and STURTRIDGE, G. (eds) (1982) *Individualisation.* London: Modern English Publications.

GIBBS, G. (1992) *Improving the Quality of Student Learning.* Bristol: Technical and Educational Services Ltd.

GILLIGAN, C. (1988) 'Remapping the moral domain: new images of the self in relationship'. In T.C. Heller, M. Sosna and D.E. Wellbery (eds) *Reconstructing Individualism: Autonomy, Individuality, and the Self in Western Thought.* Stanford: Stanford University Press, pp.237–52.

GIROUX, H.A. (1983) *Theories and Resistance in Education.* London: Heinemann Educational Books.

GIROUX, H.A. (1988) *Schooling and the Struggle for Public Life: Critical Pedagogy in the Modern Age.* Minneapolis: University of Minnesota Press.

GRAMSCI, A. (1938/1971) *Prison Notebooks.* London: Lawrence and Wishart.

GREMMO, M.J. and ABÉ, D. (1985) 'Teaching learning: redefining the teacher's role'. In P. Riley (ed.) *Discourse and Learning.* London: Longman, pp.233–47.

GREMMO, M.J. and RILEY, P. (1995) 'Autonomy and self-direction in language learning: the history of an idea', *System*, 23:2 pp.151–64.

GREMMO, M.J., HOLEC, H. and RILEY, P. (1985) 'Interactional structure: the role of role'. In P. Riley (ed.) *Discourse and learning.* London: Longman, pp.35–46.

HALLIDAY, M.A.K. (1979) *Language as Social Semiotic.* London: Edward Arnold.

HAMMOND, M. and COLLINS, R. (1991) *Self-directed Learning: Critical Practice*, London: Kogan Page.

HANKS, P. (1987) 'Definitions and explanations'. In J.M. Sinclair (ed.) *Looking up: An Account of the COBUILD Project in Lexical Computing*. London: Collins COBUILD, pp.116–36.

HARDING-ESCH, E.M. (ed.) (1977) *Self-Directed Learning and Autonomy*. Report of a Seminar held at Cambridge, 13–15 December 1976, Mimeo. University of Cambridge, Department of Linguistics and CRAPEL.

HARDING-ESCH, E.M. (1982) 'The open access sound and video library of the University of Cambridge: progress report and development', *System*, 10:1, pp.13–28.

HARRI-AUGSTEIN, S. and THOMAS, L. (1991) *Learning Conversations*. London: Routledge.

HARRIS, K. (1994) 'Turning Japanese-English into English', *The Language Teacher*, 18:7, pp.45–6.

HAWISHER, G.E. and LeBLANC, P. (eds) (1992) *Re-imagining Computers and Composition*. London: Heinemann.

HELLER, T.C. and WELLBERY, D.E. (1986) 'Introduction'. In T.C. Heller, M. Sosna and D.E. Wellbery (eds) *Reconstructing Individualism: Autonomy, Individuality, and the Self in Western Thought*. Stanford: Stanford University Press, pp.1–15.

HIGGS, J. (1988) 'Planning learning experiences to promote autonomous learning'. In D. Boud (ed.) *Developing Student Autonomy in Learning*, 2nd edn. London: Kogan Page, pp.40–58.

HILL, T.E., JR. (1991) *Autonomy and Self-respect*. Cambridge: Cambridge University Press.

HOFSTEDE, G. (1983) 'The cultural relativity of organizational practices and theories', *Journal of International Business Studies*, Fall 1983, pp.75–89.

HOLEC, H. (1980) 'Learner training: meeting needs in self-directed learning'. In H.B. Altman and C. Vaughan James (eds) *Foreign Language Learning: Meeting Individual Needs*. Oxford: Pergamon, pp.30–45.

HOLEC, H. (1981) *Autonomy in Foreign Language Learning*. Oxford: Pergamon. (First published 1979, Strasbourg: Council of Europe.)

HOLEC, H. (1985) 'On autonomy: some elementary concepts'. In P. Riley (ed.) *Discourse and Learning*. London: Longman, pp.173–90.

HOLEC, H. (ed.) (1988) *Autonomy and Self-directed Learning: Present Fields of Application*. Strasbourg: Council of Europe.

HOLLIDAY, A. (1994) *Appropriate Methodology and Social Context*. Cambridge: Cambridge University Press.

HOLZNER, B. and MARX, J.H. (1979) *Knowledge Application: The Knowledge System in Society*. Boston: Allyn and Bacon.

HOOKS, B. (1988) *Talking Back: Thinking Feminist, Thinking Black*. Toronto: Between the Lines.

HOUGHTON, D., LONG, C. and FANNING, P. (1988) 'Autonomy and

individualisation in language learning: the role and responsibilities of the EAP tutor'. In A. Brookes and P. Grundy (eds) *Individualization and Autonomy in Language Learning.* ELT Documents 131. London: Modern English Publications/British Council, pp.75–87.

HOWELL, S. (1988) 'From child to human: Chewong concepts of self'. In G. Jahoda and I.M. Lewis (eds) *Acquiring culture: Cross-cultural Studies in Child Development.* London: Routledge, pp.147–68.

HUTTUNEN, I. (1988) 'Towards learner autonomy in a school context'. In H. Holec (ed.) *Autonomy and Self-directed Learning: Fields of Application.* Strasbourg: Council of Europe, pp.31–40.

HYMES, D. (1972) 'On communicative competence'. In J.B. Pride and J. Holmes (eds) *Sociolinguistics,* Harmondsworth, Penguin, pp.269–93.

ILLICH, I. (1971) *Deschooling Society.* New York: Harper and Row.

*Independence.* Newsletter of the IATEFL Special Interest Group on Learner Independence.

ITEANU, A. (1990) 'The concept of the person and the ritual system: an Orokaiva view', *Man,* 25:1, pp.35–53.

JANICKI, K. (1990) *Towards Non-essentialist Sociolinguistics.* CSL 56, Berlin, New York: Mouton de Gruyter.

JOHNS, T. (1988) 'Whence and whither classroom concordancing?' In T. Boengaerts, T. van Els and H. Wekker (eds) *Computer Applications in Language Learning.* Dordrecht: Foris, pp.9–33.

JOHNS, T. (1991) 'Should you be persuaded: two examples of data-driven learning'. In T. Johns and P. King (eds) *Classroom Concordancing.* (*ELR journal* 4). Birmingham: Centre for English Language Studies, pp.1–16.

JOHNS, T. (1994) 'From printout to handout: grammar and vocabulary teaching in the context of Data-driven Learning'. In T. Odlin (ed.) *Perspectives on Pedagogical Grammar.* Cambridge: Cambridge University Press, pp.293–313.

JOHNS, T. and KING, P. (eds) (1991) *Classroom Concordancing.* (*ELR journal* 4). Birmingham: Centre for English Language Studies.

JOHNSON, K. (1982) *Communicative Syllabus Design and Methodology.* Oxford: Pergamon.

JOHNSTON, M. (1985) 'ESL development and self-directed learning'. In R. Mason (ed.) *Self-Directed Learning and Self-Access in Australia: From Practice to Theory.* Melbourne: Council of Adult Education, pp.173–214.

JORDAN, G. (1993) Concordancers: research findings and learner processes. Unpublished MA paper. University of London Institute of Education.

JUDD, E.L. (1984) 'TESOL as a political act: a moral question'. In J. Handscombe *et al.* (eds), *On TESOL '83: The Question of Control.* Washington: TESOL, pp.265–73.

KACHRU, B.B. (1991) 'Liberation linguistics and the Quirk concern', *English Today,* 25, pp.3–13.

KELLY, L.G. (1976) *25 Centuries of Language Teaching.* Rowley, Mass.: Newbury House.

KELLY, R. (1996) 'Language Counselling for learner autonomy: the skilled helper in self-access language learning'. In R. Pemberton *et al.* (eds) *Taking Control: Autonomy in Language Learning.* Hong Kong: Hong Kong University Press, pp.93–114.

KJISIK, F. (1994) 'The changing role of the teacher in self-access language learning'. Paper presented at the International Conference on *Autonomy in Language Learning,* University of Science and Technology and Chinese University, Hong Kong, June 1994.

KNOWLES, M. (1975) *Self-directed Learning: A Guide for Learners and Teachers.* New York: Cambridge, The Adult Education Company.

KNOWLES, M. (1986) *Using Learner Contracts.* San Francisco: Jossey-Bass.

KOHONEN, V. (1992) 'Experiential language learning: second language learning as cooperative learner education'. In D. Nunan (ed.) *Collaborative Language Learning and Teaching.* Cambridge: Cambridge University Press, pp.14–39.

KRAPELS, A.R. (1990) 'An overview of second language writing process research'. In B. Kroll (ed.) *Second Language Writing: Research Insights for the Classroom,* Cambridge University Press, pp.37–56.

KRASHEN, S.D. (1985) *The Input Hypothesis: Issues and Implications.* London: Longman.

KRESS, G.R. and HODGE, R.W. (1979) *Language as Ideology.* London: Routledge and Kegan Paul.

LARSEN-FREEMAN, D. and LONG, M.H. (eds) (1991) *An Introduction to Second Language Acquisition Research.* London: Longman.

*Learner Autonomy in Language Learning.* Newsletter of the AILA Scientific Commission on Learner Autonomy.

*Learning Learning.* Japan Association of Language Teachers Learner Development N-SIG Forum.

LEGUTKE, M. and THOMAS, H. (1991) *Process and Experience in the Language Classroom.* London: Longman.

LINDLEY, R. (1986) *Autonomy.* London: Macmillan.

LITTLE, D. (1988) 'Autonomy and self-directed learning: an Irish experiment'. In H. Holec (ed.) *Autonomy and Self-directed Learning: Fields of Application.* Strasbourg: Council of Europe, pp.77–84.

LITTLE, D. (ed.) (1989) *Self-Access Systems for Language Learning.* (With contributions from E. Esch, M.-J. Gremmo, D. Little, H. Moulden, P. Riley and D. Singleton.) Dublin: Authentik/CILT.

LITTLE, D. (1991) *Learner Autonomy. 1: Definitions, Issues and Problems,* Dublin: Authentik.

LITTLE, D. (1994a) 'Words and their properties: arguments for a lexical approach to pedagogical grammar'. In T. Odlin (ed.) *Perspectives on Pedagogical Grammar.* Cambridge: Cambridge University Press, pp.99–122.

LITTLE, D. (1994b) 'Learner autonomy: a theoretical construct and its practical application', *Die Neueren Sprachen*, 93:5, pp.430–42.

LITTLE, D. (1994c) 'Interactive videocassette for self-access: a preliminary report on the implementation of Autotutor II', *Computers in Education*, 23:1/2, pp.165–70.

LITTLE, D. and DEVITT, S. (1991) *Authentik: The User's Guide*. Dublin: Authentik.

LITTLE, D. and SINGLETON, D. (1992) 'Authentic texts, pedagogical grammar and Language Awareness in foreign language learning'. In C. James and P. Garrett (eds) *Language Awareness in the Classroom*. London and New York: Longman, pp.123–32.

LITTLE, D., DEVITT, S. and SINGLETON, D. (1989) *Learning Foreign Languages from Authentic Texts*. Dublin: Authentik, in association with CILT, London.

LITTLEJOHN, A. (1992) *Why are English Language Teaching Materials the way they are?* PhD thesis, University of Lancaster.

LITTLEJOHN, A.P. (1995) 'Language teaching in schools: what do students learn?'. In D.H. Hill (ed.) *Bologna '94: English Language Teaching*. Milan: British Council, pp.36–41.

LITTLEJOHN, A. and WINDEATT, S. (1989) 'Beyond language learning: perspectives of materials design'. In R.K. Johnson (ed.) *The Second Language Curriculum*. Cambridge: Cambridge University Press, pp.155–75.

LITTLEWOOD, W.T. (1981) *Communicative Language Teaching*. Cambridge: Cambridge University Press.

LITTLEWOOD, W.T. (1992) *Teaching Oral Communication: A Methodological Framework*. Oxford: Blackwell.

LITTLEWOOD, W.T. (1993) 'Cognitive principles underlying task-centred foreign language learning'. In N. Bird, J. Harris and M. Ingham (eds) *Language and Content*. Hong Kong: Institute of Language in Education, pp.39–55.

LITTLEWOOD, W.T. (1994) 'Language teaching methods'. In R.E. Asher (ed.) *The Encyclopedia of Language and Linguistics*. Oxford: Pergamon Press, pp.2027–35.

LOUW, B. (1993) 'Irony in the text or insincerity in the writer? The diagnostic potential of semantic prosodies'. In M. Baker, G. Francis and E. Tognini-Bonelli (eds), *Text and Technology*. Amsterdam: Benjamin, pp.157–76.

LUM, L.Y. and BROWN, R. (1994) 'Guidelines for the production of in-house self-access materials', *ELT Journal*, 48:2, pp.150–6.

MA WAI YIN, E. (1993) My relationship to English. Unpublished undergraduate paper, Hong Kong University.

MACDONALD-SMITH, F. (1993) Learner preferences in a self access language lab. Unpublished MSc paper, Aston University.

MANN, S.J. (1987) Revealing and understanding reading: an investigation with eighteen readers. Unpublished PhD thesis, University of Lancaster.

MANNHEIM, K. (1936) *Ideology and Utopia*. London: Routledge and Kegan Paul.

MARTYN, E. (1994) 'Self-access logs: promoting self-directed learning'. In D. Gardner and L. Miller (eds) *Directions in Self-access Language Learning*. Hong Kong: Hong Kong University Press, pp.65–78.

MARTYN, E. and HUSAIN, P. (1993) 'A task-based negotiated syllabus for nurses'. In T. Boswood, R. Hoffman and P. Tung (eds) *Perspectives on English for Professional Communication*. Hong Kong: City Polytechnic, pp.289–303.

MARTYN, E. and VOLLER, P. (1993) 'Teachers' attitudes to self-access learning', *Hong Kong Papers in Linguistics and Language Teaching*, 16, 103–10.

MARX, K. and ENGELS, F. (1968) *The German Ideology*. Moscow: Progress Publishers.

MASEMANN, V. (1986) 'Critical ethnography in the study of comparative education'. In P. Altbach and G. Kelly (eds) *New Approaches to Comparative Education*. Chicago: University of Chicago Press, pp.11–25.

McCAFFERTY, J. (undated) *A consideration of a Self-access Approach to the Learning of English*, mimeo. London: The British Council.

McCALL, J. (1992) *Self-access: Setting up a Centre*. Manchester: British Council.

McCARTHY, M. and CARTER, R. (1993) *Language as Discourse*. London: Longman.

MEYER, J.W. (1988) 'Myths of socialization and of personality'. In T.C. Heller, M. Sosna and D.E. Wellbery (eds) *Reconstructing Individualism: Autonomy, Individuality, and the Self in Western Thought*. Stanford: Stanford University Press, pp.208–21.

MEZIROW, J. (1985) 'A critical theory of self-directed learning'. In S. Brookfield (ed.) *Self-directed Learning: From Theory to Practice*. San Francisco: Jossey-Bass, pp.17–30.

MILLER, L. and ROGERSON-REVELL, P. (1993) 'Self-access systems'. *ELT Journal*, 47, pp.228–33.

MILTON, J. and CHOWDURY, N. (1994) 'Tagging the interlanguage of Chinese learners of English'. In L. Flowerdew and A. Tong (eds) *Entering Text*. Hong Kong: Hong Kong University of Science and Technology, pp.127–43.

MILTON, J., SMALLWOOD, I. and PURCHASE, J. (1996) 'From word processing to text processing.' In R. Pemberton *et al.* (eds) *Taking Control: Autonomy in Language Learning*. Hong Kong: Hong Kong University Press, pp.233–48.

MOULDEN, H. (1988) 'Self-directed learning of English for French students of computer applications in business management'. In H. Holec (ed.) *Autonomy and Self-directed Learning: Fields of Application*. Strasbourg: Council of Europe, pp.85–92.

MPARUTSA, C., LOVE, A. and MORRISON, A. (1991) 'Bringing concord to the ESP classroom'. In T. Johns and P. King (eds) *Classroom Concordancing* (*ELR Journal* 4). Birmingham: Centre for English Language Studies, pp.115–34.

MÜLLER, M., SCHNEIDER, G. and WERTENSCHLAG, L. (1988) 'Apprentissage autodirigé en tandem à l'Université'. In H. Holec (ed.) *Autonomy and Self-directed Learning: Fields of Application.* Strasbourg: Council of Europe, pp.65–76.

NAMENWIRTH, E. (1994) 'Lever l'ambiguité au sujet de l'autonomie'. CERCLES 1994 Hull Conference. CERCLES, Bochum.

NATIONAL CENTRE FOR ENGLISH LANGUAGE TEACHING AND RESEARCH (NCELTR) (1994) *It's Over to You. Stage 3.* Sydney: NCELTR.

NEUSTUPNY, J.V. (1987) *Communicating with the Japanese.* Tokyo: The Japan Times.

NUNAN, D. (1988) *The Learner-centred Curriculum: A Study in Second Language Teaching.* Cambridge: Cambridge University Press.

NUNAN, D. (1989) *Designing Tasks for the Communicative Classroom.* Cambridge: Cambridge University Press.

NUNAN, D. (ed.) (1992) *Collaborative Language Learning and Teaching.* Cambridge: Cambridge University Press.

NUNAN, D. (1995a) 'Closing the gap between learning and instruction', *TESOL Quarterly*, 29:1, pp.133–58.

NUNAN, D. (1995b) *ATLAS. Learning-centred Communication.* Boston: Heinle and Heinle/International Thomson Publishing.

NUNAN, D. and LAMB, C. (1995) *The Self-Directed Teacher: Managing the Learning Process.* New York: Cambridge University Press.

O'DELL, F. (1992) 'Helping teachers to use a self-access centre to its full potential', *ELT Journal*, 46:2, pp.153–9.

O'MALLEY, J.M and CHAMOT, A.U. (1990) *Learning Strategies in Second Language Acquisition.* Cambridge: Cambridge University Press.

O'MALLEY, J.M., CHAMOT, A.U., STEWNER-MANZARES, G., KUPPER, L. and RUSSO, R.P. (1985) 'Learning strategies used by beginning and intermediate ESL students', *Language Learning*, 35:1, pp.21–46.

O'NEILL, R. (1991) 'The plausible myth of learner-centredness: or the importance of doing things well', *ELT Journal*, 45:4, pp.293–304.

OVERING, J. (1988) 'Personal autonomy and the domestication of the self in Piaroa society'. In G. Jahoda and I.M. Lewis (eds) *Acquiring Culture: Cross-cultural Studies in Child Development.* London: Routledge, pp.169–92.

OXFORD, R. (1990) *Language Learning Strategies: What Every Teacher Should Know.* Rowley, Mass.: Newbury House.

OXFORD, R. and SCARCELLA, R. (1993) *The Tapestry of Language Learning.* Boston: Heinle and Heinle.

PANG, T. (1994) 'A self-directed project: a critical humanistic approach to self-access'. In D. Gardner and L. Miller (eds) *Directions in Self-access Language Learning.* Hong Kong: Hong Kong University Press, pp.29–38.

PAWLEY, A. and SYDER, F. (1983) 'Two puzzles for linguistic theory: nativelike selection and nativelike fluency'. In J. Richards and R. Schmidt (eds) *Language and Communication.* London: Longman, pp.191–226.

PEIRCE, B.N. (1989) 'Toward a pedagogy of possibility in the teaching of English internationally: People's English in South Africa', *TESOL Quarterly*, 23:3, pp.401–20.

PEMBERTON, R., LI, E., OR, W. and PIERSON, H. (eds) (1996) *Taking Control: Autonomy in Language Learning.* Hong Kong: Hong Kong University Press.

PENNINGTON, M. (1991) 'Computer based text analysis and the non-proficient writer: can the technology deliver on its promise?' In J. Milton and K.S. Tong (eds) *Text Analysis in Computer Assisted Language Learning.* Hong Kong: Hong Kong University of Science and Technology, pp.89–108.

PENNYCOOK, A. (1990) 'Towards a critical applied linguistics for the 1990s', *Issues in Applied Linguistics*, 1:1, pp.8–28.

PENNYCOOK, A. (1994) *The Cultural Politics of English as an International Language.* London: Longman.

PHILLIPSON, R. (1992) *Linguistic Imperialism.* Oxford: Oxford University Press.

PIERSON, H. (1996) 'Learner culture and learner autonomy in the Hong Kong Chinese context'. In R. Pemberton *et al.* (eds) *Taking Control: Autonomy in Language Learning.* Hong Kong: Hong Kong University Press, pp.49–58.

PORCHER, L. (1988) 'Formation de formateurs en Français langue étrangère: autonomies et technologies'. In H. Holec (ed.) *Autonomy and Self-directed Learning: Fields of Application.* Strasbourg: Council of Europe, pp.129–36.

POWELL, J. (1988) 'Reducing teacher control'. In D. Boud (ed.) *Developing Student Autonomy in Learning*, 2nd edn. London: Kogan Page, pp.109–18.

PRODROMOU, L. (1988) 'English as cultural action', *ELT Journal*, 42:2, pp.73–83.

RAIMES, A. (1983) 'Tradition and revolution in ESL teaching', *TESOL Quarterly*, 17:4, pp.535–52.

RÉGENT, O. (1993) 'Communication, strategy and language learning'. In J.L. Otal and M.L. Villanueva (eds) *Primeves Jornades Sobre Auto-aprenentatge de Llengües.* Castello Publicacions de la Universitat Jaume I, pp.29–39.

RICHARDS, J.C. (1990) *The Language Teaching Matrix.* Cambridge: Cambridge University Press.

RICHARDS, J.C. and RODGERS, T.S. (1986) *Approaches and Methods in Language Teaching.* Cambridge: Cambridge University Press.

RILEY, P. (1982) 'Learners' lib: experimental autonomous learning scheme'. In M. Geddes and G. Sturtridge (eds) *Individualisation.* London: Modern English Publications, pp.61–3.

RILEY, P. (ed.) (1985) *Discourse and Learning*. London: Longman.

RILEY, P. (1986) 'Who's who in self-access', *TESOL France News*, 6:2, pp.23–35.

RILEY, P. (1988a) 'The ethnography of autonomy'. In A. Brookes and P. Grundy (eds) *Individualisation and Autonomy in Language Learning.* ELT Documents 131. London: Modern English Publications in association with the British Council (Macmillan), pp.12–34.

RILEY, P. (1988b) ' "Who do you think you're talking to?" Perception, categorisation and negotiation processes in exolinguistic interaction'. In V. Bickley (ed.) *Languages in Education in a Bilingual or Multilingual Setting.* Hong Kong: Hong Kong Institute for Language in Education, pp.118–33.

RILEY, P. (1989a) 'Negociation et anarchie: la sociologie du savoir et les modèles discursifs'. *Verbum* XII, pp.59–72.

RILEY, P. (1989b) 'Social identity and intercultural communication'. *Levende Talen* 443, pp.488–93.

RILEY, P. (1993) 'The competence-performance distinction: poisoned chalice, mixed blessing or two-edged sword?' Paper presented at the Cambridge Summer Institute in English and Applied Linguistics. In G. Brown *et al.* (forthcoming) *Performance and Competence in Second Language Acquisition.* Cambridge: Cambridge University Press.

RILEY, P. (1994) 'Aspects of learner discourse; why listening to learners is so important'. In E.M. Esch (ed.) *Self Access and the Adult Learner.* London: CILT, pp.7–19.

RILEY, P., GREMMO, M.-J. and MOULDEN, H. (1989) 'Pulling yourself together: the practicalities of setting up and running self-access systems'. In D. Little (ed.) (1989) *Self-access Systems for Language Learning.* Dublin: Authentik, pp.34–65.

RIVERS, W.M. (1964) *The Psychologist and the Foreign Language Teacher.* Chicago: Chicago University Press.

ROGERS, C. (1969) *Freedom to Learn.* Columbus, Ohio: Charles E. Merrill.

ROST, M. (1990) *Listening in Language Learning.* London: Longman.

RUIZ, R. (1991) 'The empowerment of language-minority students'. In C. Sleeter (ed.) *Empowerment through Multicultural Education.* New York: SUNY Press, pp.217–18.

SCOLLON, R. and SCOLLON, S.W. (1980) *Narrative, Literacy and Face in Interethnic Communication.* Norwood, New Jersey: Ablex.

SCOLLON, R. and SCOLLON, S.W. (1992) *Individualism and Binarism: A Critique of American Intercultural Communication Analysis.* Research Report No. 22. Department of English, City Polytechnic of Hong Kong.

SCOLLON, R. and SCOLLON, S.W. (1993) *Discourse in Intercultural Professional Communication. An interactive sociolinguistic framework.* Department of English, City Polytechnic of Hong Kong.

SCOTT, M. and JOHNS, T. (1993) *MicroConcord.* Oxford: Oxford University Press.

SEARLE, C. (1983) 'A common language', *Race and Class*, 25:2, pp.65–74.

SELF, J. (1985) *Microcomputers in Education*. Brighton: Harvestor Press.

SHEERIN, S. (1989) *Self-access*. Oxford: Oxford University Press.

SHEERIN, S. (1991) 'State of the art: self-access', *Language Teaching*, 24:3, pp.153–7.

SILVA, T. (1990) 'Second language composition instruction: developments, issues and directions in ESL'. In B. Kroll (ed.) *Second Language Writing: Research Insights for the Classroom*. Cambridge: Cambridge University Press, pp.11–23.

SIMON, R. (1987) 'Empowerment as a pedagogy of possibility', *Language Arts*, 64:4, pp.370–82.

SIMON, R. (1992) *Teaching Against the Grain: Texts for a Pedagogy of Possibility*. Toronto: OISE Press/Bergin and Garvey.

SINCLAIR, J.M. (1991) *Corpus, Concordance, Collocation*. Oxford: Oxford University Press.

SKEHAN, P. (1989) *Individual Differences in Second Language Learning*. London: Edward Arnold.

SKILBECK, M. (1976) 'Three educational ideologies'. In *Curriculum Design and Development, Unit 3: Ideologies and Values*. Milton Keynes: The Open University Press, pp.28–41.

SKUTNABB-KANGAS, T. and PHILLIPSON, R. (eds) (1994) *Linguistic Human Rights: Overcoming Linguistic Discrimination*. Berlin: Mouton de Gruyter.

STERN, H.H. (1983) *Fundamental Concepts of Language Teaching*. Oxford: Oxford University Press.

STERN, H.H. (1990) 'Analysis and experience as variables in second language pedagogy'. In B. Harley, P. Allen, J. Cummins and M. Swain (eds) *The Development of Second Language Proficiency*. Cambridge: Cambridge University Press, pp.93–109.

STEVICK, E.W. (1976) *Memory, Meaning and Method: Some Psychological Perspectives on Language Learning*. Rowley Mass.: Newbury House.

STURTRIDGE, G. (1982) 'Individualised learning: what are the options for the classroom teacher?' In M. Geddes and G. Sturtridge (eds) *Individualisation*. London: Modern English Publications, pp.8–14.

STURTRIDGE, G. (1992) *Self-access: Preparation and Training*. Manchester: British Council.

TARONE, E. and YULE, G. (1989) *Focus on the Language Learner*. Oxford: Oxford University Press.

TOOKER, D.E. (1992) 'Identity systems of Highland Burma: "belief", Akna Zan, and a critique of interiorised notions of ethnoreligious identity', *Man*, 27:4, pp.799–820.

TOUGH, A. (1971) *The Adult's Learning Projects*. Ontario Institute for Education Studies.

TRIBBLE, C. and JONES, G. (1990) *Concordances in the Classroom*. London: Longman.

TRIM, J.L.M. (1977). 'Some possibilities and limitations of learner autonomy'. In E.M. Harding-Esch (Ed.) *Self-Directed Learning and Autonomy*, Cambridge, 13–15 December 1976, University of Cambridge, Department of Linguistics.

TUDOR, I. (1993) 'Teacher roles in the learner-centred classroom', *ELT Journal*, 47:1, pp.22–31.

TUMPOSKY, N. (1982) 'The learner on his own'. In M. Geddes and G. Sturtridge (eds) *Individualisation*. London: Modern English Publications, pp.4–7.

VAN LIER, L. (1995) *Interaction in the Language Curriculum: Awareness, Autonomy and Authenticity*. London: Longman.

VOLLER, P. and PICKARD, V. (1996) 'Conversation exchange: a way towards autonomous language learning'. In R. Pemberton *et al.* (eds) *Taking Control: Autonomy in Language Learning*. Hong Kong: Hong Kong University Press, pp.115–32.

WAITE, S. (1994) 'Low-resourced self-access with EAP in the developing world: the great enabler?', *ELT Journal*, 48:3, pp.233–42.

WALSH, C. (1991) *Pedagogy and the Struggle for Voice: Issues of Language, Power and Schooling for Puerto Ricans*. Toronto: OISE Press/Bergin and Garvey.

WENDEN, A. (1991) *Learner Strategies for Learner Autonomy*. London: Prentice-Hall.

WEST, J. (1992–4) *Progressive Grammar of German 1–6*. Dublin: Authentik.

WHITE, R. (1988) *The ELT Curriculum: Design, Innovation and Management*. Oxford: Blackwell.

WIDDOWSON, H.G. (1978) *Teaching Language as Communication*. Oxford: Oxford University Press.

WIDDOWSON, H.G. (1983) *Learning Purpose and Language Use*. Oxford: Oxford University Press.

WIDDOWSON, H.G. (1984) *Explorations in Applied Linguistics 2*. Oxford: Oxford University Press.

WILLING, K. (1987) 'Learning strategies as information management', *Prospect*, 2:3, pp.273–91.

WILLING, K. (1989) *Teaching How to Learn*. Sydney, National Centre for English Language Teaching and Research.

WRIGHT, T. (1987) *Roles of Teachers and Learners*. Oxford: Oxford University Press.

YALDEN, J. (1987) *Principles of Course Design for Language Teaching*. Cambridge: Cambridge University Press.

YOUNG, R. (1986) *Personal Autonomy: Beyond Negative and Positive Liberty*. London: Croom Helm.

ZNANIECKI, F. (1965) *The Social Role of the Man of Knowledge*. New York: Harper and Row.

# Index

advising, 169, 171, 184 *see* counselling
  for language learning
Allwright, 41
Apple, 182
approaches to language learning
  as natural growth, 85
  as skill learning, 84–5
  audio-lingual method, 79
  behaviourist, 26–7, 79
  constructivist, 6, 21, 23
  naturalistic, 26–7
assessment
  as mystification, 139
  disempowering effects of formal
    assessment procedures, 138–9
  self-assessment, 179, 220
Australian Migrant Education
  Programme, 29–30
authenticity
  authentic texts and self-access,
    231–5
  communicative purpose of
    authentic texts, 226–7
  definition of authentic text, 225
  of learner response, 179, 225
  of materials, 179
  relevance of authentic texts for
    autonomy, 33, 231
  techniques for exploiting authentic
    texts, 229
autonomous language learner
  development of, 192–5, 201
  idealised characteristics of, 134–6
autonomous language learning
  and materials design, 192, 196–203
  and skills training, 165, 177
  experience of, 132
  history of, 5–8

indirect benefits of, 133
misconceptions about, 165–8
reasons for teacher interest in,
  140–1
role of learner in, 73–6, 76–8,
  93–7, 120–1
through resources beyond the
  classroom, 215–16, 224
through self-access work, 188–91,
  204
autonomy
  and authentic texts, 226, 230–1
  and 'cultural alternatives', 15,
    35–53
  and interdependence, 109
  and language content goals, 194,
    201–2
  and learning process goals, 178,
    194, 201–2
  and motivation, 134, 230
  and philosophies of learning,
    19–25
  and self-access, 6, 9, 16–17, 41–2,
    54–65, 181, 184–5, 188–91
  and self-awareness, 134–5, 167,
    232
  and technology, 166, 180, 237–8,
    247
  and theories of knowledge, 19–25
  as a relative concept, 192–3, 203
  concepts of, 3, 14, 18–25, 81–4,
    164, 230–1
  consequences of mainstreaming, 11,
    39–44, 164
  cultural specificity of, 9, 43–4, 56
  definitions of, 1, 4, 25, 165–6, 193,
    230
  desirability of, 133, 230

265

Ellis & Sinclair, 174–5
empowerment, 45–6
  lack of in formal assessment, 138–9
  lack of in self-access work, 181–8
  of EFL learners, 215
English as a colonial language, 50–2
error correction, 243
Eurocentre Learning Centre, 151–63
experiential learning, 7

Freire, 45–6

gender, discourses of, 52
Gilligan, 38
Giroux, 48
goals, 73–4
  language learning and learning
    process, 56, 178, 194
  personal and social, 32–3
Gramsci, 22
Gremmo, 129

Hammond & Collins, 42–3, 45
Heller & Wellberry, 37
Higgs, 106
Hill, 36
Hofstede, 44
Holec, 1, 12, 193
Hong Kong, 36, 50–1

ideology, 29
  and classroom practice, 182–4
  and knowledge, 182–3
  and language, 22
  and methodology, 183
  curriculum, 181–3
  in materials, 178
Illich, 40
independent learning *see* autonomous
    language learning
  activities involved in, 57
  and writing skills, 238
  readiness for, 58–9
individualization, 6–7, 55, 167, 182
Internet, as a virtual language
    community, 180, 235
isolation, 167, 184

Japan, 216–24
Johnston, 193
Judd, 25, 27

Kant, 36–7
Kelly, 104

knowledge
  ideology of, 182–3
  schematic, 210
  theories of, 19–25
Knowles, 56

language education, political nature
    of, 7, 32–3, 189, 195–6
language laboratories, 79
language learning
  and authentic texts, 226
  and culture, 166–7, 173, 196
  and curriculum ideology, 181–4
  and social inequalities, 27
  contrasted with language use,
    226–7
  data-driven, 241–2
  goals and learning process goals,
    178, 194
  interdependence with language use,
    227–9, 232–6
  skills in self-access, 177
  technologies, 180
language teaching
  'analytic' and 'experiential'
    strategies, 84–5
  'integrated model' of, 85–6
language use
  and authentic texts, 226
  contrasted with language learning,
    226–7
  interdependence with language
    learning, 232–6
learner autonomy *see* autonomy
'learner-based teaching', 7
learner-centredness, 7, 40, 42–3,
    193–4
learner control, 33, 46, 111
learner development *see* learner
    training
  as a gradual process, 194
  as awareness raising, 194, 196–8,
    218–19, 221–2
  as learner intervention, 199
  as learner involvement, 198–9
  as skills development, 220–1,
    223
  importance of non-directivity in,
    173
  importance of self-selection in,
    169–70
  levels of, 194–5
  requirements for autonomy, 164–5,
    168–9